T0192182

Lecture Notes in Computer Science　14291

Founding Editors

Gerhard Goos
Juris Hartmanis

The series Lecture Notes in Computer Science (LNCS), including its subseries Lecture Notes in Artificial Intelligence (LNAI) and Lecture Notes in Bioinformatics (LNBI), has established itself as a medium for the publication of new developments in computer science and information technology research, teaching, and education.

LNCS enjoys close cooperation with the computer science R & D community, the series counts many renowned academics among its volume editors and paper authors, and collaborates with prestigious societies. Its mission is to serve this international community by providing an invaluable service, mainly focused on the publication of conference and workshop proceedings and postproceedings. LNCS commenced publication in 1973.

Carole H. Sudre · Christian F. Baumgartner ·
Adrian Dalca · Raghav Mehta · Chen Qin ·
William M. Wells
Editors

Uncertainty for Safe Utilization of Machine Learning in Medical Imaging

5th International Workshop, UNSURE 2023
Held in Conjunction with MICCAI 2023
Vancouver, BC, Canada, October 12, 2023
Proceedings

 Springer

Editors

Carole H. Sudre ⓘ
University College London, London, UK
King's College London
London, UK

Adrian Dalca ⓘ
Harvard Medical School,
Charlestown, MA, USA

Massachusetts Institute of Technology
Cambridge, MA, USA

Chen Qin ⓘ
Imperial College London
London, UK

Christian F. Baumgartner ⓘ
University of Tübingen
Tübingen, Germany

Raghav Mehta
McGill University
Montreal, QC, Canada

William M. Wells
Department of Radiology
Brigham and Women's Hospital
Boston, USA

Harvard Medical School
Cambridge, MA, USA

ISSN 0302-9743   ISSN 1611-3349 (electronic)
Lecture Notes in Computer Science
ISBN 978-3-031-44335-0   ISBN 978-3-031-44336-7 (eBook)
https://doi.org/10.1007/978-3-031-44336-7

This Springer imprint is published by the registered company Springer Nature Switzerland AG
The registered company address is: Gewerbestrasse 11, 6330 Cham, Switzerland

Paper in this product is recyclable.

Preface

The Fifth Workshop on UNcertainty for Safe Utilization of machine lEarning in mEdical imaging (UNSURE 2023) was a satellite event of the 26th International Conference on Medical Image Computing and Computer Assisted Intervention (MICCAI 2023). With an ever-increasing diversity in machine learning techniques for medical imaging applications, the need to quantify and acknowledge the limitations of such techniques has now become a mainstream area of research for the MICCAI community. Since its first edition, the aim of this workshop has been to develop awareness and encourage research in the field of uncertainty modelling to enable safe implementation of machine learning tools in the clinical world.

The proceedings of UNSURE 2023 include 21 high-quality papers selected among 32 submissions through a double-blind review process. Each submission was reviewed by 3 members of the Program Committee, formed by 32 experts in the field of deep learning, Bayesian theory and uncertainty modeling. The accepted papers cover the fields of uncertainty estimation and modeling, as well as those of distribution management, domain shift robustness, Bayesian deep learning and uncertainty calibration.

The accepted manuscripts again cover a large range of imaging acquisition techniques (CT, XRay, MRI...) and a large range of organs such as knee, carotid or brain.

Two keynote presentations, from experts Anastasios Angelopoulos, University of California Berkeley, USA and James Moon, University College London, UK, further contributed to place this workshop at the interface between methodological advances and practical considerations. This fifth edition was further complemented by a panel discussion including our two keynote speakers, as well as Tal Arbel and William M. Wells. We hope this workshop highlighted both new theoretical advances and reflections on practical challenges in quantifying and communicating uncertainties, and will foster new research to improve safety in the application of machine learning tools and assist in the translation of such tools to clinical practice. We would like to thank all the authors for submitting their manuscripts to UNSURE, as well as the Program Committee members for the quality of their feedback and dedication to the review process.

August 2023

Carole H. Sudre
Christian F. Baumgartner
Adrian Dalca
Raghav Mehta
Chen Qin
William M. Wells

Organization

General Chair

Robert Bai   University of Cambridge, UK

Program Committee Chairs

Christian F. Baumgartner	University of Tübingen, Germany
Adrian Dalca	Massachusetts Institute of Technology and Massachusetts General Hospital, USA
Raghav Mehta	McGill University, Canada
Chen Qin	Imperial College London, UK
Carole H. Sudre	University College London and King's College London, UK
William M. Wells	Harvard Medical School, USA

Program Committee

Adrian Galdran	Universitat Pompeu Fabra, Spain
Cheng Ouyang	Imperial College London, UK
Chloe He	University College London, UK
Di Qiu	Chinese University of Hong Kong, China
Dimitri Hamzaoui	INRIA, France
Evan Yu	Cornell University, USA
Fons van der Sommen	Eindhoven University of Technology, The Netherlands
Hariharan Ravishankar	GE Healthcare, India
Hongwei Li	Technical University of Munich, Germany
Hongxiang Lin	Zheijiang Lab, China
Isaac Llorente Saguer	University College London, UK
Ishaan Bhat	University Medical Center Utrecht, The Netherlands
Jacob Carse	University of Dundee, UK
Jinwei Zhang	Cornell University, USA
Leo Joskowicz	Hebrew University of Jerusalem, Israel

Liane Canas	King's College London, UK
Luke Whitbread	University of Adelaide, Australia
Mark Graham	King's College London, UK
Matthew Baugh	Imperial College London, UK
Max-Heinrich Laves	Leibniz Universität Hannover, Germany
Neil Oxtoby	University College London, UK
Parinaz Roshanzamir	Concordia University, Canada
Pedro Borges	King's College London, UK
Pradad Sudhakar	GE Healthcare, India
Prerak Mody	Leiden University Medical Centre, Belgium
Robin Camarasa	Erasmus Medical Centre, The Netherlands
Stephen J. McKenna	University of Dundee, UK
Tim Adler	DKFZ, Germany
Tristan Glatard	Concordia University, Canada
William Consagra	Harvard Medical School, USA
Won Hwa Kim	POSTECH, South Korea
Yiming Xiao	Concordia University, Canada
Yipeng Hu	University College London, UK

Additional Reviewers

Peter Ahn	Laura Ha
Martin Ali	Bruno Hall
Christian Almeida	William Han
Marco Bauer	Zhang Hou
Andrea Becker	Christophe Hsieh
Mark Brown	Michel Hsu
Richard Chen	Victor Ito
Marc Cheng	Jens Jain
Eric Cheung	Yang Jang
Chris Chung	Igor Jin
Jonathan Cohen	Fabio Jing
Nicolas Costa	Gabriel Johnson
Florian De Souza	Philipp Kim
Tobias Deng	Sven King
Alberto Ding	Jürgen Klein
Matthew Fernandes	Sara Lam
Pedro Fernández	Hiroshi Lau
Luca Ferreira	Joseph Le
Jorge Ghosh	Olga Lim
Alex Gomes	Guillaume Lima
Vladimir Gómez	Claudia Lin

Ralf Ludwig
Frédéric Luo
Charles Ma
Anton Miller
Alejandro Min
Ioannis Mishra
Andrzej Nguyen
Claudio Ni
Simone Nie
Petr Patel
Davide Paul
Johan Pei
Dmitry Qian
Silvia Qiao
Holger Qin
Yuki Ribeiro
Takeshi Roberts
Julia Robinson
Walter Sánchez
Marcel Santos
Jean Sato
Alexey Shao
Dimitris Sharma
Mikhail Shen

Nikolaos Singh
Edward Smith
Jonas Son
Catherine Tanaka
Masahiro Tang
Sylvain Tao
Timo Tsai
René Tseng
Omar Tu
Lorenzo Weiss
Gilles Wen
Mauro Weng
Christina Xiang
Jacques Xiao
Tony Xie
Grzegorz Yang
Ryan Yao
Elizabeth Ye
Guido Young
Antoine Yu
Andrés Yuan
Gregory Zheng
Aaron Zhong
Anders Zhou

Contents

Propagation and Attribution of Uncertainty in Medical Imaging Pipelines

Leonhard F. Feiner[1,2]($\boxtimes$)(iD), Martin J. Menten[2,3](iD), Kerstin Hammernik[2](iD), Paul Hager[2](iD), Wenqi Huang[2](iD), Daniel Rueckert[2,3](iD), Rickmer F. Braren[1,4](iD), and Georgios Kaissis[1,2,5](iD)

[1] Institute of Diagnostic and Interventional Radiology, Klinikum rechts der Isar, Technical University of Munich, Munich, Germany
[2] AI in Medicine and Healthcare, Klinikum rechts der Isar, Technical University of Munich, Munich, Germany
leo.feiner@tum.de
[3] BioMedIA, Imperial College London, London, England
[4] German Cancer Consortium DKTK, Partner Site Munich, Munich, Germany
[5] Institute for Machine Learning in Biomedical Imaging, Helmholtz-Zentrum Munich, Munich, Germany

Abstract. Uncertainty estimation, which provides a means of building explainable neural networks for medical imaging applications, have mostly been studied for single deep learning models that focus on a specific task. In this paper, we propose a method to propagate uncertainty through cascades of deep learning models in medical imaging pipelines. This allows us to aggregate the uncertainty in later stages of the pipeline and to obtain a joint uncertainty measure for the predictions of later models. Additionally, we can separately report contributions of the aleatoric, data-based, uncertainty of every component in the pipeline. We demonstrate the utility of our method on a realistic imaging pipeline that reconstructs undersampled brain and knee magnetic resonance (MR) images and subsequently predicts quantitative information from the images, such as the brain volume, or knee side or patient's sex. We quantitatively show that the propagated uncertainty is correlated with input uncertainty and compare the proportions of contributions of pipeline stages to the joint uncertainty measure.

1 Introduction

Deep learning has become the state-of-the-art tool for the reconstruction, segmentation and interpretation of medical images. When applied to clinical practice, multiple deep learning models are commonly combined in a cascade of tasks

---

Supplementary Information The online version contains supplementary material available at https://doi.org/10.1007/978-3-031-44336-7_1.

C. H. Sudre et al. (Eds.): UNSURE 2023, LNCS 14291, pp. 1–11, 2023.
https://doi.org/10.1007/978-3-031-44336-7_1

across the imaging pipeline. Hereby, the output of an upstream model is subsequently used as input of a downstream model. For example, deep learning may be used to first reconstruct magnetic resonance (MR) images from raw k-space data before the reconstructed images are interpreted by another algorithm for signs of disease. At the same time, the application of deep learning models in clinical practice requires an estimate of their uncertainty. Ideally, the algorithm informs its user about unsure predictions in order to prevent harmful medical decisions based on incorrect predictions [31]. Many solutions to estimate the uncertainty of a single deep learning model have been introduced [4,7,14].

Integrating uncertainty estimation with imaging pipelines consisting of cascading deep learning models comes with additional challenges. The uncertainty of upstream models directly affects the output of downstream models. The *propagation of uncertainty* through the cascade has to be explicitly modeled in order to obtain a *joint* uncertainty measure for the entire pipeline. This also allows for *attribution* of the total uncertainty to the pipeline's individual components. To address these unmet needs, we make the following contributions in this work:

- We propose a novel method to propagate uncertainty through a pipeline with multiple deep learning components using Monte Carlo sampling.
- The proposed strategy allows the calculation of a joint uncertainty measure for the whole pipeline, and the attribution of the contributions to the pipeline's individual models for both classification and regression tasks.
- The utility of the proposed strategy is demonstrated on realistic medical image processing pipelines, in which the upstream models reconstruct magnetic resonance (MR) images from undersampled k-space data with varying, controllable amounts of aleatoric uncertainty. Different downstream models predict the brain volume, the knee side or the patient's sex. The code is available at github.com/LeonhardFeiner/uncertainty_propagation.

2   Related Work

In general, two sources of uncertainty can be distinguished: *epistemic* (or model) uncertainty and *aleatoric* uncertainty, i.e. noise and missing information in the data [14]. Recently, Bayesian methods have been developed to estimate epistemic uncertainty in machine learning models, such as Dropout during inference [7], learning weight distributions using backpropagation [4], and model ensembling [15]. To estimate the aleatoric uncertainty, previous works have suggested modeling the deterministic network output and intermediate activation functions by distributions [8], to perform test-time augmentation [32] or estimating the mean and variance of the target distribution [21]. Shaw et al. separate aleatoric uncertainty sources by removing components during training [28].

Uncertainty estimation has been applied to various tasks in medical image processing. In MR image reconstruction, pixel-wise epistemic uncertainty was estimated by drawing model parameters from a learned multivariate Gaussian distribution [20] or applying posterior sampling using Langevin Dynamics with a deep generative prior [11]. Another approach used Monte Carlo dropout and a heteroscedastic loss to model aleatoric and epistemic uncertainty [27]. Many works have evaluated uncertainty in medical image classification [10,13] and regression [6,16]. Uncertainty estimation has also been integrated with models for MR image super-resolution [29] or medical image registration [5]. However, all these works are limited to the uncertainty estimation of a single model and do not consider a cascade of models across a typical imaging pipeline.

Techniques for uncertainty propagation include Monte Carlo sampling [1, 12,32], unscented transforms [2,22], linearizing the non-linearities of the network partially [3] or fully [25,30], as well as performing assumed density filtering [8,9]. They estimate uncertainty by assuming constant image noise as input uncertainty [3,8,12,30], generating the uncertainty within the model layers [8,9,25,30], interpreting augmentations as distribution [32], or using the output of classical language recognition models [1,2,22]. None of these works use a pipeline of deep learning models or combine the predicted uncertainty of multiple models into a joint uncertainty metric.

The following works have specifically investigated uncertainty estimation in medical imaging pipelines [17,18,23]. They use a cascade of models that each output uncertainty estimations in addition to their prediction. However, their methods cannot quantify the influence of the uncertainty of upstream tasks on the uncertainty of the downstream task. This is because their methods concatenate uncertainty maps and the prediction as input channels for downstream models. Consequently, it is impossible to attribute the output uncertainty to either the input uncertainty and individual components of the pipeline. Revealing this dependence would require the propagation of probability distributions through the network, which we propose in our work.

3   Methods

Our novel technique for propagation of aleatoric uncertainty can be applied to a model cascade of arbitrary length. For simplicity, we here limit the explicit presentation of our method to one upstream model g and one downstream model f. The latter uses the output of g as input (see Fig. 1). In the following, $\mathbf{z}$ denotes the input data of the pipeline, $\mathbf{x}$ expresses the random variable of possible intermediate outputs of the upstream model, and y is a random variable of possible outputs of the entire pipeline. Without loss of generality, we assume that $\mathbf{z}$ and $\mathbf{x}$ are vectors (bold), whereas y is a single variable. Both $\mathbf{x}$ and y are associated with a single data point $\mathbf{z}$ of the dataset, whereas $p(\mathbf{x}|\mathbf{z})$ and $p(y|\mathbf{z})$ are the distributions of the random variables that are predicted by the pipeline up to a certain model stage. We assume the distribution of $p(y|\mathbf{x})$ to be normal in the case of regression and categorical in the case of classification. We estimate the mean and variance of the target normal distributions using the technique by Nix et al. [21], whereas the parameters of categorical distributions are given by softmax outputs. We choose the variance or entropy of y, respectively, as an uncertainty measure. In the following, we describe the composition of our pipeline in more detail.

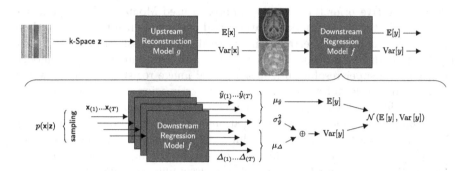

Fig. 1. An example of an imaging pipeline consisting of an upstream MR image reconstruction model g, and a downstream regression model f. Both models predict a measure of aleatoric uncertainty. Our method allows for the propagation of the mean and variance outputs of the upstream model through the downstream regression model.

3.1   Upstream Model

The upstream model g outputs a prediction and its uncertainty in the form of the parameters of a distribution $p(\mathbf{x}|\mathbf{z})$ from which we can sample. In our case, the upstream model produces images as outputs. We follow the common practice to model image uncertainty as pixel-wise variance [14], recognizing that this neglects potential higher order spatial correlations [19]. Spatial correlations in medical images can be associated with various factors, including similar tissue types across the image, local neighborhoods of voxels, or reconstruction artifacts. As the model g uses a heteroscedastic loss for training and outputs a tuple of arrays containing the mean image $\mathbb{E}[x]$ and the variance image $\mathrm{Var}[x]$, the image $\mathbf{x}$ is distributed as a diagonal multivariate normal distribution over predictions.

3.2   Downstream Model and Joint Pipeline

Next, the downstream model f processes $\mathbb{E}[x]$ and $\mathrm{Var}[x]$. As part of our contributions, we introduce a method to aggregate the uncertainties of the upstream model g and the downstream model f to a joint uncertainty measure. We propagate the uncertainty of the intermediate result, given by the distribution $p(\mathbf{x}|\mathbf{z})$, and obtain its contribution to the uncertainty of the final prediction $p(y|\mathbf{z})$. The joint uncertainty measure can be calculated by marginalizing the distribution of possible predictions $\mathbf{x}$ of the upstream model $p(y|\mathbf{z}) = \int p(y|\mathbf{x})p(\mathbf{x}|\mathbf{z})\mathrm{d}\mathbf{x}$. We approximate this integral by Monte Carlo sampling. The form of the joint uncertainty is different for regression and classification downstream tasks. We describe both cases below.

Regression Downstream Model: In the regression case, we assume that the prediction is normally distributed. Its mean is given by the expectation over the output value $\mathbb{E}[y]$. Its variance describing the joint aleatoric uncertainty can be denoted as the variance of the output value $\mathrm{Var}[y]$. Hence, the plausible predictions y are distributed as $y \sim \mathcal{N}(\mathbb{E}[y], \mathrm{Var}[y])$. However, the joint variance of the pipeline is the uncertainty of the upstream model propagated through the downstream model $\mathrm{Var}[x_{\mathrm{prop}}]$ and the uncertainty of the downstream model itself $\mathrm{Var}[y_{\mathrm{ds}}]$. The uncertainty of the downstream model $\mathrm{Var}[y_{\mathrm{ds}}]$ can not easily be computed in closed form, but is in general correlated with the propagated uncertainty of the first model $\mathrm{Var}[x_{\mathrm{prop}}]$.

The downstream model f does not output $\mathbb{E}[y]$ and $\mathrm{Var}[y_{\mathrm{ds}}]$ directly, but rather returns a tuple of outputs $(\hat{y}, \Delta)$. To perform variance propagation, we obtain T Monte Carlo samples $(\mathbf{x}_{(1)}, \ldots, \mathbf{x}_{(T)})$ from the distribution $p(\mathbf{x}|\mathbf{z})$. In Fig. 1, the T copies of the downstream model f denote simultaneous forward passes using the same model but with different samples as inputs. We use these Monte Carlo samples to approximate the expectation of the predictive distribution using the empirical mean $\mathbb{E}[y] \approx \mu_{\hat{y}}$ and the joint variance $\mathrm{Var}[y]$ by the empirical variance $\sigma_{\hat{y}}^2$ and the empirical mean μ_Δ in the following form:

$$\mathrm{Var}[y] = \underbrace{\mathrm{Var}[x_{\mathrm{prop}}]}_{} \quad + \underbrace{\mathrm{Var}[y_{\mathrm{ds}}] + 2\,\mathrm{Cov}[x_{\mathrm{prop}}, y_{\mathrm{ds}}]}_{}$$

$$= \underbrace{\frac{1}{T-1}\left(\sum_{t=1}^{T}\hat{y}_{(t)}^2 - \left(\sum_{t}\hat{y}_{(t)}\right)^2\right)}_{\sigma_{\hat{y}}^2} + \underbrace{\frac{1}{T}\sum_{t=1}^{T}\Delta_{(t)}}_{\mu_\Delta}$$

$$= \qquad\qquad \sigma_{\hat{y}}^2 \qquad\qquad + \qquad \mu_\Delta \qquad .$$

Classification Downstream Model: In the classification case, the prediction of the pipeline is given as a categorical distribution over classes c of a one-hot-encoded vector y. The downstream model outputs a vector of class confidences $\hat{y}$. To approximate the pipeline's expectation of the predictive distribution, we calculate the empirical mean of the model output $\mathbb{E}[y] \approx \mu_{\hat{y}}$. The resulting categorical distribution specifies a certain class confidence by $p(y = c|\mathbf{x}) = \mathbb{E}[y]_c$. One measure to express the joint uncertainty of a categorical distribution is the entropy of the prediction. The entropy for this pipeline is calculated as follows:

$$\mathrm{H}[y|\mathbf{z}] = -\sum_{c=1}^{C}\mathbb{E}[p(y = c|\mathbf{x})]\log\mathbb{E}[p(y = c|\mathbf{x})].$$

As the joint entropy consists of the combined uncertainty from the upstream and downstream model, we want to separate the part of the uncertainty contributed by the propagation. Hence, the mutual information I of the propagated aleatoric uncertainty and the aleatoric uncertainty of the downstream model is derived from the entropy H as follows: $\mathrm{I}[y, \mathbf{x}|\mathbf{z}] = \mathrm{H}[\mathbb{E}[y|\mathbf{z}]] - \mathbb{E}[\mathrm{H}[y|\mathbf{x}, \mathbf{z}]]$. Further details can be found in the supplementary material.

3.3   Loss and Parametrization

Instead of predicting the variance σ^2 of the upstream model and the residual uncertainty Δ of the downstream regression model directly, we reparametrize σ^2

as $\sigma^2 = e^s$ and Δ as $\Delta = e^\delta$, where s and δ are the respective outputs of the models. This ensures that σ^2 and Δ are positive. For both training and evaluation of the downstream model, we have to minimize the negative log likelihood of the joint distribution $p(y|\mathbf{z})$ for each input data point $\mathbf{z}$. Since the input of the downstream task is a probability distribution over images, we empirically chose to take 8 Monte Carlo samples during training and 256 Monte Carlo samples during evaluation to approximate the expectation. While the lower number of samples during training sacrifices accuracy for efficiency, we feel that the increased level of noise is mitigated over the course of repeated forward passes.

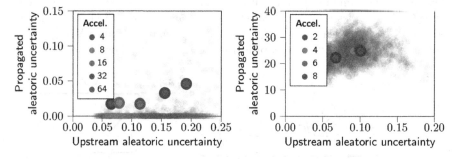

Fig. 2. Higher acceleration factors (color) lead to higher reconstruction uncertainty (x-axis) and, through propagation via our method, contribute to a higher uncertainty of the final pipeline output. The propagated portion of the output uncertainty (y-axis) is given as mutual information for knee side classification (left) and as standard deviations of brain volume predictions in ml (right). Large dots are aggregate values.

4   Experiments and Results

We test the utility of our method for three different medical pipelines with up- and downstream tasks. In all cases, the upstream task is to reconstruct MR images from undersampled k-space data. Different undersampling rates represent a varying source of aleatoric uncertainty. The downstream task is either a classification or regression task based on the reconstructed images. We demonstrate how our method propagates the uncertainty stemming from different undersampling factors to the ultimate prediction. Additionally, we show how it facilitates the attribution of the joint uncertainty to the individual models of the pipeline.

Reconstruction and Classification of Knee MR Images: Our first experiments are based on the fastMRI single-coil knee MR dataset [33]. The dataset contains reference images and raw k-space data, which we undersample with varying acceleration rates (Accel.) of 4, 8, 16, 32 and 64 by randomly removing columns from the k-space data. A fraction of the most centered columns in k-space is always used during reconstruction (C. Frac.). We use a physics-based reconstruction model based on an unrolled neural network [26,27]. In addition to the reconstructed 2D MR image, the model also outputs a map of the heteroscedastic aleatoric uncertainty. The upstream model's output is subsequently processed by a downstream model, a modified ResNet-50, that classifies the side of the knee (i.e. left or right knee). Based on the outputs of the downstream model, the pipeline calculates the parameters of a joint categorical distribution over possible predictions containing the uncertainty information. We use the fastMRI validation set containing 199 images as test set and split the original training set containing 973 images patient-wise into two parts to train the upstream and downstream model, respectively. Each model is trained with 80% of its data split and validated on the remaining 20%.

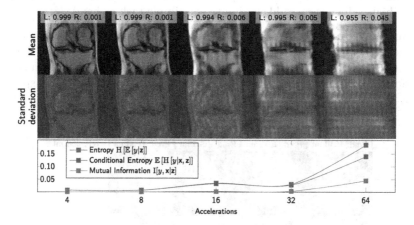

Fig. 3. Representative example (left knee) of a reconstructed knee MR images from k-space data with varying undersampling factors. Shown are the mean (top) and standard deviation maps (middle) as well as the accompanying uncertainty measures of the downstream network's knee side predictions (bottom).

Table 1. Quantitative measures characterizing the input k-space data, reconstructed images from the upstream model and final output from the downstream model.

k-space		Reconstructed image		Classification output (knee side)			
Accel.	C. Frac.	SSIM	$\sqrt{\mathrm{Var}[\mathbf{x}]}$	ACC	$I[y, \mathbf{x}\,|\,\mathbf{z}]$	$\mathbb{E}[\mathrm{H}[y|\mathbf{x}, \mathbf{z}]]$	$\mathrm{H}[\mathbb{E}[y|\mathbf{z}]]$
4	0.16	0.823	0.065	0.992	$0.32 \cdot 10^{-2}$	$1.63 \cdot 10^{-2}$	$1.95 \cdot 10^{-2}$
8	0.08	0.757	0.079	0.997	$0.32 \cdot 10^{-2}$	$1.40 \cdot 10^{-2}$	$1.71 \cdot 10^{-2}$
16	0.04	0.674	0.114	0.992	$0.34 \cdot 10^{-2}$	$1.37 \cdot 10^{-2}$	$1.71 \cdot 10^{-2}$
32	0.02	0.556	0.156	0.982	$0.76 \cdot 10^{-2}$	$2.14 \cdot 10^{-2}$	$2.90 \cdot 10^{-2}$
64	0.01	0.445	0.192	0.967	$1.74 \cdot 10^{-2}$	$5.20 \cdot 10^{-2}$	$6.93 \cdot 10^{-2}$

We observe that both the uncertainty in the reconstructed images and the propagated uncertainty in the final prediction increase with higher undersampling factors (see Fig. 2 left). Figure 3 illustrates this effect for a representative, single sample. These observations are also reflected in the quantitative results (see Table 1). With increasing undersampling, the uncertainty in the data increases, which is reflected in a higher estimated reconstruction uncertainty and lower structural similarity (SSIM) compared to the ground truth image that is obtained using the entire k-space data. The estimated reconstruction uncertainty is given as the square root of the average over the dataset and pixels ($\sqrt{\mathrm{Var}[\mathbf{x}]}$). This increased uncertainty is propagated by the downstream classification model. Higher upstream uncertainty yields a higher joint entropy ($\mathrm{H}\left[\mathbb{E}\left[y|\mathbf{z}\right]\right]$), as well as a higher mutual information ($\mathrm{I}\left[y, \mathbf{x}|\mathbf{z}\right]$) between the joint entropy and propagated uncertainty. For all undersampling factors, the prediction accuracy (ACC) is very high, which is most likely due to the simple task at hand.

Reconstruction of Brain MR Images: For the second set of experiments, we use the Alzheimer's Disease Neuroimaging Initiative (ADNI) brain MR image dataset [24]. We calculate the complex-valued k-space data by applying a Fourier transform to the images and add Gaussian noise to the synthetic k-space to mimic the MR imaging process.

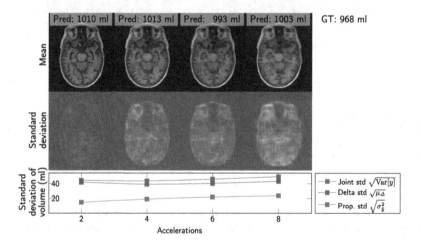

Fig. 4. Representative example of a reconstructed brain MR images from synthetic k-space data with varying undersampling factors. Shown are the mean (top) and standard deviation maps (middle) as well as the accompanying uncertainty measures in scale of ml of the downstream network's volume predictions (bottom).

We again simulate undersampling with acceleration factors of 2, 4, 6, and 8. We perform two different tasks on this dataset: regression of the brain volume and classification of the patient's sex. For the classification task, we use the same pipeline as for the fastMRI dataset, whereas for regression, we change the downstream model's output and loss accordingly. This dataset of 818 MR images is split patient-wise. We use 20% as a test set and split the remaining 80% into

Table 2. Quantitative measures characterizing the input k-space data, reconstructed images from the upstream model and final output from the downstream model.

k-space				Reconstructed image	Regression output (brain volume)				
Accel.	C. Frac.	SSIM	$\sqrt{\mathrm{Var}[\mathbf{x}]}$	L_1	L_2	$\sqrt{\sigma_{\hat{y}}^2}$	$\sqrt{\mu_\Delta}$	$\sqrt{\mathrm{Var}[y]}$
2	0.16	0.714	0.0642	63.6	78.9	22.0	59.9	64.2
4	0.08	0.567	0.0880	64.3	80.9	24.6	60.7	65.9
6	0.06	0.502	0.0957	64.3	81.6	25.1	62.3	67.6
8	0.04	0.450	0.0973	66.1	83.7	24.6	65.6	70.4

four subsets to train and validate the up- and downstream models separately, as described above.

The brain volume regression model also demonstrates that both the uncertainty in the image and the propagated uncertainty in the final prediction are positively correlated with the acceleration factor (see Fig. 2 right and Fig. 4). Higher acceleration rates lead to increasing uncertainty in the data, which returns in a higher variance of the prediction and lower structural similarity compared to the ground truth image (see Table 2). This increased uncertainty is propagated by the downstream regression model. Higher upstream uncertainty yields a higher propagated variance $\sigma_{\hat{y}}^2$ and a higher joint variance $\mathrm{Var}[y]$. Both of them are given as the square root of the average over the dataset ($\sqrt{\sigma_{\hat{y}}^2}$ and $\sqrt{\mathrm{Var}[y]}$). Beyond the uncertainty estimations, the sparser input data also leads to reduced model performance, as the average L_1 (Manhattan) and L_2 (Euclidean) distances between the prediction and the ground truth brain volumes rise with higher undersampling factors. We show the results for the patient sex classification pipeline in the material.

5 Conclusions

To the best of our knowledge, this is the first work to demonstrate how uncertainty can be propagated through medical imaging pipelines consisting of cascades of deep learning models. Our method quantifies the models' individual contributions to the joint uncertainty and be consequently aggregates them to a joint uncertainty measure. In extensive experiments, we have shown that our method can be integrated into real-world clinical image processing pipelines.

At the moment, our method does not capture the spatial correlation between the uncertainty of pixels. Future work could extend our method to handle probability distributions beyond pixel-wise independent normal distributions. Additionally, it would be valuable to incorporate epistemic uncertainty into the method. One major challenge that remains unresolved is the calibration of the pipeline's uncertainty. Moreover, to ensure meaningful comparisons between uncertainty propagation techniques and effectively evaluate different pipelines, the establishment of a well-defined metric is imperative.

Ultimately, we envision that our method will allow clinicians to assess and apportion all sources of aleatoric uncertainty within the medical imaging pipeline, increasing their confidence when deploying deep learning in clinical practice.

Acknowledgments. This research has been funded by the German Federal Ministry of Education and Research under project "NUM 2.0" (FKZ: 01KX2121). Data collection and sharing for this project was funded by the Alzheimer's Disease Neuroimaging Initiative (ADNI) (National Institutes of Health Grant U01 AG024904) and DOD ADNI (Department of Defense award number W81XWH-12-2-0012).

References

1. Abdelaziz, A.H., Watanabe, S., Hershey, J.R., Vincent, E., Kolossa, D.: Uncertainty propagation through deep neural networks. In: Annual Conference of the International Speech Communication Association, pp. 3561–3565 (2015)
2. Astudillo, R.F., Da Silva Neto, J.P.: Propagation of uncertainty through multilayer perceptrons for robust automatic speech recognition. Annual Conference of the International Speech Communication Association pp. 461–464 (2011)
3. Bibi, A., Alfadly, M., Ghanem, B.: Analytic expressions for probabilistic moments of PL-DNN with gaussian input. In: Computer Society Conference on Computer Vision and Pattern Recognition, pp. 9099–9107 (2018)
4. Blundell, C., Cornebise, J., Kavukcuoglu, K., Wierstra, D.: Weight uncertainty in neural network. In: International Conference on Machine Learning, pp. 1613–1622 (2015)
5. Dalca, A.V., Balakrishnan, G., Guttag, J., Sabuncu, M.R.: Unsupervised learning of probabilistic diffeomorphic registration for images and surfaces. Med. Image Anal. **57**, 226–236 (2019)
6. Feng, X., Li, T., Song, X., Zhu, H.: Bayesian scalar on image regression with nonignorable nonresponse. J. Am. Stat. Assoc. **115**(532), 1574–1597 (2020)
7. Gal, Y., Ghahramani, Z.: Dropout as a Bayesian approximation: representing model uncertainty in deep learning. Int. Conf. Mach. Learn. **3**, 1651–1660 (2016)
8. Gast, J., Roth, S.: Lightweight probabilistic deep networks. In: Computer Society Conference on Computer Vision and Pattern Recognition, pp. 3369–3378 (2018)
9. Ghosh, S., Delle Fave, F.M., Yedidia, J.: Assumed density filtering methods for learning Bayesian neural networks. In: Conference on Artificial Intelligence, pp. 1589–1595 (2016)
10. Ghoshal, B., Tucker, A., Sanghera, B., Lup Wong, W.: Estimating uncertainty in deep learning for reporting confidence to clinicians in medical image segmentation and diseases detection. Comput. Intell. **37**(2), 701–734 (2021)
11. Jalal, A., Arvinte, M., Daras, G., Price, E., Dimakis, A.G., Tamir, J.: Robust compressed sensing MRI with deep generative priors. Adv. Neural. Inf. Process. Syst. **34**, 14938–14954 (2021)
12. Ji, W., Ren, Z., Law, C.K.: Uncertainty propagation in deep neural network using active subspace. arXiv preprint (2019)
13. Ju, L., et al.: Improving medical images classification with label noise using dual-uncertainty estimation. Trans. Med. Imaging **41**(6), 1533–1546 (2022)
14. Kendall, A., Gal, Y.: What uncertainties do we need in Bayesian deep learning for computer vision? Neural Inf. Process. Syst. **30**, 5575–5585 (2017)

15. Lakshminarayanan, B., Pritzel, A., Blundell, C.: Simple and scalable predictive uncertainty estimation using deep ensembles. Neural Inf. Process. Syst. **30**, 1–12 (2017)
16. Laves, M.H., Ihler, S., Fast, J.F., Kahrs, L.A., Ortmaier, T.: Well-calibrated regression uncertainty in medical imaging with deep learning. In: Medical Imaging with Deep Learning, pp. 393–412 (2020)
17. Mehta, R., et al.: Propagating uncertainty across cascaded medical imaging tasks for improved deep learning inference. Trans. Med. Imaging. **41**, 360–373 (2021)
18. Mehta, R., Christinck, T., Nair, T., Lemaitre, P., Arnold, D., Arbel, T.: Propagating uncertainty across cascaded medical imaging tasks for improved deep learning inference. UNSURE/CLIP Conjunct. MICCAI **2019**, 23–32 (2019)
19. Monteiro, M., et al.: Stochastic segmentation networks: modelling spatially correlated aleatoric uncertainty. Neural Inf. Process. Syst. **33**, 12756–12767 (2020)
20. Narnhofer, D., Effland, A., Kobler, E., Hammernik, K., Knoll, F., Pock, T.: Bayesian uncertainty estimation of learned variational MRI reconstruction. Trans. Med. Imaging **41**(2), 279–291 (2022)
21. Nix, D.A., Weigend, A.S.: Estimating the mean and variance of the target probability distribution. Int. Conf. Neural Netw. **1**, 55–60 (1994)
22. Novoa, J., Fredes, J., Poblete, V., Yoma, N.B.: Uncertainty weighting and propagation in DNN-HMM-based speech recognition (2018)
23. Ozdemir, O., Woodward, B., Berlin, A.A.: Propagating uncertainty in multi-stage Bayesian convolutional neural networks with application to pulmonary nodule detection. arXiv preprint (2017)
24. Petersen, R.C., et al.: Alzheimer's disease neuroimaging initiative (ADNI): clinical characterization. Neurology **74**(3), 201–209 (2010)
25. Postels, J., Ferroni, F., Coskun, H., Navab, N., Tombari, F.: Sampling-free epistemic uncertainty estimation using approximated variance propagation. In: International Conference on Computer Vision, pp. 2931–2940 (2019)
26. Schlemper, J., Caballero, J., Hajnal, J.V., Price, A.N., Rueckert, D.: A deep cascade of convolutional neural networks for dynamic MR image reconstruction. Trans. Med. Imaging **25**(2), 491–503 (2018)
27. Schlemper, J., et al.: Bayesian deep learning for accelerated MR image reconstruction. In: Knoll, F., Maier, A., Rueckert, D. (eds.) MLMIR 2018. LNCS, vol. 11074, pp. 64–71. Springer, Cham (2018). https://doi.org/10.1007/978-3-030-00129-2_8
28. Shaw, R., Sudre, C.H., Ourselin, S., Cardoso, M.J.: A heteroscedastic uncertainty model for decoupling sources of MRI image quality. In: Medical Imaging with Deep Learning, pp. 733–742 (2020)
29. Tanno, R., et al.: Bayesian image quality transfer with CNNs: Exploring uncertainty in dMRI super-resolution. CoRR (2017)
30. Titensky, J.S., Jananthan, H., Kepner, J.: Uncertainty propagation in deep neural networks using extended Kalman filtering. In: MIT Undergraduate Research Technology Conference (2018)
31. Tschandl, P., et al.: Human-computer collaboration for skin cancer recognition. Nat. Med. **26**(8), 1229–1234 (2020)
32. Wang, G., Li, W., Aertsen, M., Deprest, J., Ourselin, S., Vercauteren, T.: Aleatoric uncertainty estimation with test-time augmentation for medical image segmentation with convolutional neural networks. Neurocomputing **338**, 34–45 (2019)
33. Zbontar, J., et al.: fastMRI: An open dataset and benchmarks for accelerated MRI. arXiv preprint (2018)

RR-CP: Reliable-Region-Based Conformal Prediction for Trustworthy Medical Image Classification

Yizhe Zhang[1]([✉]), Shuo Wang[2,3], Yejia Zhang[4], and Danny Z. Chen[4]

[1] School of Computer Science and Engineering, Nanjing University of Science and Technology, Nanjing, Jiangsu 210094, China
yizhe.zhang.cs@gmail.com
[2] Digital Medical Research Center, School of Basic Medical Sciences, Fudan University, Shanghai 200032, China
shuowang@fudan.edu.cn
[3] Shanghai Key Laboratory of MICCAI, Shanghai 200032, China
[4] Department of Computer Science and Engineering, University of Notre Dame, Notre Dame, IN 46556, USA
{yzhang46,dchen}@nd.edu

Abstract. Conformal prediction (CP) generates a set of predictions for a given test sample such that the prediction set almost always contains the true label (e.g., 99.5% of the time). CP provides comprehensive predictions on possible labels of a given test sample, and the size of the set indicates how certain the predictions are (e.g., a set larger than one is 'uncertain'). Such distinct properties of CP enable effective collaborations between human experts and medical AI models, allowing efficient intervention and quality check in clinical decision-making. In this paper, we propose a new method called Reliable-Region-Based Conformal Prediction (RR-CP), which aims to impose a stronger statistical guarantee so that an extremely low error rate (e.g., 0.5%) can be achieved in the test time, and under this constraint, the size of the prediction set is optimized to be small. We consider a small prediction set size an important measure only when the low error rate is achieved. Experiments on five public datasets show that our RR-CP performs well: with a reasonably small-sized prediction set, it achieves the user-specified low error rate significantly more frequently than exiting CP methods.

Keywords: Conformal Prediction · Reliable Regions · Extremely Low Error Rate · Computer-Aided Diagnosis · Trustworthy Medical AI

1 Introduction

Deep learning (DL) models nowadays have become go-to approaches for medical image classification in computer-aided diagnosis. Despite their successes in many medical AI benchmarks, the reliability and trustworthiness of DL models are still one of the major concerns and obstacles in applying DL-based methodologies in clinical practice. Recently, conformal prediction (CP) has drawn lots of attention

C. H. Sudre et al. (Eds.): UNSURE 2023, LNCS 14291, pp. 12–21, 2023.
https://doi.org/10.1007/978-3-031-44336-7_2

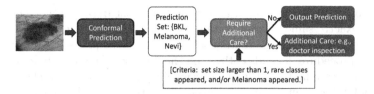

Fig. 1. Illustrating a practical CP-based workflow for trustworthy medical image classification: Conformal prediction works together with medical doctors.

for improving the trustworthiness of medical AI [2,10,11]. CP generates not only a single prediction label but a set of possible labels (containing one or multiple labels) for a given test image sample, and the true label is guaranteed (in the statistical sense) to be within the prediction set. CP enables effective collaborations between human experts and AI models [5], allowing efficient intervention and quality check in clinical decision-making (see Fig. 1).

More formally, given an image sample x to a classification model f, we first obtain a probability output vector $\pi = f(x)$. A CP method then performs on top of this output to generate a prediction set of possible labels to which the sample x's true label y may belong: $PS(x) = CP(f(x))$. Traditionally, a CP method is designed to achieve the following goal:

$$1 - \alpha \leq P(Y_{test} \in PS(X_{test})) \leq 1 - \alpha + \epsilon, \qquad (1)$$

where Y_{test} is the true labels of test samples X_{test}, α is a user-specified error rate and should be set to a small value for critical applications (e.g., medical image classification), and $\epsilon > 0$ is a small value for making the coverage tight.

A trivial solution for constructing a CP model is to let it produce all the possible class labels for any given sample with a $1 - \alpha$ probability. Clearly, this would give little useful information on any test sample as the model almost always generates the same full prediction set for a test sample. To avoid such a trivial solution, the size of the prediction set must be considered when designing a CP model. A general goal that includes the prediction set size is to satisfy the constraints in Eq. (1) using a prediction set of the smallest possible size.

Suppose a calibration set $D_{cali} = (X_{cali}, Y_{cali})$, with $X_{cali} = \{x_1, x_2, \ldots, x_n\}$ and $Y_{cali} = \{y_1, y_2, \ldots, y_n\}$, is given for a K-class classification problem ($y_i \in \{1, 2, \ldots, K\}$). For a classifier f (e.g., a ResNet classifier), a classic CP method [14] computes a score for each sample x_i using $s(x_i, y_i) = 1 - \pi_i[y_i]$, where $\pi_i = f(x_i)$ and $\pi_i[y_i]$ is the predicted probability of the ground truth y_i. The method then collects all the scores for the samples in D_{cali} and finds the $1 - \alpha$ quantile of the collected scores, denoted as q_α. For a new sample x_{test}, with the classifier f applied on top of it, the prediction set is generated by selecting any class label k ($k \in \{1, 2, \ldots, K\}$) with the score $\pi_{test}[k] \geq 1 - q_\alpha$. In [14], it was shown that using the above procedure, when the samples in a test set $D_{test} = (X_{test}, Y_{test})$ and the samples in the set D_{cali} are independent and identically distributed (i.i.d.), then $1 - \alpha \leq P(Y_{test} \in PS(X_{test}))$ holds. Although this is a great theoretical result, two key issues remain: (1) The i.i.d.

assumption is often too strong, and in practice, test data may not be sampled from the exactly same distribution of the data used to find q_α. (2) No explicit control on the size of the prediction set: The size of the prediction set yielded in the above procedure depends entirely on the quality of the score function, which depends on the quality of the class probability output from the classifier f. If the probability output is entirely random, then the size of the prediction set can be arbitrarily large (up to K).

Recently, Adaptive Prediction Set (APS) [4,12] modified the classic CP method by accumulating class probabilities when computing scores. More formally, for each sample (x_i, y_i) in D_{cali}, APS first sorts the class probabilities in each π_i (from high to low) and obtains $\tau_i = argsort([\pi_i[1], \pi_i[2], \ldots, \pi_i[K]])$, where τ_i is a permutation of $\{1, \ldots, K\}$ resulted from the sorting. The score for a sample (x_i, y_i) is computed as $s(x_i, y_i) = \sum_{k=1}^{k^*} \pi_i[\tau(k)]$, with $\tau_i(k^*) = y_i$. With this new score function, the remaining procedure for computing q_α and using the computed q_α for getting the prediction set on a new sample in the test set D_{test} is largely the same as the above classic CP method. APS aims to improve the robustness of CP by improving the score function and making a fuller utilization of the probability output. For multi-label classification tasks where a sample can be associated with more than one true label, a method [8] proposed to reduce false positives in the prediction set by trading with coverage, and demonstrated practical usage of this design in screening molecule structures. Recently, the CP formula was generalized using a more general term/formula ("risk") to represent terms such as the error rate in classification [3].

In medical image analysis, a most critical consideration of CP is to ensure that the actual error rate in deployment is no bigger than the user-specified one when constructing a CP method. If the user-specified error rate is not attained in test time, a smaller-sized prediction set is meaningless when the true label is not in the prediction set. Hence, we propose a new method called Reliable-Region-based Conformal Prediction (RR-CP), which puts satisfying the user-specified error rate as the first priority and reducing the prediction set size as the second one. We estimate a set of reliable regions for set predictions to ensure when a prediction set falls into a particular reliable region, this prediction set is guaranteed (statistically) to contain the true label. Overall, RR-CP can be viewed as a constrained optimization approach in which the constraint is to satisfy the user-specified error rate and the objective is to minimize the set size.

This paper contributes to trustworthy medical AI in the following ways. (1) We identify a crucial aspect of applying conformal prediction in medical AI, which is the expectation that a CP method should achieve an extremely low error rate (e.g., 0.5%) during deployment. Such an extremely low error rate had not been addressed by previous CP methods. (2) In order to fulfill the low error rate requirement, we develop a novel method called reliable-region-based conformal prediction (RR-CP) which by design exerts a stronger correctness guarantee for achieving the desired minimal error rate. (3) Theoretical analyses demonstrate the distinct value of our proposed RR-CP, and experimental results show that RR-CP satisfies the desired low error rates significantly more often than known CP methods.

2   Reliable-Region-Based Conformal Prediction

In Sect. 2.1, we first give a high-level elucidation of the overall goal, principles, and ideas of our proposed RR-CP. We then give detailed descriptions of the process and algorithm in Sect. 2.2. In Sect. 2.3, we provide further theoretical analyses and justifications for our RR-CP method.

2.1   Principles and Overall Ideas

We aim to produce a prediction set for test samples to attain the following goal:

$$1 - \alpha \leq P(Y_{test} \in PS(X_{test})). \tag{2}$$

Note that Eq. (2) is different from the original goal in Eq. (1) as we drop the constraint of $P(Y_{test} \in PS(X_{test})) \leq 1 - \alpha + \epsilon$, where ϵ is a small term. In [14], it was shown that the classic CP method satisfies this constraint with $\epsilon = \frac{1}{n+1}$, where n is the number of samples used in estimating the parameters of the CP method. Usually in critical applications such as medical image classification, the value of α is expected to be small (e.g., 0.005). Suppose we set $\alpha = 0.005$; then $1 - \alpha$ is already very close to 1, which makes it less meaningful/useful to impose the constraint of $P(Y_{test} \in PS(X_{test})) \leq 1 - \alpha + \epsilon$.

More importantly, dropping this constraint will allow more flexibility in designing a practically effective CP method. Previously, a CP method was designed and built to be not too conservative and not too relaxed as the gap between the lower and upper constraints in Eq. (1) is often quite small. In critical applications, satisfying the lower end of the constraints is a more essential consideration. Therefore, we aim to impose a stricter criterion when building a CP method to achieve a better guarantee for satisfying Eq. (2) in practice.

The high-level idea of our RR-CP method is to find a reliable region in the prediction set confidence score space for each prediction set size option, where the samples in that region strictly satisfy the correctness constraint in Eq. (2). In test time, generating a prediction set for a given sample is conducted by testing its prediction set confidence scores against the reliable regions thus found, and for the prediction sets in these reliable regions, we choose a prediction set with the smallest size. Below we first describe what the reliable regions are in the prediction set confidence score space and how to estimate the reliable regions using calibration data. Then we discuss how to use reliable regions for conformal prediction, and finally provide theoretical analyses of our RR-CP method.

2.2   Algorithms and Details

Given a trained classifier f and a calibration set $D_{cali} = (X_{cali}, Y_{cali})$, with $X_{cali} = \{x_1, x_2, \ldots, x_n\}$ and $Y_{cali} = \{y_1, y_2, \ldots, y_n\}$, we aim to estimate K reliable regions, each corresponding to a set size option for conformal prediction.

Preparation. For each sample $x_i \in X_{cali}$, we apply the classifier f and obtain a vector output π_i, where each element in $\pi_i[k]$, for $k = 1, 2, \ldots, K$, describes the likelihood of the sample x_i belonging to the class k. We then sort the class probabilities in π_i from high to low and obtain $\tau_i = argsort([\pi_i[1], \pi_i[2], \ldots, \pi_i[K]])$, where τ_i is a permutation of $\{1, \ldots, K\}$ obtained from the sorting. For a set size option w, the prediction set is computed as:

$$PS_i^w = \begin{cases} \{\tau_i[1]\} & \text{if } w = 1, \\ \{\tau_i[1], \ldots, \tau_i[w]\} & \text{if } 2 \leq w \leq K. \end{cases} \tag{3}$$

The prediction set confidence score is computed as:

$$C_i^w = \sum_{q=1}^{w} \pi_i[\tau_i[q]]. \tag{4}$$

For each sample $x_i \in D_{cali}$, we obtain its prediction set PS_i^w and its corresponding confidence C_i^w, for $i = 1, 2, \ldots, n$ and $w = 1, 2, \ldots, K$.

Estimation. For each prediction set size option, we aim to find a reliable region (for a user-specified error rate α) in the prediction set confidence score space. In total, we find K reliable regions. For a given α and a set size option w, we collect all the corresponding PS_i^w and C_i^w, for $i = 1, 2, \ldots, n$. We then find C^w with a probability no less than $1 - \alpha$, such that **every sample** that satisfies $C_i^w \geq C^w$ has its true label y_i in PS_i^w. Note that this criterion is stronger than the following one: With a probability no less than $1 - \alpha$, the true label y_i is in PS_i^w for a sample x_i that satisfies $C_i^w \geq C^w$. Below we describe how to find/estimate C^w for each set size option w. For each value of w, given a confidence score C_{i*}^w, we apply Bootstrapping [7] (using B rounds of sampling with replacement) to check whether with probability $1 - \alpha$, PS_i^w contains its true label y_i for **every** sample x_i that has $C_i^w \geq C_{i*}^w$. If yes, we record the value C_{i*}^w in a list L^w. We repeat the above process for each value of C_{i*}^w, for $i* = 1, 2, \ldots, n$. We then generate C^w using $C^w = min(L^w)$. Finding the lowest confidence level in this list means to encourage the corresponding reliable region to be large so that in the subsequent inference, the yielded prediction set will be small. We repeat this process to find C^w for each prediction set size option w, with $w = 1, 2, \ldots, K$. The pseudo-code for this part is given in Algorithms 1 and 2.

Algorithm 1: Find_RR	**Algorithm 2: RRCP_Build**
Function Find_RR(scores, conf, alpha, B):	**Function** RRCP_Build(D_cali, f, K, alpha):
index ← argsort(conf, 'descend');	conf ← [[] for w in xrange(K)];
c ← 1.0;	scores ← [[] for w in xrange(K)];
for id ← 0 to len(index)-1 **do**	RR ← [];
pool ← scores [index [0:id+1];	**for** x, y in D_cali **do**
s_pool ← [];	pi ← f (x);
for b ← 0 to B-1 **do**	tau ← argsort (pi, 'descend');
poolB ←	**for** w ← 0 to K-1 **do**
random.choice(pool,	c_t ← sum (pi [tau [0:w+1])];
len(pool));	conf[w].append(c_t);
stats ← min(poolB);	**if** y ∈ tau [0:w+1] **then**
s_pool.append(stats);	scores[w].append(1) ;
lower ← quantile(s_pool,	**else**
alpha);	scores[w].append(0) ;
if lower = 1 **then**	**for** w ← 0 to K-1 **do**
c ← conf[index [id]];	c ← Find_RR (scores[w], conf[w], alpha,
return c;	100); RR.append(c);
	return RR;

Inference. For a new test sample x_{test}, we apply f on top of it to obtain $\pi_{test} = f(x_{test})$. We then compute the prediction sets PS_{test}^w and confidence scores C_{test}^w for each set size option (for $w = 1, 2, \ldots, K$) using Eq. (4). With the reliable regions thus found (indicated by C^w), we find the smallest possible set size w^* which satisfies $C^{w^*} \geq C^w$, and use the obtained w^* to report the prediction set $P_{test}^{w^*}$ as the final output. The pseudo-code for using RR-CP to infer the prediction set for a given test sample is given in Algorithm 3 below.

Algorithm 3: RRCP_Inference

Function RRCP_Inference(x_test, f, K, RR, alpha):
  pi ← f (x_test);
  tau ← argsort (pi, 'descend');
  for w ← *0* to K-*1* **do**
    c_t ← sum (pi [tau [0:w+1]]);
    if c_t ≥ RR [w] **then**
      return tau [0:w+1];
  return tau;

2.3   Theoretical Analyses

Proposition: Suppose the samples in D_{cali} and D_{test} are independent and identically distributed. Then the prediction sets obtained by the RR-CP method (estimated by D_{cali}) satisfy

$$1 - \alpha \leq P(Y_{test} \in PS(X_{test})) \leq 1 - \frac{\alpha}{n}, \tag{5}$$

where n is the number of samples in D_{cali}. The Bootstrapping loop (line 5 in Listing 1.1) explicitly checks the correctness of the samples in the candidate regions for determining the reliable regions, where the correctness check considers all the prediction sets (PSs) in a given candidate confidence score region. If the α quantile (line 9 in Listing 1.1) obtained from the statistics of the Bootstrapping loop is equal to 1 (line 10 in Listing 1.1), then it means that with a $1 - \alpha$ chance, all the PSs in this region are correct (i.e., containing true labels). As a result, the $1 - \alpha \leq P(Y_{test} \in PS(X_{test}))$ part is enforced in the worst case scenario: for the α chance when not all the PSs in the region are correct, all the PSs are incorrect. In this worst case, $P(Y_{test} \in PS(X_{test})) = 1 - \alpha$. In the best case scenario, for the α chance when not all the PSs in the region are correct, only 1 PS is incorrect. Hence, the best case gives the part $P(Y_{test} \in PS(X_{test})) \leq 1 - \frac{\alpha}{n}$. Note that with more samples in D_{cali} (n getting larger), the upper-bound of $P(Y_{test} \in PS(X_{test}))$ is approaching 1. Although the gap between the lower-bound and upper-bound in Eq. (5) is not as tight as the bounds from the previous CP methods (e.g., Eq. (1) from [14]), RR-CP still gives a pair of bounds that is practically tight enough for small values of α.[1] More importantly, RR-CP

---

[1] The user-specified error rate α should be very small for medical application cases.

considers the worst-case scenario for the reliable regions when establishing the lower-bound of the coverage (with $1 - \alpha$), making it more viable to achieve such a bound.

2.4 Limitations

The proposed RR-CP method is designed to achieve an extremely low actual error rate in model deployment for critical applications, such as medical diagnosis. However, the limitation of RR-CP becomes evident in situations where the user-set error rate is high, such as 5% or 10%. This issue arises because the gap between the lower and upper bounds in Eq. 5 increases as α grows larger. Consequently, when dealing with a large user-specified error rate (α), RR-CP might yield an actual error rate that is significantly smaller than the user-specified rate. This particular aspect of RR-CP could be considered a drawback from the conventional perspective of CP methods.

3 Experiments

3.1 Datasets and Setups

Five public medical image classification datasets, OrganAMNIST (11 classes) [6], OrganCMNIST (11 classes) [6], OrganSMNIST (11 classes) [6], BloodMNIST (8 classes) [1], and DermaMNIST (7 classes) [13] (all obtained from the MedMNIST benchmark [16]) are utilized for the experiments. The numbers of samples in the train/val/test sets are 34581/6491/17778 for OrganAMNIST, 13000/2392/8268 for OrganCMNIST, 13940/2452/8829 for OrganSMNIST, 11959/1712/3421 for BloodMNIST, and 7007/1003/2005 for DermaMNIST. For a particular dataset, its training set is used to train a classifier. Here, we use ResNet18 [9] as the classifier for all the experiments. Model weights are obtained from the official release[2]. The validation set is used as the set D_{cali} for estimating the parameters in a CP method, and the test set is used to evaluate the CP method for the actual error rate and its corresponding prediction set size. We compare our RR-CP with the classic CP method [14], the recently developed Regularized Adaptive Prediction Set (RAPS) [4], and Ensemble-RAPS [15]. As discussed above, α (the user-specified/chosen error rate) should be set as a small value for medical use cases. We set $\alpha = 0.005$ for all the methods utilized in the experiments.

3.2 Results

On Achieving the User-Specified Error Rate. In Table 1, we show that our RR-CP achieves the desired error rate (0.005) on four (out of five) datasets, and the competing methods failed to achieve the desired error rate for most of the experiments. Particularly, on OrganAMNIST, RR-CP achieves almost half of the error rates compared to the competing methods. On BloodMNIST, RR-CP

---

[2] https://github.com/MedMNIST/experiments.

gives 54%, 47%, and 34% reductions in the error rate compared to the classic CP, ERAPS, and RAPS, respectively. On OrganCMNIST, all the known CP methods failed to achieve the user-chosen error rate. On OrganSMNIST, RR-CP achieves the desired error rate, and its actual error rate is also significantly lower than those of the competing methods. On DermaMNIST, the classic CP and ERAPS failed to meet the user-specified error rate, while both RR-CP and RAPS satisfy the specified error rate on this dataset.

On Prediction Set Size. Due to the stronger guarantee of satisfying the user-specified error rate, RR-CP is observed to give a relatively large prediction set (see the "PSS" columns in Table 1). As discussed and emphasized in the previous sections, smaller-sized prediction sets are meaningful only when the desired error rate is honored and achieved in deployment. This is especially true and critical for medical and diagnostic use cases, where trading accuracy for smaller prediction set sizes is often unacceptable. The larger-sized prediction sets from RR-CP are needed for the strong guarantee of satisfying the user-specified low error rate (and RR-CP achieves it in most of the experiments). It is worth noting that when RR-CP and RAPS yield a similar level of actual error rate (see the "Derma" column in Table 1), their prediction set sizes are almost the same. This indicates that the sizes of prediction sets generated by RR-CP are reasonably small with respect to the actual error rates it attains. In addition, on OrganA/C/S, we observe that ERAPS yields prediction sets with sizes bigger than half of the largest possible set size. Too relaxed prediction sets, as in the ERAPS case, can make CP less effective for computer-aided diagnosis.

Table 1. Performance comparisons of our RR-CP and known CP methods. The user-specified error rate α is set to be 0.5%. All the methods are evaluated using the test sets of the datasets. The actual error rates that are equal to or smaller than 0.5% are marked in **bold**. AER: actual error rate (%). PSS: prediction set size.

Method	OrganA		Blood		OrganC		OrganS		Derma	
	AER	PSS	AER	PSS	AER	PSS	AER	PSS	AER	PSS
CP [14]	0.78	1.5	0.85	1.2	2.09	1.8	2.25	2.7	0.85	3.2
RAPS [4]	0.79	1.7	0.59	1.3	2.19	1.8	1.60	3.2	**0.16**	4.27
ERAPS [15]	0.96	6.2	0.74	2.0	0.82	8.3	0.88	7.1	0.55	5.2
RR-CP (ours)	**0.42**	2.4	**0.39**	1.6	1.38	2.1	**0.49**	4.8	**0.15**	4.28

4   Conclusions

In this paper, we identified the known CP methods often failed to reach a desired low error rate for medical image classification. We developed a novel, statistically sound, and effective method (RR-CP) for addressing this problem. RR-CP is designed to impose a strong correctness guarantee. Theoretical analyses showed that in the worst case scenario, RR-CP yields an error rate that is the same as the user-specified error rate. Empirical results further validated that, on real data on which the i.i.d. assumption is not exactly held, RR-CP achieved the desired low error rate significantly more often than the known CP methods.

Acknowledgement. This work was supported in part by National Natural Science Foundation of China (62201263) and Natural Science Foundation of Jiangsu Province (BK20220949). S.W. is supported by Shanghai Sailing Programs of Shanghai Municipal Science and Technology Committee (22YF1409300).

References

1. Acevedo, A., Merino, A., Alférez, S., Molina, Á., Boldú, L., Rodellar, J.: A dataset of microscopic peripheral blood cell images for development of automatic recognition systems. Data Brief **30** (2020)
2. Angelopoulos, A.N., Bates, S.: A gentle introduction to conformal prediction and distribution-free uncertainty quantification. arXiv preprint arXiv:2107.07511 (2021)
3. Angelopoulos, A.N., Bates, S., Fisch, A., Lei, L., Schuster, T.: Conformal risk control. arXiv preprint arXiv:2208.02814 (2022)
4. Angelopoulos, A.N., Bates, S., Jordan, M. Malik, J.: Uncertainty sets for image classifiers using conformal prediction. In: International Conference on Learning Representations (2021)
5. Babbar, V., Bhatt, U., Weller, A.: On the utility of prediction sets in human-AI teams. arXiv preprint arXiv:2205.01411 (2022)
6. Bilic, P., et al.: The liver tumor segmentation benchmark (LiTS). Med. Image Anal. **84**, 102680 (2023)
7. Efron, B., Tibshirani, R.J.: An Introduction to the Bootstrap. CRC Press (1994)
8. Fisch, A., Schuster, T., Jaakkola, T., Barzilay, R.: Conformal prediction sets with limited false positives. In: International Conference on Machine Learning, pp. 6514–6532. PMLR (2022)
9. He, K., Zhang, X., Ren, S., Sun, J.: Deep residual learning for image recognition. In: Proceedings of the IEEE Conference on Computer Vision and Pattern Recognition, pp. 770–778 (2016)
10. Lu, C., Angelopoulos, A.N., Pomerantz, S.: Improving trustworthiness of AI disease severity rating in medical imaging with ordinal conformal prediction sets. In Medical Image Computing and Computer Assisted Intervention-MICCAI 2022: 25th International Conference, Singapore, 18–22 September 2022, Proceedings, Part VIII, pp. 545–554. Springer, Cham (2022). https://doi.org/10.1007/978-3-031-16452-1_52
11. Charles, L., Lemay, A., Chang, K., Höbel, K., Kalpathy-Cramer, J.: Fair conformal predictors for applications in medical imaging. Proc. AAAI Conf. Artif. Intell. **36**, 12008–12016 (2022)
12. Romano, Y., Sesia, M., Candes, E.: Classification with valid and adaptive coverage. Adv. Neural. Inf. Process. Syst. **33**, 3581–3591 (2020)
13. Tschandl, P., Rosendahl, C., Kittler, H.: The HAM10000 dataset, a large collection of multi-source dermatoscopic images of common pigmented skin lesions. Sci. Data **5**(1), 1–9 (2018)

14. Vovk, V., Gammerman, A., Saunders, C.: Machine-learning applications of algorithmic randomness. In: International Conference on Machine Learning, pp. 444–453 (1999)
15. Xu, C., Xie, Y.: Conformal prediction set for time-series. arXiv preprint arXiv:2206.07851 (2022)
16. Yang, J., et al.: MedMNIST v2 - a large-scale lightweight benchmark for 2D and 3D biomedical image classification. Sci. Data **10**(1), 41 (2023)

Bayesian Uncertainty Estimation in Landmark Localization Using Convolutional Gaussian Processes

Lawrence Schobs[1]([✉]), Thomas M. McDonald[2], and Haiping Lu[1]

[1] Department of Computer Science, University of Sheffield, Sheffield, UK
`laschobs1@sheffield.ac.uk`
[2] Department of Computer Science, University of Manchester, Manchester, UK

Abstract. Landmark localization is an important step in image analysis, where the clinical definition of a landmark can be ambiguous, leading to a practical necessity for model uncertainty quantification that is rigorous and trustworthy. In this paper, we present the first Bayesian framework using Gaussian processes to capture both dataset-level landmark ambiguity and sample-level model uncertainty. Our proposed two-stage approach includes a deep learning based U-Net for coarse predictions, followed by a convolutional Gaussian process (CGP) for fine-grained predictions with uncertainty estimates, learning covariance matrices rather than using a pre-defined covariance matrix. Our Bayesian approach yields a more rigorous quantification of uncertainty compared to deep learning-based uncertainty estimation techniques, whilst still achieving comparable localization accuracy. Our results suggest that CGPs can better model the inherent uncertainties in landmark localization tasks and provide more reliable confidence estimates, making it a promising direction for future research.

Keywords: Landmark Localization · Gaussian Proccess · Uncertainty · Bayesian

1 Introduction

Automatic landmark localization is a critical component of medical image analysis, encompassing tasks such as image segmentation [2] and image registration [9,15]. However, defining anatomical landmarks with precision can be a challenging endeavor, especially for those situated on smooth edges, such as the corner of the jaw, in contrast to distinctive anatomical structures like the incisor tip [21]. In this regard, it would be preferable for a model to predict the distribution of likely landmark locations rather than a single point estimate. Quantifying the uncertainty associated with landmark predictions is crucial in a clinical setting, where explainability is essential and there is a need for human intervention to correct highly uncertain predictions [6]. Further, it is imperative that the uncertainty quantification can be trusted to represent a mathematically rigorous and

© The Author(s), under exclusive license to Springer Nature Switzerland AG 2023
C. H. Sudre et al. (Eds.): UNSURE 2023, LNCS 14291, pp. 22–31, 2023.
https://doi.org/10.1007/978-3-031-44336-7_3

transparent uncertainty of the model, which is rarely the case for deep learning based approaches.

Current state-of-the-art (SOTA) approaches for landmark localization are deep-learning based, the most popular paradigm being heatmap regression [8, 16,25]. Heatmap regression models perform landmark localization by learning an image-to-image function, where the target is a heatmap of a Gaussian function centered on the landmark of interest. It is noteworthy that conventional training methodologies in heatmap regression models fix the variance of the Gaussian function, preventing the model from modifying its output to reflect elevated or diminished uncertainty in its predictions.

Thaler *et al.* incorporated aleatoric uncertainty directly during training by learning anisotropic Gaussian heatmaps for each landmark. The study demonstrated that the learned heatmap shapes correspond to inter-observer variability from multiple annotators [21]. However, this method only models the homoscedastic aleatoric uncertainty of the dataset, whereby a single covariance matrix is learned over the entire dataset for each landmark during training. At inference, a Gaussian function is fitted to each individual prediction to model heteroscedastic aleatoric uncertainty. Nonetheless, this measure heavily depends on the learned homoscedastic uncertainty, and its post-hoc nature makes it challenging to rely on for a true reflection of model uncertainty. Other existing approaches to estimate landmark uncertainty include using the variance between an ensemble of convolutional neural networks (CNNs) [20], and utilizing Bayesian CNNs to predict confidence intervals [12]. However, these methods rely on deep neural networks, which have been notoriously criticized for their unreliability in terms of calibration [5] and interpretability.

In this study, we depart from the conventional practice of utilizing deep learning and instead employ a Bayesian methodology for landmark localization, relying on Gaussian processes (GPs). GPs are nonparametric statistical models which are robust to both the presence of noisy data and overfitting, even in low-data regimes which can prove challenging for neural network-based techniques [18]. Specifically, we use convolutional Gaussian processes (CGPs), which offer an attractive alternative to deep neural networks for the task of landmark localization. CGPs are constructed using a covariance function which is heavily inspired by the efficient convolutional structure of the kernels used in CNNs [24]. CGPs offer us a mathematically rigorous Bayesian framework for predicting the distribution of likely landmark locations and quantifying model uncertainty. The intrinsically Gaussian nature of the uncertainty estimates generated by CGPs render them an intriguing alternative to the conventional deep learning approaches that aim to predict a Gaussian heatmap (either fixed or learned).

Our contributions are threefold: **(1)** A two stage coarse-to-fine approach using a multi-task CGP for fine predictions and uncertainty estimates, which is the first of its kind for regression. **(2)** A novel approach to initialize inducing patches for the CGP using first-stage prediction information. **(3)** Evaluation of CGP uncertainty estimates against a deep learning baseline CNN method.

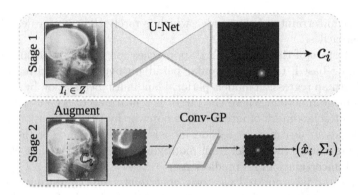

Fig. 1. Overview of our two stage coarse-to-fine framework. We utilize deep learning in Stage 1 to obtain coarse predictions, and refine them in Stage 2 with a convolutional Gaussian process and obtain an uncertainty estimate (covariance).

2 Methods

Due to limitations with the scalability of convolutional Gaussian processes (CGPs), we use a two stage coarse-to-fine approach, outlined in Fig. 1. The first stage uses a CNN to obtain a coarse prediction of the landmark location. Then, the CGP predicts the final landmark distribution using the corresponding cropped patch of the image.

2.1 Stage 1: Coarse Prediction Using U-Net

To obtain our coarse predictions, we design a vanilla U-Net following the template of the original U-Net [19] and nnU-Net [7]. The U-Net follows the standard configuration of two blocks per resolution layer, with each block consisting of a 3×3 convolution, instance normalization [22], and leaky ReLU (negative slope, 0.01). Downsampling is achieved through strided convolutions and upsampling through transposed convolutions. The initial number of feature maps is set to 32, doubling with each downsample to a maximum of 512 and halving at each upsample step. We automatically configure the number of resolution layers by adding encoder steps until any dimension of the feature map resolution hits a minimum of 4. The objective for the model is to learn a Gaussian heatmap image for each landmark, with the centre of the heatmap on the target landmark. For a landmark i with 2D coordinate position $\mathbf{x}_i$, the 2D heatmap image is defined as the 2D Gaussian function:

$$g_i\left(\mathbf{x} \,\|\, \boldsymbol{\mu} = \mathbf{x}_i; \sigma\right) = \frac{1}{(2\pi)\sigma^2} \exp\left(-\frac{\|\mathbf{x} - \boldsymbol{\mu}\|_2^2}{2\sigma^2}\right), \tag{1}$$

where $\mathbf{x}$ is the 2D coordinate vector of each pixel and σ is a user-defined standard deviation. The network learns weights $\mathbf{w}$ and biases $\mathbf{b}$ to predict the heatmap

$h_i(\mathbf{x}; \mathbf{w}, \mathbf{b})$. The objective function is the mean squared error (MSE) between the Gaussian target heatmap and the predicted heatmap. We train on images of size $H \times W$ at this stage, obtaining the coarse predictions of our landmarks, $\mathbf{C}$. For each landmark $\mathbf{x}_i$, we obtain $\mathbf{c}_i$ by selecting the pixel with the highest activation in each heatmap.

2.2   Stage 2: Fine Prediction Using CGP

Following the initial prediction, we extract cropped patches of size $H' \times W', (H' < H, W' < W)$ around each image using our *Stage 1* predictions, $\mathbf{C}$. We then use a multi-task CGP for the final, sub-pixel prediction and uncertainty estimate.

Multi-task Convolutional Gaussian Processes. Gaussian processes (GPs) are powerful nonparametric Bayesian models, gaining popularity due to their ability to provide a rigorous quantification of predictive uncertainty. A GP defines a distribution over functions and is completely specified by a covariance function $k(\cdot, \cdot)$ and a mean function which is commonly assumed to be zero. For an input $\mathbf{I} \in \mathbb{R}^{D_{\text{in}}}$ (e.g. an image), a GP is denoted by $u(\mathbf{I}) \sim \mathcal{GP}(0, k(\mathbf{I}, \mathbf{I}'))$ [18]. The choice of covariance function (also called the *kernel*) affects the variation of the function over the input domain, and many options for the kernel exist. The CNN-inspired *image convolutional kernel* [24] has become the standard tool for applying GPs to computer vision tasks. A GP with this kernel (i.e. a CGP) can be written as,

$$u \sim \mathcal{GP}\left(0, \sum_{p=1}^{P}\sum_{p'=1}^{P} k_g\left(\mathbf{I}^{[p]}, \mathbf{I}'^{[p']}\right)\right), \tag{2}$$

where k_g is a base kernel (e.g. RBF or Matérn) which generates a real-valued response value for a square patch of pixels within the image $\mathbf{I}$. P denotes the total number of patches we can extract from our input image, and is therefore determined by the patch size, which we define to be (5×5). Specifically, we use the weighted kernel proposed by the authors, whereby each patch is additionally assigned a learnable weighting parameter. As in the original work, we take a stochastic variational approach to performing inference, using a set of *inducing patches*. The intuition behind the overall approach is that the inducing patches can be considered as analogous to the filters in a conventional CNN. For further details on the approach we refer the reader to the original work [24] and material on variational inducing points-based inference in GPs [13].

Typically, CGPs are used with a single output. However, for our problem setting, we require a multi-output GP as we wish to predict a 2D coordinate associated with each landmark. To achieve this, we firstly model each output using independent GPs, each with their own separate convolutional kernel, sharing the inducing patches across both outputs. We instantaneously mix the outputs of these two GPs $\mathbf{u} \in \mathbb{R}^2$ using the *linear model of coregionalization* (LMC) [1,10], such that $\mathbf{f} = \mathbf{W}\mathbf{u}$, where $\mathbf{f} \in \mathbb{R}^2$ are our correlated outputs, and $\mathbf{W} \in \mathbb{R}^{2 \times 2}$ is a learnable mixing matrix.

As this is a regression problem, we use a Gaussian likelihood with independent likelihood noise for each spatial dimension, denoted by l_x and l_y. Therefore, for each prediction we obtain the final sub-pixel coordinate prediction $\hat{\mathbf{x}}_i$ from the CGP mean prediction $\mathbf{m}_i$ and a covariance matrix $\boldsymbol{\Sigma}_i$, which is the summation of the LMC covariance and the likelihood noise:

$$\hat{\mathbf{x}}_i = \mathbf{m}_i, \quad \boldsymbol{\Sigma}_i = \mathbf{W}\mathbf{u} + \begin{pmatrix} l_x & 0 \\ 0 & l_y \end{pmatrix}. \tag{3}$$

Inducing Patch Initialization. To initialize the inducing patches, we introduce a bias towards inducing patches proximal to the anticipated landmark location, given by *Stage 1*. We do so because regions in the image near the landmark tend to contain more salient information about its location as compared to regions further away. Therefore, this initialisation sets up a simpler optimisation problem as opposed to choosing the initial patches purely at random. For each inducing patch P, we randomly select an image from the training set and sample a 5×5 patch, selecting a patch centre point P_c by sampling from a Gaussian distribution over the image:

$$P_c \sim g\left(\mu = \mathbf{c}_i; \sigma\right), \tag{4}$$

where g is a 2D Gaussian Distribution (see Eq. (1)), $\mathbf{c}_i$ is the coarse prediction for landmark $\mathbf{x}_i$ from *Stage 1*, and σ is defined by the user.

Neural Network Baseline. To serve as a deep learning baseline for *Stage 2* predictions, we replace the CGP with a compact U-Net architecture. Specifically, we adopt the identical design to the U-Net used in *Stage 1*, with the only difference being a smaller number of layers (due to the use of smaller 64×64 input images). To obtain a comparable likelihood distribution to the CGP, we follow the approach by Thaler *et al.* [21] to fit a 2D Gaussian function to the heatmap prediction, robust least squares fitting method [3], obtaining the sub-pixel mean prediction $\hat{\mathbf{x}}_i$ and covariance matrix $\boldsymbol{\Sigma}_i$.

Training Procedure. We train using mini-batching, maximising the evidence lower bound (ELBO) at each iteration step (or the MSE for the CNN baseline). At each step, we extract a batch of $H' \times W'$ patches from the image batch, centred around the *Stage 1* predictions, $\mathbf{C}$. To prevent overfitting and improve robustness, we implement data augmentation by randomly selecting a new centre point for each patch, $\hat{\mathbf{c}}_i$, each time the data is seen using the following equation:

$$\hat{\mathbf{c}}_i = \mathbf{c}_i + \mathbf{u}, \quad \mathbf{u} \sim U(-D, D)^2, \tag{5}$$

where U is Uniform distribution and $D < \frac{H'}{2}, \frac{W'}{2}$, ensuring the *Stage 1* prediction $\mathbf{c}_i$ is always present in the image patch.

3   Experiments and Analysis

3.1   Dataset

We show results on the publicly available Cephalometric dataset [23], which consists of 400 cephalograms with 19 landmarks, each annotated by a senior and junior expert. We select 3 landmarks representing various difficulty levels: the tip of the chin, the corner of the jaw, and the tip of the incisor (exemplified in Fig. 2). The images are a resolution of 1935×2400 pixels, where each pixel represents 0.1 mm. The images are resized to a resolution of 512×512 pixels, and the final sub-pixel coordinate predictions are scaled to the original resolution. We report results of a 4-fold cross validation (CV) over all 400 images, using the junior annotations only, following convention [14,17,21].

3.2   Metrics

To evaluate the quality of uncertainty estimates in our predictive model, we report the negative log predictive density (NLPD):

$$NLPD = -\log p\left(\mathbf{y}_i | \mathbf{X}_i, \boldsymbol{\Sigma}_i\right) = -\sum_{j=1}^{N} \log p\left(y_i^{(j)} | \hat{\mathbf{x}}_i^{(j)}, \boldsymbol{\Sigma}_i^{(j)}\right), \qquad (6)$$

where $\hat{\mathbf{x}}_i^{(j)}$ is the predicted coordinate for landmark i in image j, $\mathbf{y}_i$ represents the target landmarks for landmark i, $\mathbf{X}_i$ the predicted point-wise estimates, and $\boldsymbol{\Sigma}_i$ the predicted covariances. The NLPD quantifies the likelihood that the predictive distribution contains the true landmark location. Lower NLPD values indicate a better model fit to the data, and thus better uncertainty estimates.

For completeness, we evaluate localization performance using point-to-point error, defined by the Euclidean distance from the predicated coordinate for landmark i in image j, $\hat{\mathbf{x}}_i^{(j)}$, to the target coordinate $\mathbf{x}_i^{(j)}$: $PE(\mathbf{x}_i^{(j)}) = \|\mathbf{x}_i^{(j)} - \hat{\mathbf{x}}_i^{(j)}\|$.

3.3   Implementation Details

All hyperparameter tuning was performed on the first fold of landmark L_1, the tip of the incisor.

Stage 1: For the target Gaussian heatmap in Eq. (1), we use $\sigma = 8$. We train for 500 epochs using stochastic gradient descent with an initial learning rate of 0.01, decaying it using the 'poly' scheme, $(1 - epoch/epoch_{max})^{0.9}$ [4]. One epoch consists of 150 mini-batches, where each mini-batch is 12 samples. We employ early stopping using a hold-out validation set (20% of training set), stopping training if the validation set's localization error does not drop for 150 epochs. We employ data augmentations with a probability of 0.5, uniformly sampling from a continuous range $[\alpha, \omega]$: Random scaling $[0.8, 1.2]$, translation $[-0.07\%,$ $0.07\%]$, rotation $[-45°, 45°]$, shearing $[-16, 16]$ and vertical flipping.

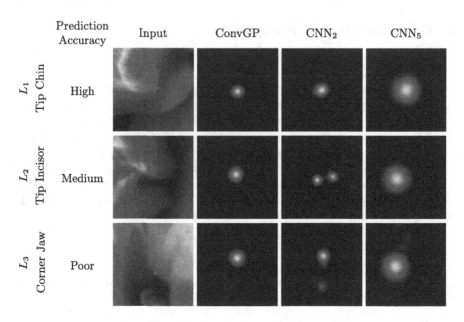

Fig. 2. Figure showing 3 landmarks of varying difficulty and predictions from our method with learned covariances (ConvGP), and 2 deep learning baselines with fixed covariances (CNN$_5$ and CNN$_2$).

Stage 2: We set $H' = W' = 64$ to select a 64×64 patches around the *Stage 1* predictions C, reaching a compromise between capturing enough context in the image patch and computational limitations. For the data augmentation, we select $D = 32$ for Eq. 5, enabling the model to train on a diverse set of images. We do not perform further data augmentation. At test time, we choose the model checkpoint with the lowest validation loss during training.

For the convolutional Gaussian process, we use a stride of 5 when extracting the 5×5 patches, since a stride of 1 is to demanding in terms of memory. We train for 6000 epochs with minibatches of size 6, using the Adam optimizer [11] for stochastic gradient descent with an initial learning rate of 0.01, reducing it after 3000 epochs to 0.001. To prevent the likelihood variance from growing large during optimization and dominating the posterior covariance, we fix it for 3000 epochs. For the inducing patch sampling, we set $\sigma = 1$ for the sampler in Eq. (4), heavily biasing the patch initializations to parts of the image near the *Stage 1* prediction. For the base kernel within the CGP, we use an automatic relevance determination (ARD) Matérn 1/2 kernel, initialized with a lengthscale of 1 for each input dimension, and a variance of 20.

For the CNN baseline, we use the same minibatch size, training length and learning rate schedule as the CGP. We experiment using $\sigma = 2$ and $\sigma = 5$ for Eq. (1) to compare the sensitivity of uncertainty estimates depending on the target heatmap size. The values respectively represent a high and low precision choice for the target heatmap, typically selected through a hyper-parameter search.

Table 1. Localization results from 3 landmarks of the Cepalmetric dataset [23] over a 4-fold CV. The Negative Log Predictive Density is reported (NLPD, lower is better), the mean point-to-point error (PE), in millimeters. Our non deep-learning (DL) method, convolutional Gaussian process (CGP), is compared to two DL baseline methods: CNN_2, CNN_5, which use a heatmap label $\sigma = 2$, $\sigma = 5$, respectively.

	Metric	CGP	CNN_2	CNN_5
		(Learned Covariance)	(Fixed Covariance)	(Fixed Covariance)
All	**NLPD**($\downarrow$)	5.54 ± 2.24	6.83 ± 17.64	5.51 ± 1.87
	PE ($\downarrow$)	1.81 ± 1.11	1.36 ± 1.84	1.15 ± 1.28
L_1	**NLPD** ($\downarrow$)	4.67 ± 1.33	4.30 ± 3.22	5.25 ± 0.23
	PE ($\downarrow$)	1.26 ± 0.76	0.91 ± 0.75	0.87 ± 0.58
L_2	**NLPD** ($\downarrow$	5.35 ± 1.73	5.50 ± 14.14	5.27 ± 0.85
	PE ($\downarrow$)	1.72 ± 1.00	0.84 ± 1.58	0.68 ± 0.93
L_3	**NLPD**($\downarrow$)	6.57 ± 3.55	10.67 ± 35.56	6.02 ± 4.52
	PE ($\downarrow$)	2.46 ± 1.55	2.33 ± 3.19	1.90 ± 2.34

3.4   Results and Discussion

Table 1 shows that our CGP is capable of reliably quantifying predictive uncertainty, achieving an NLPD of 5.54. The CNN with a target heatmap of $\sigma = 5$ (CNN_5) achieves a marginally lower NLPD score of 5.51, despite achieving much better localization error of 1.15 mm compared to the CGP error of 1.84 mm. Notably, an improved mean estimate (PE) will in turn improve the NLPD. Therefore, the fact that the CGP achieves an NLPD within approximately 0.03 of CNN_5 is encouraging.

Moreover, the performance of the CNN model, in terms of both the PE and NLPD, is highly dependent on the hyperparameter σ, resulting in significant variations between CNN_5 and CNN_2. This reflects the limitations of deep learning methods in measuring uncertainty, as the NLPD score is almost entirely dependent on the mean estimate. This is exemplified by the results of CNN_2 on L_3, where a poor PE of 2.33 mm leads to extremely poor uncertainty estimations, resulting in an NLPD score of 10.67. In contrast, the CGP, with a higher PE error of 2.46 mm, still manages to produce more reliable uncertainty estimates, achieving an NLPD score of 6.57. Unlike the CNNs, the covariance of the CGP is learned during training and mathematically grounded, making it a more trustworthy and stable measure of the model's confidence.

Figure 2 highlights how the distribution of the CNN's output heatmap is highly dependent on the value of σ from the target function in Eq. (1), and is uniform across all landmarks. Note, that CNN_2 even has multiple hallucinated covariances. In contrast, the covariances learned by the CGP are distinct for each landmark, but unfortunately show a relatively uniform pattern across predictions of the same landmark. This uniformity is due to the fact that the covariance function was dominated by the likelihood noise during training, resulting in more homogeneous uncertainty estimates than optimal.

4 Conclusion

We showed that convolutional Gaussian processes (CGPs) can be applied to the complex vision task of landmark localization, allowing us to quantify the uncertainty associated with predictions using a nonparametric approach. Empirically, the localization error obtained with CGPs are not yet competitive with those of a CNN. This is attributed to optimization challenges related to the GP likelihood noise, which dominates the output covariance matrices, resulting in relatively uniform uncertainty estimates. Despite this, the CGP obtains a similar NLPD to the CNN baseline, suggesting that if this optimisation issues can be addressed and the predictive error decreased, the uncertainty quantification provided by the CGP would be far superior to that of the CNN. Furthermore, the uncertainty estimates provided by GPs are more rigorous mathematically and more interpretable in practice than those of deep learning. A promising avenue for future work could address the uniformity of the uncertainty estimates by incorporating a heteroscedastic likelihood that produces different likelihood variance outputs for each image.

Acknowledgements. This work was supported by EPSRC (2274702) and the Wellcome Trust (215799/Z/19/Z and 205188/Z/16/Z). Thomas M. McDonald would like to thank the Department of Computer Science at The University of Manchester for their financial support.

References

1. Alvarez, M.A., Lawrence, N.D.: Computationally efficient convolved multiple output Gaussian processes. J. Mach. Learn. Res. **12**, 1459–1500 (2011)
2. Beichel, R., Bischof, H., Leberl, F., Sonka, M.: Robust active appearance models and their application to medical image analysis. IEEE Trans. Med. Imaging **24**(9), 1151–1169 (2005)
3. Branch, M.A., Coleman, T.F., Li, Y.: A subspace, interior, and conjugate gradient method for large-scale bound-constrained minimization problems. SIAM J. Sci. Comput. **21**(1), 1–23 (1999)
4. Chen, L.C., Papandreou, G., Kokkinos, I., Murphy, K., Yuille, A.L.: DeepLab: semantic image segmentation with deep convolutional nets, atrous convolution, and fully connected CRFs. IEEE Trans. Pattern Anal. Mach. Intell. **40**(4), 834–848 (2017)
5. Guo, C., Pleiss, G., Sun, Y., Weinberger, K.Q.: On calibration of modern neural networks. In: Proceedings ICML, pp. 1321–1330. PMLR (2017)
6. Holzinger, A.: Interactive machine learning for health informatics: when do we need the human-in-the-loop? Brain Inf. **3**(2), 119–131 (2016)
7. Isensee, F., Jaeger, P.F., Kohl, S.A., Petersen, J., Maier-Hein, K.H.: nnU-net: a self-configuring method for deep learning-based biomedical image segmentation. Nat. Methods **18**(2), 203–211 (2021)
8. Jiang, Y., Li, Y., Wang, X., Tao, Y., Lin, J., Lin, H.: CephalFormer: incorporating global structure constraint into visual features for general cephalometric landmark detection. In: Wang, L., Dou, Q., Fletcher, P.T., Speidel, S., Li, S. (eds.) Proceedings MICCAI, pp. 227–237. Springer, Cham (2022). https://doi.org/10.1007/978-3-031-16437-8_22

9. Johnson, H.J., Christensen, G.E.: Consistent landmark and intensity-based image registration. IEEE Trans. Med. Imaging **21**(5), 450–461 (2002)
10. Journel, A.G., Huijbregts, C.J.: Mining geostatistics (1976)
11. Kingma, D.P., Ba, J.: Adam: a method for stochastic optimization. arXiv preprint arXiv:1412.6980 (2014)
12. Lee, J.H., Yu, H.J., Kim, M.J., Kim, J.W., Choi, J.: Automated cephalometric landmark detection with confidence regions using Bayesian convolutional neural networks. BMC Oral Health **20**(1), 1–10 (2020)
13. Leibfried, F., Dutordoir, V., John, S., Durrande, N.: A tutorial on sparse Gaussian processes and variational inference. arXiv preprint arXiv:2012.13962 (2020)
14. Lindner, C., Wang, C.W., Huang, C.T., Li, C.H., Chang, S.W., Cootes, T.F.: Fully automatic system for accurate localisation and analysis of cephalometric landmarks in lateral cephalograms. Sci. Rep. **6**(1), 1–10 (2016)
15. Murphy, K., et al.: Semi-automatic construction of reference standards for evaluation of image registration. Med. Image Anal. **15**(1), 71–84 (2011)
16. Payer, C., Štern, D., Bischof, H., Urschler, M.: Integrating spatial configuration into heatmap regression based CNNs for landmark localization. Med. Image Anal. **54**, 207–219 (2019)
17. Payer, C., Urschler, M., Bischof, H., Štern, D.: Uncertainty estimation in landmark localization based on Gaussian heatmaps. In: Sudre, C.H., et al. (eds.) UNSURE/GRAIL -2020. LNCS, vol. 12443, pp. 42–51. Springer, Cham (2020). https://doi.org/10.1007/978-3-030-60365-6_5
18. Rasmussen, C.E.: Gaussian processes in machine learning. In: Bousquet, O., von Luxburg, U., Rätsch, G. (eds.) ML -2003. LNCS (LNAI), vol. 3176, pp. 63–71. Springer, Heidelberg (2004). https://doi.org/10.1007/978-3-540-28650-9_4
19. Ronneberger, O., Fischer, P., Brox, T.: U-Net: convolutional networks for biomedical image segmentation. In: Navab, N., Hornegger, J., Wells, W.M., Frangi, A.F. (eds.) MICCAI 2015. LNCS, vol. 9351, pp. 234–241. Springer, Cham (2015). https://doi.org/10.1007/978-3-319-24574-4_28
20. Schöbs, L., Swift, A.J., Lu, H.: Uncertainty estimation for heatmap-based landmark localization. IEEE Trans. Med Imaging, 1 (2022)
21. Thaler, F., Payer, C., Urschler, M., Štern, D., et al.: Modeling annotation uncertainty with Gaussian heatmaps in landmark localization. J. Mach. Learn. Biomed. Imaging **1**, 1–10 (2021)
22. Ulyanov, D., Vedaldi, A., Lempitsky, V.: Instance normalization: the missing ingredient for fast stylization. arXiv preprint arXiv:1607.08022 (2016)
23. Wang, C.W., et al.: A benchmark for comparison of dental radiography analysis algorithms. Med. Image Anal. **31**, 63–76 (2016)
24. Van der Wilk, M., Rasmussen, C.E., Hensman, J.: Convolutional Gaussian processes. In: Advances in Neural Information Processing Systems, vol. 30 (2017)
25. Zhong, Z., Li, J., Zhang, Z., Jiao, Z., Gao, X.: An attention-guided deep regression model for landmark detection in cephalograms. In: Shen, D., et al. (eds.) MICCAI 2019. LNCS, vol. 11769, pp. 540–548. Springer, Cham (2019). https://doi.org/10.1007/978-3-030-32226-7_60

TriadNet: Sampling-Free Predictive Intervals for Lesional Volume in 3D Brain MR Images

Benjamin Lambert[1,2(✉)], Florence Forbes[3], Senan Doyle[2], and Michel Dojat[1]

[1] University Grenoble Alpes, Inserm, U1216, Grenoble Institut Neurosciences,
38000 Grenoble, France
benjamin.lambert@univ-grenoble-alpes.fr
[2] Pixyl, Research and Development Laboratory, 38000 Grenoble, France
[3] University Grenoble Alpes, Inria, CNRS, Grenoble INP, LJK,
38000 Grenoble, France

Abstract. The volume of a brain lesion (e.g. infarct or tumor) is a powerful indicator of patient prognosis and can be used to guide the therapeutic strategy. Lesional volume estimation is usually performed by segmentation with deep convolutional neural networks (CNN), currently the state-of-the-art approach. However, to date, few work has been done to equip volume segmentation tools with adequate quantitative predictive intervals, which can hinder their usefulness and acceptation in clinical practice. In this work, we propose **TriadNet**, a segmentation approach relying on a multi-head CNN architecture, which provides both the lesion volumes and the associated predictive intervals simultaneously, in less than a second. We demonstrate its superiority over other solutions on BraTS 2021, a large-scale MRI glioblastoma image database. Our implementation of TriadNet is available at https://github.com/benolmbrt/TriadNet.

Keywords: Brain MRI · Uncertainty · Segmentation · Deep Learning

1 Introduction

The lesional volume is a powerful and commonly used biomarker in brain MRI analysis and interpretation. Such an imaging biomarker is a guide to predict the patient's neurological outcome in Stroke [8] or to assess the grade of a Glioblastoma [3]. For Multiple Sclerosis (MS), the evolution of the lesional load between two patient's visits helps to assess the progress of the disease and to personalize his/her treatment [14] and even to predict the disability [19]. For neurodegenerative diseases such as Alzheimer's disease, the brain atrophy is quantified by estimating the volume of different anatomical regions (e.g. hippocampus or amygdala) compared to normative values [5].

Volume estimation is usually carried out through image segmentation, relying on Deep Convolutional Neural Networks (CNNs) trained on an annotated database, comprising both images and their corresponding manual delineations

C. H. Sudre et al. (Eds.): UNSURE 2023, LNCS 14291, pp. 32–41, 2023.
https://doi.org/10.1007/978-3-031-44336-7_4

[10]. CNNs provide a mask, which is generally correct for easy detectable regions or lesions, but whose accuracy may be more uncertain when the zone to segment is disputable even for an expert. To help clinicians to focus on the more subtle regions, we propose to associate quantitative Predictive Intervals (PIs) to volume estimation. Such PIs can straightforwardly be interpreted as uncertainty markers and facilitate the acceptance of advanced computerized tools by practitioners.

PI construction has been mainly studied in the context of 1D regression tasks [12,17,22] and applications in the context of medical image processing are very scarce. To compute PIs for lesion counting in 2D medical images, reference work proposes either a sampling approach or a regression model [6]. In the former, several plausible and diverse segmentation masks are generated for the same input image, forming a distribution over the quantity of interest (e.g. lesion volume or number), from which the mean and the standard deviation can be extracted to define a PI. This Uncertainty Quantification (UQ) methodology offers several variants to generate the diverse set of predictions. Popular UQ methods include the Monte Carlo Dropout (MC) [7], Deep Ensemble [13], or Test Time Augmentation (TTA) [23]. Based on sampling, UQ methods are associated with an important computational burden to obtain the predictions. With the regression approach, a network is trained to directly predict the PI's components: the mean value as well as the lower and upper bounds from the data themselves. As no assumptions are made regarding the distribution of the regressed variable, this approach is referred to as Distribution-Free Uncertainty Quantification (DFUQ) [17]. In this direction, we introduce a sampling-free approach based on an original CNN architecture called TriadNet which exhibits the following assets:

- It enhances the 3D volume estimation with associated fast and reliable PIs.
- The methodology is simple to implement and can be applied to any encoder-decoder segmentation architecture.

2 Problem Definition

We consider a 3D segmentation problem with N classes. Excluding the background class, we aim at estimating the true unknown volumes $Y \in \mathbb{R}^{N-1}$ of each foreground classes based on the predicted segmentation. In this context, for an estimation X of the volume, seen as a random variable, we define a predictive interval $\Gamma_\alpha(X)$ as a range of values that are conditioned to contain Y, the actual volume, with a certain degree of confidence $1 - \alpha$ (e.g. 90% or 95%). That is, given a series of estimated volumes $X_1 \ldots X_n$ and their associated ground truth volumes $Y_1 \ldots Y_n$, $\Gamma_\alpha(\cdot)$ should be learned as to satisfy:

$$P(Y_{\text{test}} \in \Gamma_\alpha(X_{\text{test}})) \geq 1 - \alpha \tag{1}$$

for any $(Y_{\text{test}}, X_{\text{test}})$ following the same distribution as the (Y_i, X_i)'s. This property is called the *marginal coverage*, as the probability is marginal over the entire test dataset [1].

Sampling-based PI estimation methods rely on the hypothesis that X follows a normal distribution for each predicted class. Under this assumption, the mean value μ_X and standard deviation σ_X of the distribution are estimated by sampling several distinct predictions for the same input, and PI are constructed as $\Gamma_\alpha(X) = [\mu_X - z\sigma_X, \mu_X + z\sigma_X]$ where z is the number of standard deviation, stipulating the degree of confidence of the interval. For instance, for a 90% confidence interval, z corresponds to 1.65. In contrast, direct PI estimation techniques (including regression approaches and our proposed TriadNet) directly output the mean value μ, the lower bound l_b and the upper bound u_b ($l_b \leq \mu \leq u_b$), without sampling.

3   Our Solution: TriadNet

Overview: TriadNet corresponds to a CNN model modified in order to produce three outputs for each segmented class: the mean, lower bound and upper bound masks (see Fig. 1). To obtain these distinct masks, we propose a multi-head architecture as well as a novel learning objective, the TriadLoss. The masks are then used to directly estimate the class-wise mean volume as well as the lower and upper bounds, by summing the segmented voxels.

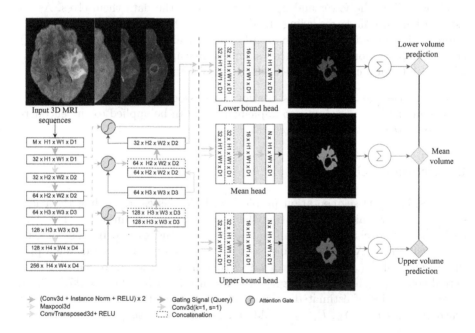

Fig. 1. The Triadnet architecture. Each head yields a distinct mask for each class: lower bound, mean and upper bound masks. For ease of visualization, we only represent for a Glioblastoma application, the masks for the *edematous* class.

TriadNet: The Architecture relies on the Attention Unet 3d (AttUNet3d) [16] as backbone. We modified it by duplicating the output convolutional block in order to obtain a total of 3 separate and identical heads. Each head generates a specific mask: respectively, one corresponding to the lower bound, one to the upper bound, and one for the mean value, by predicting a probabilistic distribution $p_{n,i}$ over the N classes and for each voxel i. This modification only slighly increase the complexity of the segmentation model, raising the number of parameters from 5 millions to 5.3 millions.

TriadLoss: The Objective Function is built on the observation that the lower bound mask should be more restrictive (*i.e.* higher precision and lower recall) than the mean mask. Similarly, the upper bound mask should be more permissive (*i.e.* higher recall and lower precision). To achieve this, we propose to rely on the Tversky loss [20], which provides a direct control on the trade-off between recall and precision. The Tversky loss $T_{\alpha,\beta}$ is an extension of the popular Dice loss [15], with 2 extra hyperparameters α and β which respectively control the weighting of False Positives (FP) and False Negatives (FN). With $\alpha = \beta = 0.5$, the Tversky loss is strictly equivalent to the standard Dice loss.

Writing p_{lower}, p_{mean} and p_{upper} the outputs of each head and y the ground-truth segmentation, we defined the Triad loss as:

$$\text{TriadLoss} = T_{1-\gamma,\gamma}(p_{lower,y}) + T_{0.5,0.5}(p_{mean,y}) + T_{\gamma,1-\gamma}(p_{upper,y}) \qquad (2)$$

with γ an hyperparameter in the range $[0, 0.5]$ controlling the penalties applied to FP and FN during the training of the lower and upper bound heads. In other words, the mean decoder was trained with a standard Dice Loss. To obtain more restrictive masks (and lower volumes), the lower bound decoder was trained to minimize FP at the expense of a higher FN rate. Similarly, to obtain more permissive masks (and larger volumes), the upper bound decoder sought to minimize FN at the expense of a higher number of FP.

4   Material and Methods

4.1   Datasets

We illustrate our framework on a brain tumor segmentation task, using the open-source part of the BraTS 2021 dataset [2] containing 1251 patients. Four MRI sequences are available for each patient: FLAIR, T1, T2, and T1ce (T1w with contrast agent). The ground truth segmentation masks contain 4 classes: the background, the necrotic tumor core, the edematous, and the GD-enhancing (GDE) tumor. We randomly split the data into a training fold (651), a calibration fold (200), and a testing fold (400).

4.2   Comparison with Known Approaches

We compared TriadNet with 3 sampling-based approaches: Confidence Thresholding (CT), Monte Carlo dropout (MC), and Test Time Augmentation (TTA), as well as a sampling-free PI estimation framework based on the training of a regression CNN (RegCNN).

Confidence Thresholding (CT) is a simple approach to obtain PI's from the output probability estimates produced by a trained segmentation model. For each class, the probability map is binarized with progressively increasing thresholds. As the threshold increases, fewer voxels are segmented, thus the volume decreases. As this method relies on the calibration of the output probabilities, we perform Temperature Scaling [9] on the trained segmentation model before performing CT.

Monte Carlo Dropout (MC) is based on the Dropout technique [21] which consists of turning a subset of the model parameters off, to prevent overfitting. The MC dropout technique proposes to keep dropout activated during inference, meaning that T forward steps of the same image through the MC dropout model will lead to T different segmentations (and thus volume estimates), as the dropout mask is randomly sampled at each step.

Test Time Augmentation (TTA) consists in using data augmentation to generate alternative versions of the input images. Each augmented image is processed by the segmentation model, yielding to a distinct estimation of the volumes. By repeating this process, a distribution over volumes can be obtained, from which the PI is derived.

Regression CNN (RegCNN) proposes to train a regression neural network to directly predict the lower, mean and upper bounds of the target quantity from the data itself [1,6]. To achieve this, the Pinball loss P_t can be used to train the model to predict a desired quantile t. In our study, the regressor took as input the MRI sequences and automated segmentation produced by a segmentation model and was trained to predict three scores for each segmentation class, namely the $q_{\alpha/2}$, $q_{0.5}$ and $q_{1-\alpha/2}$ quantiles, allowing the construction of $(1-\alpha)\%$ confidence intervals. To do so, the regressor was trained with a compound loss $L = P_{\alpha/2} + P_{0.5} + P_{1-\alpha/2}$ to learn each quantile.

4.3   Post-hoc PI Calibration

In practice, the predicted PIs may be inaccurate and not respect the desired *marginal coverage* property. To alleviate this, PI post-hoc calibration is usually performed using a set-aside calibration dataset [1]. This calibration step aims at finding the optimal corrective value q such that the calibrated PIs achieve the desired $(1-\alpha)\%$ coverage on the calibration dataset.

In the case of sampling-based PI, the corrective value takes the form of a multiplicative factor applied to the standard deviation (Eq. 3). Alternatively, if the PI estimation is direct, q corresponds to an additive factor applied to the lower and upper bounds (Eq. 4):

$$\Gamma_{\alpha,\text{cal}}(X) = [\mu_X - q\sigma_X, \mu_X + q\sigma_X] \tag{3}$$

$$\Gamma_{\alpha,\text{cal}}(X) = [l_b - q, u_b + q] \tag{4}$$

4.4 Evaluation

We performed all our experiments with $\alpha = 0.1$, meaning that we focussed on 90% PIs. Segmentation performance was assessed using the Dice score (DSC) between the predicted segmentation and the ground truth delineations (for TriadNet, the Dice was computed using the *mean* predicted mask). We also used the Mean Average Error (MAE) between the estimated mean volumes and the true volumes to assess the reliability of the volume prediction.

Useful PIs should have two properties. They should i) achieve the desired *marginal coverage* and ii) be the narrowest possible in order to be informative. To verify this, we computed two scores for PIs: the coverage error (Δf) and the interval width (W). Δf is defined as the distance between the empirical coverage and target coverage (90%). W is the average distance between the lower and upper bounds. Note that a successful PI calibration should ensure $\Delta f \geq 0$. However, as the width of intervals tend to augment with Δf, a value close to 0 is preferred. To estimate computational efficiency, we also reported the average time to produce a segmentation and PI for one input MRI volume.

To assess the impact of the choice of the γ hyper-parameter in the TriadLoss on PI quality, we trained Triadnet models with varying γ values, ranging from 0.1 to 0.4. To obtain robust statistics, each model is trained 5 times and we reported the average and standard deviation for each metrics.

4.5 Implementation Details

Three types of segmentation models are used in this study. First, *Baseline* AttUnet3d was trained to serve as a common basis for the implementation of CT, TTA and RegCNN approaches. For MC, we trained a dedicated *Dropout* AttUnet3ds by adding a dropout rate of 20% in each layer of the encoder and decoder. The last type of segmentation model was our proposed TriadNet. All models were trained with the ADAM optimizer [11], with a learning rate of $2e^-4$, using the Dice loss for *Baseline* and *Dropout* models and the TriadLoss for TriadNet. For CT-based PIs, we used 20 different thresholds uniformly distributed in the range $[0.01, 0.99]$ to binarize the probability maps. For MC dropout, we performed $T = 20$ forward passes of the same input image with dropout activated to obtain the PIs. To implement the TTA baseline, we generated 20 random augmentations for each input MRI using flipping, rotation, translation and contrast augmentation with randomized parameters, implemented using the TorchIO Data Augmentation library [18]. Finally for RegCNN, we used an open-source regressor CNN implementation [4].

5   Results and Discussion

Table 1 presents the performance of segmentation (DSC) and PIs for each app-roach and for all 3 segmented tumor tissues; and Table 2, the average computa-tion time for each method. Finally, Fig. 2 provides an illustration of PI computed by our proposed TriadNet on the test dataset.

Table 1. Performances for each tumor tissue for each method. Δf: coverage error, W: average interval width. Mean scores obtained over 5 runs. SD: standard deviation.

	Method	Δf (%±SD)	W ↓ (mL±SD)	MAE ↓ (mL±SD)	DSC ↑ (±SD)
Necrotic	CT	5.6 ± 1.5	32.3 ± 5.3	3.4 ± 0.1	**0.76 ± 0.00**
	TTA	6.3 ± 1.1	25.0 ± 3.7	3.5 ± 0.1	**0.76 ± 0.00**
	RegCNN	6.1 ± 1.7	25.8 ± 5.7	6.3 ± 3.6	**0.76 ± 0.00**
	MC dropout	5.6 ± 0.6	20.6 ± 2.1	3.3 ± 0.1	**0.76 ± 0.00**
	TriadNet ($\gamma = 0.1$)	4.5 ± 0.8	14.5 ± 1.4	3.4 ± 0.1	0.75 ± 0.00
	TriadNet ($\gamma = 0.2$)	**3.4 ± 0.6**	**13.7 ± 1.1**	**3.2 ± 0.1**	**0.76 ± 0.00**
	TriadNet ($\gamma = 0.3$)	4.1 ± 0.9	15.0 ± 0.4	3.3 ± 0.1	**0.76 ± 0.01**
	TriadNet ($\gamma = 0.4$)	4.4 ± 0.4	16.6 ± 0.8	3.4 ± 0.1	0.75 ± 0.00
Edematous	CT	1.4 ± 1.2	54.4 ± 12.3	8.2 ± 0.9	**0.85 ± 0.01**
	TTA	-1.3 ± 2.3	34.9 ± 2.5	7.7 ± 0.2	**0.85 ± 0.01**
	RegCNN	1.7 ± 0.9	41.9 ± 1.7	9.2 ± 0.4	**0.85 ± 0.01**
	MC dropout	**-0.01 ± 1.4**	32.0 ± 2.0	7.5 ± 0.2	0.84 ± 0.01
	TriadNet ($\gamma = 0.1$)	0.9 ± 0.7	31.8 ± 0.8	7.4 ± 0.5	**0.85 ± 0.00**
	TriadNet ($\gamma = 0.2$)	1.6 ± 1.2	**30.2 ± 1.7**	7.2 ± 0.2	**0.85 ± 0.00**
	TriadNet ($\gamma = 0.3$)	3.2 ± 1.6	35.7 ± 4.3	**7.1 ± 0.2**	**0.85 ± 0.00**
	TriadNet ($\gamma = 0.4$)	1.4 ± 0.7	31.1 ± 2.2	7.5 ± 0.3	0.84 ± 0.01
GDE	CT	3.6 ± 1.4	17.8 ± 3.5	2.0 ± 0.0	**0.85 ± 0.01**
	TTA	3.0 ± 1.8	10.6 ± 1.0	2.0 ± 0.1	**0.85 ± 0.01**
	RegCNN	**0.7 ± 0.5**	22.2 ± 5.9	3.2 ± 0.3	**0.85 ± 0.01**
	MC dropout	3.5 ± 1.3	10.0 ± 0.5	1.9 ± 0.1	**0.85 ± 0.01**
	TriadNet ($\gamma = 0.1$)	3.7 ± 1.1	11.0 ± 0.6	**1.8 ± 0.1**	**0.85 ± 0.00**
	TriadNet ($\gamma = 0.2$)	4.2 ± 1.4	**8.9 ± 0.5**	**1.8 ± 0.1**	**0.85 ± 0.00**
	TriadNet ($\gamma = 0.3$)	4.1 ± 0.4	9.3 ± 0.6	**1.8 ± 0.1**	**0.85 ± 0.00**
	TriadNet ($\gamma = 0.4$)	4.0 ± 0.5	11.0 ± 0.4	1.9 ± 0.1	**0.85 ± 0.00**

Table 2. Average prediction time to obtain a segmentation of a 3D MRI volume associated to predictive intervals on the volumes. SD=standard deviation

	CT	TTA	RegCNN	MC	TriadNet
Time (s±SD) ↓	1.1 ± 0.1	14.3 ± 1.2	**0.3 ± 0.1**	6.4 ± 0.1	0.6 ± 0.1

Most methods provide PIs that, after calibration, achieve the target *marginal coverage* property ($\Delta f \geq 0$). In terms of interval width (W), the narrowest inter-vals are provided by our proposed TriadNet parameterized by $\gamma = 0.2$, while MC dropout ranks as the second best approach. To estimate the significance of this result, two-sided paired t-test between both methods were performed, showing that TriadNet's PI are significantly narrower compared to MC dropout ones

($p < 0.05$ for each tumor class). The best volume estimation, computed using the MAE, is also obtained by TriadNet, while RegCNN estimation is systematically the worst. In terms of segmentation quality (DSC scores), all models achieve very similar performances. Finally, regarding computational efficiency (Table 2), RegCNN appears as the fastest approach, followed by TriadNet, both producing segmentation and associated PIs in less than one second for an input MRI volume. As expected, sampling approaches are much more time-consuming, with MC and TTA being respectively 10 and 24 times slower than our proposed TriadNet.

The choice of the γ parameter in the TriadLoss has proved to be important, with an optimal PI quality reached for $\gamma = 0.2$, equivalent to a weighting of 0.8 for FP and 0.2 for FN in the lower bound head; and 0.2 for FP and 0.8 for FN in the upper bound head. This setting allows the different masks (lower, mean and upper) to be different enough to allow a reliable PI estimation, which is not the case with higher γ values ($\gamma = 0.3$ and $\gamma = 0.4$). However when γ is lower ($\gamma = 0.1$), the penalty on FP and FN is too small, which yields to a larger amount of erroneous predictions, lowering PI quality.

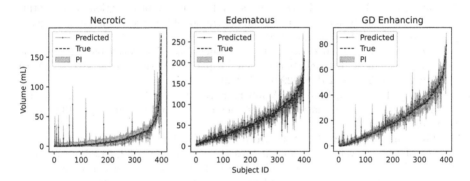

Fig. 2. Predictive intervals generated by TriadNet ($\gamma = 0.2$) on the test dataset.

6   Conclusion

In this work, we addressed the problem of constructing PIs associated to 3D brain MR segmented volumes. Our proposed TriadNet provides narrower and thus more informative intervals in practice compared to competing methods, while preserving the desired *marginal coverage* property. Interestingly, it is also 10 times faster than the second best baseline, MC dropout, making it suitable for clinical routine. Finally, it only requires a minor modification of the segmentation architecture, which has no negative impact on segmentation quality. Future work will investigate the robustness of TriadNet's predictive intervals in the presence of domain shift, and evaluate how our approach behaves with respect to the size of the target region, ranking from very small targets (e.g. the hippocampus region or MS lesions) to very large (e.g. the overall grey matter volume).

References

1. Angelopoulos, A.N., Bates, S.: A gentle introduction to conformal prediction and distribution-free uncertainty quantification. arXiv preprint arXiv:2107.07511 (2021)
2. Baid, U., Ghodasara, S., et al.: The RSNA-ASNR-MICCAI BraTS 2021 benchmark on brain tumor segmentation and radiogenomic classification. arXiv preprint arXiv:2107.02314 (2021)
3. Baris, M.M., Celik, A.O., et al.: Role of mass effect, tumor volume and peritumoral edema volume in the differential diagnosis of primary brain tumor and metastasis. Clin. Neurol. Neurosurg. **148**, 67–71 (2016)
4. Cardoso, M.J., et al.: MONAI: an open-source framework for deep learning in healthcare. arXiv preprint arXiv:2211.02701 (2022)
5. Contador, J., Pérez-Millán, A., et al.: Longitudinal brain atrophy and CSF biomarkers in early-onset Alzheimer's disease. NeuroImage Clin. **32**, 102804 (2021)
6. Eaton-Rosen, Z., Varsavsky, T., Ourselin, S., Cardoso, M.J.: As easy as 1, 2...4? Uncertainty in counting tasks for medical imaging. In: Shen, D., et al. (eds.) MICCAI 2019. LNCS, vol. 11767, pp. 356–364. Springer, Cham (2019). https://doi.org/10.1007/978-3-030-32251-9_39
7. Gal, Y., Ghahramani, Z.: Dropout as a Bayesian approximation: representing model uncertainty in deep learning. In: International Conference on Machine Learning, vol. 48, pp. 1050–1059 (2016)
8. Ghoneem, A., Osborne, M.T., et al.: Association of socioeconomic status and infarct volume with functional outcome in patients with ischemic stroke. JAMA Netw. Open **5**(4), e229178–e229178 (2022)
9. Guo, C., Pleiss, G., Sun, Y., Weinberger, K.Q.: On calibration of modern neural networks. In: International Conference on Machine Learning, pp. 1321–1330. PMLR (2017)
10. Hesamian, M.H., Jia, W., et al.: Deep learning techniques for medical image segmentation: achievements and challenges. J. Digit. Imaging **32**, 582–596 (2019)
11. Kingma, D.P., Ba, J.: Adam: a method for stochastic optimization. In: 3rd International Conference on Learning Representations, ICLR 2015 (2015)
12. Kivaranovic, D., Johnson, K.D., Leeb, H.: Adaptive, distribution-free prediction intervals for deep networks. In: International Conference on Artificial Intelligence and Statistics, pp. 4346–4356 (2020)
13. Lakshminarayanan, B., Pritzel, A., Blundell, C.: Simple and scalable predictive uncertainty estimation using deep ensembles. Adv. Neural. Inf. Process. Syst. **30**, 6402–6413 (2017)
14. Mattiesing, R.M., Gentile, G., et al.: The spatio-temporal relationship between white matter lesion volume changes and brain atrophy in clinically isolated syndrome and early multiple sclerosis. NeuroImage Clin. **36**, 103220 (2022)
15. Milletari, F., Navab, N., Ahmadi, S.A.: V-Net: fully convolutional neural networks for volumetric medical image segmentation. In: 2016 Fourth International Conference on 3D Vision (3DV), pp. 565–571 (2016)
16. Oktay, O., Schlemper, J., et al.: Attention U-Net: learning where to look for the pancreas. In: Medical Imaging with Deep Learning (MIDL) (2018)
17. Pearce, T., Brintrup, A., et al.: High-quality prediction intervals for deep learning: a distribution-free, ensembled approach. In: International Conference on Machine Learning, pp. 4075–4084 (2018)

18. Pérez-García, F., Sparks, R., Ourselin, S.: Torchio: a python library for efficient loading, preprocessing, augmentation and patch-based sampling of medical images in deep learning. Comput. Methods Programs Biomed. **208**, 106236 (2021)
19. Roca, P., Attye, A., et al.: Artificial intelligence to predict clinical disability in patients with multiple sclerosis using flair MRI. Diagn. Interv. Imaging **101**(12), 795–802 (2020)
20. Salehi, S.S.M., Erdogmus, D., Gholipour, A.: Tversky loss function for image segmentation using 3D fully convolutional deep networks. In: Wang, Q., Shi, Y., Suk, H.-I., Suzuki, K. (eds.) MLMI 2017. LNCS, vol. 10541, pp. 379–387. Springer, Cham (2017). https://doi.org/10.1007/978-3-319-67389-9_44
21. Srivastava, N., Hinton, G., et al.: Dropout: a simple way to prevent neural networks from overfitting. J. Mach. Learn. Res. **15**(1), 1929–1958 (2014)
22. Tagasovska, N., Lopez-Paz, D.: Single-model uncertainties for deep learning. In: Advances in Neural Information Processing Systems, vol. 32 (2019)
23. Wang, G., Li, W., Aertsen, M., Deprest, J., Ourselin, S., Vercauteren, T.: Aleatoric uncertainty estimation with test-time augmentation for medical image segmentation with convolutional neural networks. Neurocomputing **338**, 34–45 (2019)

Examining the Effects of Slice Thickness on the Reproducibility of CT Radiomics for Patients with Colorectal Liver Metastases

Jacob J. Peoples[1(✉)], Mohammad Hamghalam[1,2], Imani James[3],
Maida Wasim[3], Natalie Gangai[3], HyunSeon Christine Kang[4],
Xiujiang John Rong[5], Yun Shin Chun[6], Richard K. G. Do[3],
and Amber L. Simpson[1,7]

[1] School of Computing, Queen's University, Kingston, ON, Canada
jacob.peoples@queensu.ca
[2] Department of Electrical Engineering, Qazvin Branch, Islamic Azad University, Qazvin, Iran
[3] Department of Radiology, Memorial Sloan Kettering Cancer Center, New York, NY, USA
[4] Department of Abdominal Imaging, The University of Texas MD Anderson Cancer Center, Houston, TX, USA
[5] Department of Imaging Physics, The University of Texas MD Anderson Cancer Center, Houston, TX, USA
[6] Department of Surgical Oncology, The University of Texas MD Anderson Cancer Center, Houston, TX, USA
[7] Department of Biomedical and Molecular Sciences, Queen's University, Kingston, ON, Canada

Abstract. We present an analysis of 81 patients with colorectal liver metastases from two major cancer centers prospectively enrolled in an imaging trial to assess reproducibility of radiomic features in contrast-enhanced CT. All scans were reconstructed with different slice thicknesses and levels of iterative reconstruction. Radiomic features were extracted from the liver parenchyma and largest metastasis from each reconstruction, using different levels of resampling and methods of feature aggregation. The prognostic value of reproducible features was tested using Cox proportional hazards to model overall survival in an independent, public data set of 197 hepatic resection patients with colorectal liver metastases. Our results show that larger differences in slice thickness reduced the concordance of features ($p < 10^{-6}$). Extracting features with 2.5D aggregation and no axial resampling produced the most robust features, and the best test-set performance in the survival model on the independent data set (C-index = 0.65). Across all feature extraction methods, restricting the survival models to use reproducible

Supplementary Information The online version contains supplementary material available at https://doi.org/10.1007/978-3-031-44336-7_5.

features had no statistically significant effect on the test set performance ($p = 0.98$). In conclusion, our results show that feature extraction settings can positively impact the robustness of radiomics features to variations in slice thickness, without negatively effecting prognostic performance.

Keywords: Radiomics · Reproducibility · Colorectal liver metastases · Imaging biomarkers · Computed tomography · Prospective studies

1   Introduction

Radiomics is the quantitative mining of medical imaging data for insight into patient health [7]. The field has seen rapid development over the last decade [11], but clinical uptake remains limited. A deeper understanding of the robustness of radiomics models is required to see acceptance for clinical use [28]. A key aspect of ensuring the robustness of radiomics models is to understand the robustness of the model inputs – that is, to understand the stability and reliability of radiomics features. Understanding the reproducibility of radiomic features, however, is difficult given the many factors affecting the results [31]. While standardisation efforts such as Image Biomarker Standardisation Initiative (IBSI) [34] are helpful to create a common nomenclature and a standard set of well-defined features, such initiatives still leave many parameters of feature extraction unfixed.

Slice thickness is one major parameter to which computed tomography (CT) radiomics have been shown to be sensitive. Feature values have been shown to be unstable when extracted from images with different slice thicknesses in a variety of phantom studies [1,6,12,15,17,29,32]. Studies examining multiple reconstructions for each scan have reproduced this result on images from patients with lung cancer [4,5,19,21,30], and liver metastases [20]. Instability with respect to slice thickness is concerning because many retrospective or multi-site data sets include images with a range of slice thicknesses due to variations in local protocols [6]. Although image interpolation to a common, isotropic voxel size is considered a best practice for preprocessing during feature extraction [34], it appears, on its own, to be insufficient to overcome the instability of features due to slice thickness variation, except in a small subset of features [9,10].

In this work, we prospectively collected portal venous phase CT scans from 81 colorectal liver metastases (CRLM) patients across two sites, systematically varying the image reconstruction in order to study the stability of radiomics features across images with varied slice thicknesses. We extracted radiomics features using different levels of resampling, and different approaches to aggregating the feature values across slices, in order to determine if these extractor settings could improve feature stability. Finally, we included a radiomics-based survival analysis of a public CRLM data set [26] to verify that the features we identified as reproducible in our main analysis were still useful for radiomics modeling.

2   Methods

2.1   CT Imaging and Segmentation

Contrast enhanced, portal venous phase CT scans were prospectively collected from a total of 81 patients with CRLM from two institutions, Memorial Sloan Kettering Cancer Center (New York, NY) (MSK) (n=44) and MD Anderson Cancer Center (Houston, TX) (MDA) (n=37), with institutional review board approval and informed consent. Every scan was collected on a multi-detector CT scanner (Discovery CT750 HD; GE Healthcare, Madison, WI, USA) with 64 detector rows. The images were collected with kVp 120, noise index in the range of 12–16, rotation time of 0.7–0.8 ms, and reconstructed with the standard soft tissue kernel. Tube current varied between sites, with AutomA 220–380 mA for MSK and 250–565 mA for MDA. Each scan was reconstructed with different slice thicknesses (2.5 mm, 3.75 mm, 5 mm), and levels of adaptive statistical iterative reconstruction (ASiR) (0% to 60% in increments of 10%), giving a total of 3 × 7 = 21 reconstructions. A single reconstruction setting which was closest to the clinical protocol used at MSK (slice thickness 5 mm and ASiR 20%) was chosen as the reference reconstruction for each patient, for which a segmentation was generated separating voxels from the liver parenchyma, metastases, and vessels. The segmentation was completed in two phases: an automated segmentation was generated, then corrected by an experienced radiologist (R. Do (R. D.)) using 3D Slicer [14]. The initial segmentations were generated using an nnU-net [13] trained on a public database of 197 CT scans from patients with CRLM [25,26], available from the Cancer Imaging Archive [3]. Segmentations for other slice thicknesses were automatically generated using nearest-neighbour resampling.

2.2   Radiomic Feature Extraction

Features were extracted from every image using `pyradiomics` [8]. Two regions of interest (ROIs) were used: the largest liver tumor, and the liver parenchyma (with all tumors and vessels excluded). The `pyradiomics` library has seven default classes of features: shape, first order, gray level co-occurrence matrix (GLCM), gray level dependence matrix (GLDM), gray level size zone matrix (GLSZM), gray level run length matrix (GLRLM), neighboring gray-tone difference matrix (NGTDM). We used all default features from all classes with the exception of 10 excluded unnormalized features (explained below), giving a total of 83 features from each ROI, broken down by class in Table 1(a). Shape features were excluded because there was only one reference segmentation per patient.

For every image, features were extracted with eight distinct approaches to image resampling and texture feature aggregation, as shown in Table 1(b). We considered three different levels of resampling: $1 \times 1 \times 1$ mm, $0.85 \times 0.85 \times 0.85$ mm, and $0.85 \times 0.85 \times 2.5$ mm, where 0.85 mm was chosen as the median in-plane pixel spacing in the data set. In the naming scheme in Table 1, the letters L (large), S (small), and A (anisotropic) refer respectively to these resampling settings. For each resampling we took two approaches to texture feature aggregation: one full

Table 1. (a) Feature class breakdown. (b) Feature extraction methods.

Class	Count	Aggregation 2.5D	3D
First order	17		
GLCM	24	JJUI	ITBB
NGTDM	2	62GR	KOBO
GLDM	12	62GR	KOBO
GLRLM	14	JJUI	ITBB
GLSZM	14	62GR	KOBO

(a)

Name	In-plane	Axial	Aggregation
L2i	1	None	2.5D
L2	1	1	2.5D
L3	1	1	3D
S2i	0.85	None	2.5D
S2	0.85	0.85	2.5D
S3	0.85	0.85	3D
A2	0.85	2.5	2.5D
A3	0.85	2.5	3D

Resampling (mm)

(b)

3D approach, and the other 2.5D, as classified by IBSI [33,34], and indicated by the numbers 3 and 2 respectively in the naming scheme. The details of the 2.5D and 3D aggregation methods vary by feature class, but the key difference is that in computing the matrices underlying each feature class, 3D methods treat voxels in adjacent slices as potential neighbours, while 2.5D aggregation only considers neighboring pixels inside the current slice. The IBSI reference manual [33] abbreviations for the aggregation methods used are given in Table 1(a). Finally, we explored resampling the images in-plane only, indicated by a lower case "i" in the naming scheme. All feature extractions were completed using a discretisation level of 24 bins for texture features, and a resegmentation window of $[-50, 350]$ Hounsfield units (HU). Images were interpolated using B-splines.

As recommended by IBSI [34], 3D aggregation was avoided when not resampling all three dimensions. Furthermore, because several features are known to be unnormalized with respect to voxel volume and voxel count [9], we implemented a custom procedure to detect unnormalized features. Using the reference image from each patient, we generated an identical image with 2.5 mm slice thickness by splitting every voxel in half, axially. These image pairs are identical in space, so normalized 2.5D features should be equal between the two. We used this test to identify 10 unnormalized features, listed in supplementary Table S1, which were removed from the feature sets before doing the reproducibility analysis.

2.3 Reproducibility Analysis

The first phase of the analysis was restricted to the reference ASiR level of 20%, and used the concordance correlation coefficient (CCC) [18] to measure reproducibility of features. Taking 5 mm as the reference slice thickness, the pairwise CCC was computed for every feature comparing the reference with both the 2.5 mm and 3.75 mm reconstructions. The Wilcoxon signed-rank test was used to test the significance of the change in CCC between slice thicknesses.

The second phase of the analysis used a linear mixed model (LMM) for each feature in order to compute a generalized CCC using the data from all three slice thicknesses [2]. The reconstructions with different ASiR levels were also included, and controlled for as a fixed-effect. Because first-order features are not affected by aggregation settings, they were analyzed separately from the texture features. We removed features that had CCC < 0.7 across all extractors for parts of the analysis in order to focus on features that were plausibly reproducible.

2.4   Survival Analysis on Independent Data Set

To investigate the interaction of feature reproducibility and prognostic value we did a survival analysis on the aforementioned public data set of 197 CRLM patients [26]. The data set includes scans acquired prior to hepatic resection of CRLM, along with right-censored data on overall survival time post-operation. Features were grouped into redundant sets using hierarchical clustering based on the absolute Spearman rank correlation with threshold 0.8. The most significant feature from each group, as rated by a univariate Cox proportional hazards (CPH) model, was selected if $p < 0.1$ and used to construct a multivariate CPH model of overall survival. Feature selection and modeling was repeated in a 5-fold cross-validation in order to compute an average Harrell's C-index (C-index) for the multivariate model. To investigate the effects of using reproducible features, we completed the analysis twice: once with all radiomics features, and again with only the features with CCC > 0.9 in our prospective data set.

3   Results

Figure 1 shows the comparison of the CCCs for features when comparing 3.75 mm or 2.5 mm reconstructions to the reference slice thickness of 5 mm. The CCC with the reference 5 mm images for features extracted from the 3.75 mm images were found to be significantly higher than those for the 2.5 mm images using Wilcoxon signed-rank test ($p < 10^{-6}$ for all extraction settings).

The generalized CCCs from the LMM are summarized in Fig. 2, broken down by first order (a-b) and texture (c-d) features. For the first order feature results, L3, S3, and A3 are excluded because aggregation does not affect the first order features. Figure 2(a) plots the average voxel volume for each level of resampling, along with the boxplots of the CCC distributions, indicating an inverse relationship between voxel volume and CCC of first order features. The texture feature CCC distributions are plotted in Fig. S2 and Fig. 2(c-d), which show the results before and after applying the threshold of CCC > 0.7 in at least one extractor setting, respectively. Thresholding resulted in the removal of 13 texture features (listed in supplementary Table S2) after which the 2.5D aggregation methods outperformed all 3D aggregation methods in terms of mean CCC. The column order in Fig. 2(c-d) forms three coherent groups: a) S2i and L2i use 2.5D aggregation and no axial resampling; b) S2, L2, and A2 use 2.5D aggregation, resampling all directions; and c) L3, S3 and A3 use 3D aggregation.

The reproducibility of all features is further summarized in Table 2, which uses the column order from Fig. 2(c-d) for easier comparison. The mean CCC across all features for each extractor setting is listed before and after removing

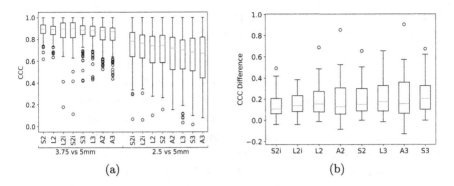

Fig. 1. (a) CCCs for features extracted with different methods. The columns are sorted in order of the mean CCC, with the 3.75 mm slice thickness on the left, and 2.5 mm slice thickness on the right. (b) Distributions of the difference of CCC between the 3.75 mm and 2.5 mm reconstructions, sorted in order of mean difference.

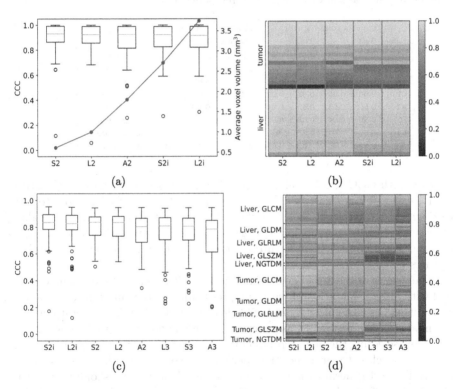

Fig. 2. Boxplots (a,c) and heatmaps (b,d) of the CCCs of features extracted with different settings, with columns sorted in order of descending mean CCC. (a-b): Results for first-order features. (c-d): Results for texture features, after thresholding. The purple line in (a) shows the average voxel volume for each extractor setting. Features in the heatmaps are grouped by ROI (b) or ROI and feature class (d). See supplementary Fig. S1 for a larger version of (b) with individual feature labels.

Table 2. Summary of the robustness of all features based on generalized CCC. Mean CCCs are given before and after thresholding, along with the number of features with CCC > 0.9 broken down by ROI and feature type (first-order vs. texture).

	S2i	L2i	S2	L2	A2	L3	S3	A3
Mean CCC	0.80	0.79	0.80	0.80	0.77	0.77	0.77	0.74
Mean after threshold	0.83	0.83	0.83	0.80	0.80	0.80	0.80	0.76
No. features CCC > 0.9	**43**	**40**	**39**	**32**	**29**	**27**	**34**	**29**
Tumor	**36**	**34**	**26**	**22**	**22**	**19**	**22**	**22**
First order	12	11	16	15	15	15	16	15
Texture	24	23	10	7	7	4	6	7
Liver Parenchyma	**7**	**6**	**13**	**10**	**7**	**8**	**12**	**7**
First order	6	6	6	6	6	6	6	6
Texture	1	0	7	4	1	2	6	1

Table 3. Survival analysis results with reproducible (left) vs. all (right) features.

Name	C-index (mean ± std) Test	Train	Mean # Features	C-index (mean ± std) Test	Train	Mean # Features
S2i	0.64 ± 0.06	0.64 ± 0.02	3.2	0.62 ± 0.07	0.65 ± 0.02	5.2
L2i	**0.65 ± 0.09**	0.65 ± 0.02	3.2	0.61 ± 0.08	0.65 ± 0.02	5.4
S2	0.59 ± 0.05	0.62 ± 0.01	3.6	0.61 ± 0.03	0.64 ± 0.01	4.8
L2	0.60 ± 0.06	0.63 ± 0.02	4.4	0.61 ± 0.04	0.65 ± 0.02	5.0
A2	0.60 ± 0.06	0.62 ± 0.01	3.2	**0.63 ± 0.04**	0.65 ± 0.02	4.8
S3	0.59 ± 0.04	0.63 ± 0.01	3.6	0.60 ± 0.03	0.67 ± 0.02	8.6
L3	0.62 ± 0.04	**0.65 ± 0.02**	4.6	0.60 ± 0.05	**0.67 ± 0.02**	8.2
A3	0.59 ± 0.04	0.62 ± 0.02	2.6	0.61 ± 0.05	0.67 ± 0.01	7.4

features with CCC < 0.7 in all settings. The number of features in each setting with CCC > 0.9 is also listed, broken down by ROI and feature type to indicate which extractor settings had the most robust features. Broadly speaking the results show better robustness from 2.5D aggregation, with S2i and L2i having the best mean CCC after thresholding, and the highest number of robust features.

The results of the 5-fold cross-validation for CPH survival models made with and without consideration of feature reproducibility are summarized in Table 3. When using only the most reproducible features (CCC > 0.9), the best performing model on the test sets was generated from the features in L2i. For L2i and S2i, when selecting the most reproducible features, the model performance on the test sets was close to, or higher than performance on the training sets, indicating relatively good generalization. In comparison, when not thresholding on CCC, all models performed worse on the test sets than on the training sets. The effect of accounting for CCC on test set performance was not significant: comparing the C-index with and without CCC thresholding across all 5 folds, a Wilcoxon signed-rank test indicated no statistically significant difference ($p = 0.98$).

4 Discussion

Although in the present study we have restricted our analysis to the stability of radiomic features when slice thickness is varied at reconstruction time, the ultimate purpose of the data collection effort from which this study draws is to look at the effects of contrast timing and reconstruction parameters using a test-retest paradigm with two portal venous phase images collected within 15 s of each other. As part of a multicenter prospective study systematically varying contrast timing and reconstruction parameters, this paper presents early results from a larger study that will be a substantial step forward in the understanding of the reproducibility of radiomics for contrast enhanced CT of CRLM.

Our results support several findings in the literature. First, we found that larger changes in slice thickness degraded the stability of features—a finding which is consistent with similar analyses in phantom studies [15,17,32], as well as lung cancer CT [5,19,21], indicating some level of generalization across anatomies. Second, with respect to differences between the ROIs, a previous retrospective study of contrast enhanced CT of liver metastases found that features extracted from liver metastases were more stable than those from the liver parenchyma across variations of all variables they considered, including pixel spacing, and contrast timing [22]. This difference in stability can also be observed in our results: Fig. 2(d) shows a visual decrease in the CCC from the tumor texture features to those of the liver parenchyma, and Table 2 shows a larger number of robust features from the tumor for all extractor settings. Third, our finding that S2i, which used 2.5D feature aggregation, had the best test set performance in the survival analysis is concordant with the findings of a previous study by Shen et al. [24], which found that a CPH model using 2D radiomics features performed better than a 3D feature-based model in a study of overall survival in non-small cell lung cancer. Given that reproducibility is known to be anatomy/disease-specific even within CT [27], it is significant that our findings are concordant with results from other cancers in the literature.

A limitation of this study is the use of only one bin count when computing the texture features; however a previous study on contrast enhanced CT of hepato-cellular carcinoma found that the optimal bin count for feature robustness when varying slice thickness was 32–64 HU [23], which is supportive of our choice of 24 HU when accounting for the study's step size. Further, though bin count has a large effect on the values of texture features, the effect may be predictable [9,10], and has been found to have a small effect on feature stability across other variables [16]. Though these considerations suggest that our findings may generalize to other bin counts, this generalization would need to be verified in future work.

In conclusion, our results demonstrate the strong effect of slice thickness on feature reproducibility for contrast enhanced CT imaging of CRLM. When slice thickness is variable, our results suggest that isotropic resampling may not be the best interpolation setting, at least when working with anisotropic CT imaging, where the slice thickness is substantially larger than the pixel spacing. Indeed, we found that the most reproducible features were produced by resampling only in 2D, leaving the axial direction unchanged, and aggregating texture features in

2.5D. This approach also produced the most generalizable prognostic models for overall survival after hepatic resection in an independent CRLM dataset. Overall, our results show that feature extraction with 2.5D aggregation, and without axial resampling, can improve the robustness of radiomic features to variations in slice thickness in CRLM CT imaging, without reducing their prognostic value.

Acknowledgements. This work was supported in part by National Institutes of Health grant R01 CA233888.

References

1. Berenguer, R., et al.: Radiomics of CT features may be nonreproducible and redundant: influence of CT acquisition parameters. Radiology **288**(2), 407–415 (2018). https://doi.org/10.1148/radiol.2018172361
2. Carrasco, J.L., Jover, L.: Estimating the generalized concordance correlation coefficient through variance components. Biometrics **59**(4), 849–858 (2003). https://doi.org/10.1111/j.0006-341x.2003.00099.x
3. Clark, K., et al.: The cancer imaging archive (TCIA): maintaining and operating a public information repository. J. Digit. Imaging **26**(6), 1045–1057 (2013). https://doi.org/10.1007/s10278-013-9622-7
4. Emaminejad, N., Wahi-Anwar, M.W., Kim, G.H.J., Hsu, W., Brown, M., McNitt-Gray, M.: Reproducibility of lung nodule radiomic features: Multivariable and univariable investigations that account for interactions between CT acquisition and reconstruction parameters. Med. Phys. **48**(6), 2906–2919 (2021). https://doi.org/10.1002/mp.14830
5. Erdal, B.S., et al.: Are quantitative features of lung nodules reproducible at different CT acquisition and reconstruction parameters? PLoS ONE **15**, e0240184 (2020). https://doi.org/10.1371/journal.pone.0240184
6. Ger, R.B., et al.: Comprehensive investigation on controlling for CT imaging variabilities in radiomics studies. Sci. Rep. **8**(1), 13047 (2018). https://doi.org/10.1038/s41598-018-31509-z
7. Gillies, R.J., Kinahan, P.E., Hricak, H.: Radiomics: images are more than pictures, they are data. Radiology **278**, 563–577 (2016). https://doi.org/10.1148/radiol.2015151169
8. van Griethuysen, J.J., et al.: Computational radiomics system to decode the radiographic phenotype. Cancer Res. **77**(21), e104–e107 (2017). https://doi.org/10.1158/0008-5472.can-17-0339
9. Shafiq-ul Hassan, M., Latifi, K., Zhang, G., Ullah, G., Gillies, R., Moros, E.: Voxel size and gray level normalization of CT radiomic features in lung cancer. Sci. Rep. **8**(1), 10545 (2018). https://doi.org/10.1038/s41598-018-28895-9
10. Shafiq-ul Hassan, M., et al.: Intrinsic dependencies of CT radiomic features on voxel size and number of gray levels. Med. Phys. **44**(3), 1050–1062 (2017). https://doi.org/10.1002/mp.12123
11. Horvat, N., et al.: A primer on texture analysis in abdominal radiology. Abdom. Radiol. (NY) **47**, 2972–2985 (2022). https://doi.org/10.1007/s00261-021-03359-3
12. Ibrahim, A., et al.: MaasPenn radiomics reproducibility score: a novel quantitative measure for evaluating the reproducibility of CT-based handcrafted radiomic features. Cancers (Basel) **14**(7), 1599 (2022). https://doi.org/10.3390/cancers14071599

13. Isensee, F., Jaeger, P.F., Kohl, S.A.A., Petersen, J., Maier-Hein, K.H.: nnU-Net: a self-configuring method for deep learning-based biomedical image segmentation. Nat. Methods **18**(2), 203–211 (2021). https://doi.org/10.1038/s41592-020-01008-z

14. Kikinis, R., Pieper, S.D., Vosburgh, K.G.: 3D slicer: a platform for subject-specific image analysis, visualization, and clinical support. In: Jolesz, F.A. (ed.) Intraoperative Imaging and Image-Guided Therapy, pp. 277–289. Springer, New York (2014). https://doi.org/10.1007/978-1-4614-7657-3_19

15. Kim, Y.J., Lee, H.J., Kim, K.G., Lee, S.H.: The effect of CT scan parameters on the measurement of CT radiomic features: a lung nodule phantom study. Comput. Math. Methods Med. **2019**, 1–12 (2019). https://doi.org/10.1155/2019/8790694

16. Larue, R.T.H.M., et al.: Influence of gray level discretization on radiomic feature stability for different CT scanners, tube currents and slice thicknesses: a comprehensive phantom study. Acta Oncol. **56**(11), 1544–1553 (2017). https://doi.org/10.1080/0284186x.2017.1351624

17. Ligero, M., et al.: Minimizing acquisition-related radiomics variability by image resampling and batch effect correction to allow for large-scale data analysis. Eur. Radiol. **31**(3), 1460–1470 (2020). https://doi.org/10.1007/s00330-020-07174-0

18. Lin, L.I.K.: A concordance correlation coefficient to evaluate reproducibility. Biometrics **45**(1), 255 (1989). https://doi.org/10.2307/2532051

19. Lu, L., Ehmke, R.C., Schwartz, L.H., Zhao, B.: Assessing agreement between radiomic features computed for multiple CT imaging settings. PLoS ONE **11**(12), e0166550 (2016). https://doi.org/10.1371/journal.pone.0166550

20. Meyer, M., et al.: Reproducibility of CT radiomic features within the same patient: influence of radiation dose and CT reconstruction settings. Radiology **293**(3), 583–591 (2019). https://doi.org/10.1148/radiol.2019190928

21. Park, S., et al.: Deep learning algorithm for reducing CT slice thickness: effect on reproducibility of radiomic features in lung cancer. Korean J. Radiol. **20**(10), 1431 (2019). https://doi.org/10.3348/kjr.2019.0212

22. Perrin, T., et al.: Short-term reproducibility of radiomic features in liver parenchyma and liver malignancies on contrast-enhanced CT imaging. Abdom. Radiol. (NY) **43**(12), 3271–3278 (2018). https://doi.org/10.1007/s00261-018-1600-6

23. Sanchez, L.E., Rundo, L., Gill, A.B., Hoare, M., Serrao, E.M., Sala, E.: Robustness of radiomic features in CT images with different slice thickness, comparing liver tumour and muscle. Sci. Rep. **11**(1), 8262 (2021). https://doi.org/10.1038/s41598-021-87598-w

24. Shen, C., Liu, Z., Guan, M., Song, J., Lian, Y., Wang, S., Tang, Z., Dong, D., Kong, L., Wang, M., Shi, D., Tian, J.: 2D and 3D CT radiomics features prognostic performance comparison in non-small cell lung cancer. Transl. Oncol. **10**(6), 886–894 (2017). https://doi.org/10.1016/j.tranon.2017.08.007

25. Simpson, A.L., et al.: Computed tomography image texture: a noninvasive prognostic marker of hepatic recurrence after hepatectomy for metastatic colorectal cancer. Ann. Surg. Oncol. **24**(9), 2482–2490 (2017). https://doi.org/10.1245/s10434-017-5896-1

26. Simpson, A.L., et al.: Preoperative CT and survival data for patients undergoing resection of colorectal liver metastases (Colorectal-Liver-Metastases) (Version 2) [Data set]. The Cancer Imaging Archive (2023). https://doi.org/10.7937/QXK2-QG03

27. van Timmeren, J.E., et al.: Test-retest data for radiomics feature stability analysis: generalizable or study-specific? Tomography **2**(4), 361–365 (2016). https://doi.org/10.18383/j.tom.2016.00208

28. Traverso, A., Wee, L., Dekker, A., Gillies, R.: Repeatability and reproducibility of radiomic features: a systematic review. Int. J. Radiat. Oncol. Biol. Phys. **102**(4), 1143–1158 (2018). https://doi.org/10.1016/j.ijrobp.2018.05.053

29. Varghese, B.A., et al.: Reliability of CT-based texture features: phantom study. J. Appl. Clin. Med. Phys. **20**(8), 155–163 (2019). https://doi.org/10.1002/acm2.12666

30. Yang, S., Wu, N., Zhang, L., Li, M.: Evaluation of the linear interpolation method in correcting the influence of slice thicknesses on radiomic feature values in solid pulmonary nodules: a prospective patient study. Ann. Transl. Med. **9**(4), 279–279 (2021). https://doi.org/10.21037/atm-20-2992

31. Zhao, B.: Understanding sources of variation to improve the reproducibility of radiomics. Front. Oncol. **11**, 826 (2021). https://doi.org/10.3389/fonc.2021.633176

32. Zhao, B., Tan, Y., Tsai, W.Y., Schwartz, L.H., Lu, L.: Exploring variability in CT characterization of tumors: a preliminary phantom study. Transl. Oncol. **7**(1), 88–93 (2014). https://doi.org/10.1593/tlo.13865

33. Zwanenburg, A., Leger, S., Vallières, M., Löck, S.: Image biomarker standardisation initiative: Reference manual. arXiv:1612.07003 [cs.CV] (2016). https://doi.org/10.48550/ARXIV.1612.07003

34. Zwanenburg, A., et al.: The image biomarker standardization initiative: standardized quantitative radiomics for high-throughput image-based phenotyping. Radiology **295**(2), 328–338 (2020). https://doi.org/10.1148/radiol.2020191145

Benchmarking Scalable Epistemic Uncertainty Quantification in Organ Segmentation

Jadie Adams[1,2(✉)] and Shireen Y. Elhabian[1,2]

[1] Scientific Computing and Imaging Institute, University of Utah, Salt Lake City, UT, USA
jadie.adams@utah.edu, shireen@sci.utah.edu
[2] School of Computing, University of Utah, Salt Lake City, UT, USA

Abstract. Deep learning based methods for automatic organ segmentation have shown promise in aiding diagnosis and treatment planning. However, quantifying and understanding the uncertainty associated with model predictions is crucial in critical clinical applications. While many techniques have been proposed for epistemic or model-based uncertainty estimation, it is unclear which method is preferred in the medical image analysis setting. This paper presents a comprehensive benchmarking study that evaluates epistemic uncertainty quantification methods in organ segmentation in terms of accuracy, uncertainty calibration, and scalability. We provide a comprehensive discussion of the strengths, weaknesses, and out-of-distribution detection capabilities of each method as well as recommendations for future improvements. These findings contribute to the development of reliable and robust models that yield accurate segmentations while effectively quantifying epistemic uncertainty.

1 Introduction

Deep learning systems have made significant strides in automating organ segmentation from 3D medical images. Segmentation networks can be efficiently integrated into image processing pipelines, facilitating research and clinical use (i.e., tumor segmentation in radiotherapy [30] and hippocampus segmentation for neurological disease analysis [6]). However, these systems also introduce new challenges and risks compared to traditional segmentation processes, including issues of bias, errors, and lack of transparency. Deep networks are prone to providing overconfident estimates and thus cannot be blindly trusted in sensitive decision-making scenarios without the safeguard of granular uncertainty quantification (UQ) [20,21]. UQ is the process of estimating and representing the uncertainty associated with predictions made by deep neural networks. UQ provides necessary insight into the reliability and confidence of the model's predicted segmentation. In the context of organ segmentation, areas near organ boundaries can be uncertain due to the low contrast between the target organ and surrounding tissues [33]. Pixel or voxel-level uncertainty estimates can be used to identify potential incorrect regions or guide user interactions for

© The Author(s), under exclusive license to Springer Nature Switzerland AG 2023
C. H. Sudre et al. (Eds.): UNSURE 2023, LNCS 14291, pp. 53–63, 2023.
https://doi.org/10.1007/978-3-031-44336-7_6

refinement [27,33]. This enables quality control of the segmentation process and the detection of out-of-distribution (OOD) samples.

Two forms of uncertainty are distinguished in deep learning frameworks: aleatoric and epistemic[14]. *Aleatoric uncertainty* refers to the inherent uncertainty in the input data distribution that cannot be reduced [16] (i.e., uncertainty resulting from factors like image acquisition noise, over-exposure, occlusion, or a lack of visual features [32]). Aleatoric uncertainty is typically quantified by adjusting the model to be stochastic (predicting a distribution rather than a point-wise estimate [16]) or by methods such as test time augmentation [31,33]. *Epistemic uncertainty* is model-based and arises from a lack of knowledge or uncertainty about the model's parameters due to limited training data or model complexity. Capturing epistemic uncertainty is considerably more difficult as it cannot be learned as a function of the input but rather requires fitting a distribution over model parameters. Several approaches have been proposed to accomplish this, but many of them significantly increase the computational cost and memory footprint and may impact prediction accuracy [7]. There is no ubiquitous method for epistemic UQ in segmentation networks, as each proposed technique has its own trade-offs and limitations.

This study benchmarks Bayesian and frequentist epistemic UQ methods for organ segmentation from 3D CT scans in terms of scalability, segmentation accuracy, and uncertainty calibration using multiple datasets. While previous benchmarks (e.g., [24,25,29]) have been conducted on small subsets of such methods, there is a need for a comprehensive evaluation. To the best of our knowledge, this work provides the most extensive benchmarking of scalable methods for epistemic UQ in medical segmentation. The key contributions are as follows:

1. We conduct a benchmark evaluation of scalable methods for epistemic UQ in medical image segmentation, including deep ensemble [28], batch ensemble [34], Monte Carlo dropout [10], concrete dropout [11], Rank-1 Bayesian Neural Net (BNN) [7], latent posterior BNN [9], Stochastic Weight Averaging (SWA) [15], SWA Gaussian (SWAG) [22], and Multi-SWAG [35].
2. We evaluate these methods in detecting out-of-distribution (OOD) instances, which is an important aspect of robust uncertainty estimation.
3. We provide a comprehensive discussion of the strengths and weaknesses of the evaluated methods, enabling a better understanding of their performance characteristics and potential improvements.
4. To facilitate further research and reproducibility, we provide an open-source PyTorch implementation of all benchmarked methods.[1]

2   Epistemic Uncertainty Quantification Techniques

Modeling epistemic uncertainty in a scalable manner poses significant challenges as it entails placing distributions over model weights. Both Bayesian and frequentist methods have been proposed, with Bayesian approaches aiming to directly

---

[1] Source code is publicly available: https://github.com/jadie1/MedSegUQ.

estimate the posterior distribution over the model's parameters, while frequentist methods use ensembles of models to approximate the posterior empirically.

In Bayesian deep learning, obtaining an analytical solution for the posterior is often intractable, necessitating the use of approximate posterior inference techniques such as variational inference [3]. The most common Bayesian technique for UQ is **Monte Carlo (MC) dropout** sampling, as it provides a fast, scalable solution for approximate variational inference [10]. In MC dropout, uncertainty is captured by the spread of predictions resulting from sampled dropout masks in inference. However, obtaining well-calibrated epistemic UQ with dropout requires a time-consuming grid search to tune layer-wise dropout probabilities. **Concrete dropout** [11] was proposed to address this limitation by automatically optimizing layer-wise dropout probabilities along with the network weights. Certain Bayesian approaches for approximate inference are excluded from this benchmark due to their limited scalability and tendency to underfit [7,10,19], such as sampling-based Markov chain Monte Carlo [5], Bayes by Backprop [4], and variational inference based methods [3]. These techniques rely on structured or factorized distributions with tied parameters, have a high computational cost, and are generally slow to converge [10]. Additionally, previous work has shown that such methods perform similarly to the much more lightweight MC dropout approach in medical image segmentation UQ [26].

Deep ensembles are an effective and popular frequentist method for UQ [13]. Ensembling involves training multiple independent networks (or ensemble members) with different initialization then aggregating predictions for improved robustness [8]. The spread or variability among the predictions of the ensemble members effectively captures the epistemic uncertainty [19]. It has been shown that deep ensemble models can provide a better approximation than standard Bayesian methods [35]. The main drawback of deep ensembles lies in their computational and memory costs, which increase linearly with the number of ensemble members. To address the trade-off between accuracy and scalability, **batch ensemble** [34] has been proposed. Batch ensemble [34] compromises between a single network and an ensemble by employing shared weight matrices and lightweight rank-1 ensemble members. The concept of batch ensembling has also been applied to improve the scalability of Bayesian Neural Networks (BNNs). **Rank-1 BNN** [7] reduces computational complexity by utilizing a rank-1 parameterization in variational inference. **Latent Posterior BNN (LP-BNN)** [9] was proposed to improve scalability further by learning the posterior distribution of lower-dimensional latent variables derived from rank-1 vectors. This is accomplished by training layer-wise variational autoencoders (VAEs) [18] on the rank-1 vectors. The latent space of these VAEs can then be sampled, providing a distribution of rank-1 weights.

Additional methods of epistemic UQ have been developed based on the stochastic weight averaging (SWA) technique [15]. SWA was proposed to enhance generalization in deep learning by estimating the mean of the stationary distribution of SGD iterates. In SWA, final model weights are defined by averaging the weights traversed during SGD after initial convergence. **SWA-Gaussian (SWAG)** [22] fits a Gaussian distribution to the traversed weights, creating an approximate posterior distribution over the weights that can be sampled for Bayesian model averaging. It has been shown that combining traditional Bayesian methods with ensembling improves the fidelity of approximate inference via multimodal marginalization, resulting in a more robust, accurate model [35]. Based on this observation, **Multi-SWAG** [35] was proposed as an ensemble of SWAG models. These approaches offer alternative ways to capture epistemic uncertainty by leveraging the ensemble characteristics and combining them with Bayesian principles. They aim to improve the fidelity of approximate inference and provide scalable solutions for epistemic UQ in deep learning tasks.

3   Experimental Design

We utilize the residual U-Net architecture originally proposed for cardiac left-ventricle segmentation [17] as a base architecture to compare the epistemic UQ techniques. This model is comprised of residual units of 3D convolutional layers with batch normalization and PReLU activation. As a baseline for UQ calibration analysis, we consider the predicted segmentation probabilities. Specifically, for the **base** model, we quantify voxel-wise UQ as: $UQ = 1 - C$, where confidence, C, is the maximum of the foreground and background softmax probabilities. This is not strictly a measure of epistemic UQ, as there is no notion of posterior approximation and marginalization. However, this formulation of UQ has been shown to correlate with prediction error and is useful for OOD detection [12] and thus provides an evaluation baseline.

We benchmark the following aforementioned scalable methods for epistemic UQ: Ensemble [19], Batch Ensemble [34], MC Dropout [10], Concrete Dropout [11], Rank1 BNN [7], LP-BNN [9], SWAG [22], and Mulit-SWAG [35]. In implementing dropout and rank1-based methods, dropout and batch ensemble are applied to every convolutional layer respectively. Models are trained on $(96 \times 96 \times 96)$ patches of the input images scaled to an intensity of $[0, 1]$. A validation set is used to assess the convergence of each model. Models are trained until the performance on the validation set has not improved in 100 epochs. The model weights resulting from the epoch with the best validation performance are used in the evaluation of held-out testing data. Implementation and tuned hyperparameter values for each model are provided in the GitHub repository.

3.1   Datasets

We utilize two open-source datasets from the Medical Segmentation Decathlon [32] in evaluation: the spleen and pancreas. These datasets comprise of 3D CT images and corresponding manual ground truth segmentations. The **spleen** dataset was selected to provide a typical medical image analysis scenario where data is scarce and varied. There are only 41 instances in the spleen dataset, and the size of the spleen versus the background varies widely. The **pancreas** dataset was selected to evaluate OOD detection accuracy. This dataset contains cancerous cases with segmentations of both the pancreas organ and tumor masses. We analyze the accuracy of joint segmentation of the pancreas and tumors, holding out the cases with the largest tumors an OOD test set.

3.2   Metrics

In 3D image segmentation, accuracy is typically assessed via the **Dice Similarity Coefficient (DSC)** between manual annotations and the model's prediction. The DSC metric captures the percentage of voxel-wise agreement between a predicted segmentation and its corresponding ground truth. In these experiments the target organs are small compared to the total image size. Because of this, we only include the foreground in DSC calculations so that the DSC value is not overwhelmed by the background signal.

To measure overall uncertainty calibration, we consider the correlation between estimated epistemic uncertainty and prediction error (100 - DSC). We report the **Pearson correlation coefficient (r)** between error and sum of the uncertainty map, where a higher r-value indicates better correlation.

Finally, we assess segmentation accuracy and uncertainty quality jointly via **error-retention curves** [19,23]. Error-retention curves depict a given error metric over a dataset as ground-truth labels replace a model's predictions in order of decreasing estimated uncertainty. The **area under the curve (AUC)** is reduced as the overall error is decreased, as well as the correlation between error and uncertainty is increased. We report the **area under the error retention curve (R-AUC)** using 100 - DSC as the error metric. Smaller R-AUC indicates both better segmentation accuracy and uncertainty calibration.

4   Results

4.1   Spleen

Because the spleen dataset is comprised of only 41 examples, we employ K-folds to define the training, validation, and test sets. The data is split into 70% train, 10% validation, and 20% held-out test using five different folds. For each fold, a separate model of every form is trained. In this manner, results are reported across the entire dataset, where the predicted segmentation of each image is acquired from the model for which the image was held out. The results are reported in Table 1, and qualitative visualizations are provided in Fig. 1. For Ensemble and Batch Ensemble models four ensemble members are used, thus four predictions are averaged and used for UQ estimation.

For methods that fit a distribution over weights, any number of weight samples can be used to provide an average prediction and UQ esti-

Table 1. Spleen results: Mean and standard deviation values across held-out data, best values in bold.

	DSC ↑	r ↑	R-AUC ↓
Base	89.15 ± 9.55	0.56	2.54 ± 4.52

Method	4 Samples			30 Samples		
	DSC ↑	r ↑	R-AUC ↓	DSC ↑	r ↑	R-AUC ↓
Ensemble [19]	$\mathbf{92.77 \pm 5.34}$	0.37	0.71 ± 1.09	N/A	N/A	N/A
Batch Ensemble [34]	86.87 ± 14.21	0.40	0.58 ± 1.09	N/A	N/A	N/A
MC Dropout [10]	86.16 ± 19.07	-0.07	1.54 ± 4.06	86.40 ± 18.33	-0.08	1.31 ± 3.79
Concrete Dropout [11]	90.21 ± 6.42	0.45	0.42 ± 0.47	90.23 ± 6.49	0.59	$\mathbf{0.28 \pm 0.35}$
Rank1 BNN [7]	55.01 ± 19.17	0.10	3.69 ± 3.47	66.36 ± 16.84	0.11	0.79 ± 1.45
LP-BNN [9]	87.77 ± 10.66	0.57	0.98 ± 1.27	87.74 ± 10.83	0.47	0.93 ± 1.48
SWAG [22]	87.80 ± 15.53	0.18	0.99 ± 2.47	87.80 ± 15.69	0.20	0.74 ± 1.71
Mulit-SWAG [35]	92.49 ± 10.18	**0.69**	0.69 ± 0.84	$\mathbf{93.11 \pm 10.07}$	**0.64**	0.57 ± 0.77

mation. Additional samples improve accuracy and calibration but also increase

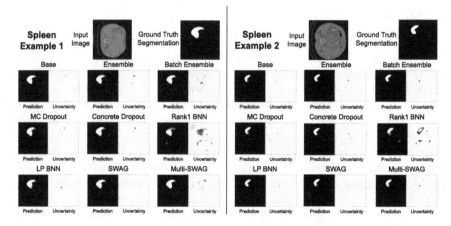

Fig. 1. Slices of two spleen examples are provided with the segmentation resulting from each model with error overlayed in red. Additionally, predicted uncertainty maps are shown where darker red indicates higher uncertainty. (Color figure online)

inference time. In evaluating such methods, we elect to use 4 and 30 samples for a comprehensive comparison.

4.2 Pancreas

The pancreas dataset is used to analyze the robustness and uncertainty calibration of the various methods in the case of OOD examples. To this end, we calculate the ratio of tumor to pancreas voxels in the ground truth segmentations. We hold out the 50 instances with the largest tumor ratio as a test set. This provides an OOD test set, as the models are trained only on examples with smaller tumors. The remaining 231 image/segmentation pairs are randomly split into a single training, validation, and in-distribution (ID) test set using a 70%, 10%, 20% split. Figure 2 displays the distributions of tumor-to-pancreas ratios in the ID and OOD test sets. The results are reported on both the ID and OOD test set in Table 2. Additionally, the correlation between the tumor-to-pancreas ratio

Table 2. Pancreas results: Mean and standard deviation values across both held-out test sets are reported with the best values marked in bold.

	In-Distribution Test Set				Out-of-Distribution Test Set			
		DSC	R	R-AUC		DSC	R	R-AUC
	Base	71.02±14.49	0.12	8.66±7.36	Base	67.32±18.35	0.04	8.95±7.03

Model	4 Samples			30 Samples			4 Samples			30 Samples		
	DSC	r	R-AUC	DSC	r	R-AUC	DSC	r	R-AUC	DSC	r	R-AUC
Ensemble [19]	72.44±13.54	0.04	4.70±3.57	N/A	N/A	N/A	**67.54±19.58**	0.15	5.65±5.64	N/A	N/A	N/A
Batch Ensemble [34]	64.04±16.49	0.24	6.30±4.38	N/A	N/A	N/A	57.08±21.51	0.12	9.77±10.02	N/A	N/A	N/A
MC Dropout [10]	70.16±13.96	0.36	9.97±7.43	70.22±13.93	0.38	8.90±6.54	67.24±18.13	0.30	10.63±9.33	67.35±18.20	0.33	9.45±9.18
Concrete Dropout [11]	**73.07±11.91**	0.32	4.67±3.13	73.06±11.98	0.33	4.29±2.64	66.99±18.40	0.08	8.39±9.17	**67.83±18.62**	0.27	7.54±8.71
Rank1 BNN [7]	12.77±11.81	−0.23	11.37±8.99	17.76±13.60	−0.2	9.07±8.91	9.20±10.17	−0.33	12.91±10.17	12.39±11.85	−0.41	9.21±4.72
LP-BNN [9]	65.28±16.18	0.36	4.92±3.05	65.31±16.10	0.21	4.66±2.94	60.39±19.34	0.14	6.34±5.03	60.16±19.78	0.19	7.26±6.95
SWAG [22]	66.68±17.27	0.36	9.32±8.24	66.69±17.29	0.49	9.34±8.14	63.20±20.90	**0.31**	10.06±8.16	63.07±21.04	0.45	9.89±7.86
Mulit-SWAG [35]	69.67±15.06	**0.39**	5.57±4.32	69.31±15.19	0.41	5.46±4.24	64.94±21.13	0.12	**6.19±5.86**	64.65±21.28	0.14	**6.01±5.71**

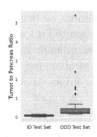

Fig. 2. Pancreas test set ratio box plots.

Table 3. Pearson correlation coefficients across both pancreas test sets are reported, where error = 100 − DSC.

Model	r values		
	Ratio/Error	UQ/Error ↑	UQ/Ratio ↑
Base	0.42	−0.08	−0.06
Ensemble [19]	0.44	0.22	−0.01
Batch Ensemble [34]	0.34	0.13	0.10
MC Dropout [10]	0.46	0.35	0.10
Concrete Dropout [11]	0.48	0.28	0.08
Rank1 BNN [7]	0.02	−0.32	0.06
LP-BNN [9]	0.38	0.2	0.06
SWAG [22]	0.34	**0.46**	**0.11**
Mulit-SWAG [35]	0.39	0.22	−0.04

and the estimated uncertainty across both test sets is reported in Table 3. We expect well-calibrated UQ to correlate with the tumor-to-pancreas ratio as the models are not exposed examples with large tumors in training. However, none of the epistemic UQ quantification methods proved a strong correlation with the ratio, suggesting these models are not effective in accurate OOD detection.

4.3 Scalability Comparison

Table 4 reports the average time and memory requirements associated with training and testing each model on the pancreas dataset. Note that for models that can be sampled, the reported inference time is for a single sample. Inference time scales linearly with the number of samples. Additionally, note "params size" refers to the memory required to store the parameters and "pass size" refers to the memory required to perform a forward/backward pass through the network.

Table 4. Scalability comparison: Time reported in seconds and memory size in MB, best values in bold.

Model	Train epochs	Train time	Inference time	Total params	Params size	Pass size
Base	222	17261	0.2587	**4808917**	**19.24**	**1211.20**
Ensemble [19]	888	69045	1.0348	19235668	76.96	4844.80
Batch Ensemble [34]	341	45409	0.8698	4824513	**19.24**	4842.81
MC Dropout [10]	**197**	**16841**	**0.2548**	**4808917**	**19.24**	**1211.20**
Concrete Dropout [11]	259	36847	0.3694	4808934	**19.24**	**1211.20**
Rank1 BNN [7]	1142	157100	0.7712	4835229	**19.24**	4844.81
LP-BNN [9]	881	121343	0.8742	4957940	19.77	4844.92
SWAG [22]	422	31615	0.2921	9617834	38.48	**1211.20**
Mulit-SWAG [35]	1688	126460	1.1684	38471336	153.92	4844.80

5   Discussion and Conclusion

We conducted a benchmark of scalable epistemic UQ techniques on two challenging organ segmentation tasks. The spleen experiment represented a low training budget scenario, while the pancreas experiment involved significant variation in the shape and size of the organ and tumor masses. These challenging scenarios, where the base model provides low prediction accuracy, served as stress tests for UQ evaluation. We discuss the performance of each model as follows:

Base Model: While the base models provided competitive accuracy and r values (suggesting instance-level UQ/error correlation) the R-AUC values were low. This indicates the voxel-level UQ did not correlate well with error and thus could not be used to accurately identify erroneous regions. The base model UQ correlates more with the organ boundary than error, as can be seen in Fig. 1.

Ensemble [19]: As expected, the ensemble model provided an accuracy improvement over the base model. However, it came at the expense of scalability, which is an important consideration in practical applications. More scalable methods outperformed ensembling in terms of R-AUC in these experiments.

Batch Ensemble [34]: While batch ensemble reduces the memory cost associated with ensembling, it did not provide the same accuracy improvement. This is likely because joint training of the rank1 members proved difficult on these challenging tasks. However, it still provided improved UQ over the base model.

MC Dropout [10]: This approach is appealing as it does not increase memory costs or impact the training objective. However, it did not perform as well as concrete dropout, highlighting the importance of tuning layer-wise dropout probabilities. For MC dropout models, we used a dropout rate of 0.1 for all layers. The concrete dropout optimization found a dropout probability of around 0.08 for shallow layers, increasing to around 0.16 for the deepest layer.

Concrete Dropout [11]: This technique arguably performed best overall and is desirable as it is scalable and only requires the addition of concrete dropout layers and a loss regularization term.

Rank1 BNN [7]: This model did not perform well on either task, especially the pancreas segmentation. While the rank1 parameterization greatly improves the scalability of the BNNs, it does not appear to solve the issue of poor convergence that BNNs are prone to suffer from.

LP-BNN [9]: Approximating the posterior in a learned latent space of the rank1 vectors improved convergence, as LP-BNN outperformed Rank1 BNN. However, LP-BNN did not perform as well as other methods with regard to any metrics, likely because training layer-wise VAEs complicates the learning task.

SWAG [22]: The SWAG models did not outperform the base models in terms of accuracy as expected. This can be attributed to the fact that the base models used in the evaluation were those resulting from the epoch with the best validation performance, whereas the SWAG weight posterior was fit across the converged SGD trajectory. This technique is desirable because it does not require adapting the architecture in any way and can be considered a post hoc process.

Mulit-SWAG [35]: Ensembling SWAG models improved the accuracy and UQ calibration but again at the expense of scalability.

This benchmark provides some insights into how UQ methods can be improved. The Multi-SWAG performance reinforces the notion that ensembling Bayesian methods can improve the fidelity of approximate inference by enabling multimodal marginalization. This could be made more scalable by combining SWAG with a batch ensemble model rather than applying naive ensembling. Existing work has also demonstrated that combining ensembling with dropout improves performance on related medical imaging tasks [1]. These experiments additionally demonstrate that LP-BNN is a desirable alternative to Rank1 BNN. However, improvements could be made to the LP-BNN process of learning a low-dimension representation of the rank1 vectors, as layer-wise VAEs increase the training burden and hyperparameters to tune. The pancreas OOD analysis reveals that none of the epistemic UQ methods were effective at detecting instances with larger tumor sizes than those seen in training. As Table 2 demonstrate, all methods provided better calibrated uncertainty estimates on in domain test data than OOD. Such failure has been noted before, as model misestimation can result in overconfidence in OOD predictions [2,36]. This illustrates the need to consider alternative test statistics and objectives in developing epistemic uncertainty estimation techniques.

In conclusion, our benchmarking study of scalable epistemic uncertainty quantification techniques for challenging organ segmentation tasks highlights the importance of accurate uncertainty estimation in medical image analysis. The insights gained from this study can guide researchers and practitioners in selecting appropriate methods to enhance the reliability and robustness of deep learning models for organ segmentation, ultimately contributing to improved diagnosis and treatment planning in clinical practice.

Acknowledgments. This work was supported by the National Institutes of Health under grant numbers NIBIB-U24EB029011, NIAMS-R01AR076120, NHLBI-R01HL135568, and NIBIB-R01EB016701. The content is solely the responsibility of the authors and does not necessarily represent the official views of the National Institutes of Health.

References

1. Adams, J., Elhabian, S.: Fully Bayesian VIB-DeepSSM. arXiv preprint arXiv:2305.05797 (2023)
2. Besnier, V., Bursuc, A., Picard, D., Briot, A.: Triggering failures: out-of-distribution detection by learning from local adversarial attacks in semantic segmentation. In: Proceedings of the IEEE/CVF International Conference on Computer Vision, pp. 15701–15710 (2021)
3. Blei, D.M., Kucukelbir, A., McAuliffe, J.D.: Variational inference: a review for statisticians. J. Am. Stat. Assoc. **112**(518), 859–877 (2017). https://doi.org/10.1080/01621459.2017.1285773

4. Blundell, C., Cornebise, J., Kavukcuoglu, K., Wierstra, D.: Weight uncertainty in neural network. In: International Conference on Machine Learning, pp. 1613–1622. PMLR (2015)
5. Chen, T., Fox, E., Guestrin, C.: Stochastic gradient Hamiltonian Monte Carlo. In: International Conference on Machine Learning, pp. 1683–1691. PMLR (2014)
6. Chupin, M., et al.: Fully automatic hippocampus segmentation and classification in Alzheimer's disease and mild cognitive impairment applied on data from ADNI. Hippocampus **19**(6), 579–587 (2009)
7. Dusenberry, M., et al.: Efficient and scalable Bayesian neural nets with rank-1 factors. In: International Conference on Machine Learning, pp. 2782–2792. PMLR (2020)
8. Fort, S., Hu, H., Lakshminarayanan, B.: Deep ensembles: a loss landscape perspective. arXiv preprint arXiv:1912.02757 (2019)
9. Franchi, G., Bursuc, A., Aldea, E., Dubuisson, S., Bloch, I.: Encoding the latent posterior of Bayesian neural networks for uncertainty quantification. arXiv preprint arXiv:2012.02818 (2020)
10. Gal, Y., Ghahramani, Z.: Dropout as a Bayesian approximation: representing model uncertainty in deep learning. In: International Conference on Machine Learning, pp. 1050–1059. PMLR (2016)
11. Gal, Y., Hron, J., Kendall, A.: Concrete dropout. In: Advances in Neural Information Processing Systems, vol. 30 (2017)
12. Hendrycks, D., Gimpel, K.: A baseline for detecting misclassified and out-of-distribution examples in neural networks. arXiv preprint arXiv:1610.02136 (2016)
13. Hu, R., Huang, Q., Chang, S., Wang, H., He, J.: The MBPEP: a deep ensemble pruning algorithm providing high quality uncertainty prediction. Appl. Intell. **49**, 2942–2955 (2019)
14. Hüllermeier, E., Waegeman, W.: Aleatoric and epistemic uncertainty in machine learning: an introduction to concepts and methods. Mach. Learn. **110**(3), 457–506 (2021)
15. Izmailov, P., Podoprikhin, D., Garipov, T., Vetrov, D., Wilson, A.G.: Averaging weights leads to wider optima and better generalization. arXiv preprint arXiv:1803.05407 (2018)
16. Kendall, A., Gal, Y.: What uncertainties do we need in Bayesian deep learning for computer vision? In: Advances in Neural Information Processing Systems, vol. 30 (2017)
17. Kerfoot, E., Clough, J., Oksuz, I., Lee, J., King, A.P., Schnabel, J.A.: Left-ventricle quantification using residual U-net. In: Pop, M., et al. (eds.) STACOM 2018. LNCS, vol. 11395, pp. 371–380. Springer, Cham (2019). https://doi.org/10.1007/978-3-030-12029-0_40
18. Kingma, D.P., Welling, M.: Auto-encoding variational bayes. Stat **1050**, 1 (2014)
19. Lakshminarayanan, B., Pritzel, A., Blundell, C.: Simple and scalable predictive uncertainty estimation using deep ensembles. In: Advances in Neural Information Processing Systems, vol. 30 (2017)
20. Li, B., et al.: Trustworthy AI: from principles to practices. ACM Comput. Surv. **55**(9), 1–46 (2023)
21. Liang, W., et al.: Advances, challenges and opportunities in creating data for trustworthy AI. Nat. Mach. Intell. **4**(8), 669–677 (2022)
22. Maddox, W.J., Izmailov, P., Garipov, T., Vetrov, D.P., Wilson, A.G.: A simple baseline for Bayesian uncertainty in deep learning. In: Advances in Neural Information Processing Systems, vol. 32 (2019)

23. Malinin, A., et al.: Shifts 2.0: extending the dataset of real distributional shifts. arXiv preprint arXiv:2206.15407 (2022)
24. Mehrtash, A., Wells, W.M., Tempany, C.M., Abolmaesumi, P., Kapur, T.: Confidence calibration and predictive uncertainty estimation for deep medical image segmentation. IEEE Trans. Med. Imaging **39**(12), 3868–3878 (2020)
25. Ng, M., et al.: Estimating uncertainty in neural networks for cardiac MRI segmentation: a benchmark study. IEEE Trans. Biomed. Eng. **70**, 1955–1966 (2022)
26. Ng, M., Guo, F., Biswas, L., Wright, G.A.: Estimating uncertainty in neural networks for segmentation quality control. In: 32nd International Conference on Neural Information Processing Systems, NIPS 2018, Montréal, Canada, pp. 3–6 (2018)
27. Prassni, J.S., Ropinski, T., Hinrichs, K.: Uncertainty-aware guided volume segmentation. IEEE Trans. Vis. Comput. Graph. **16**(6), 1358–1365 (2010)
28. Rahaman, R., et al.: Uncertainty quantification and deep ensembles. In: Neural Information Processing Systems, vol. 34, pp. 20063–20075 (2021)
29. Sahlsten, J., et al.: Application of simultaneous uncertainty quantification for image segmentation with probabilistic deep learning: performance benchmarking of oropharyngeal cancer target delineation as a use-case. medRxiv, pp. 2023–02 (2023)
30. Savjani, R.R., Lauria, M., Bose, S., Deng, J., Yuan, Y., Andrearczyk, V.: Automated tumor segmentation in radiotherapy. In: Seminars in Radiation Oncology, vol. 32, pp. 319–329. Elsevier (2022)
31. Shanmugam, D., Blalock, D., Balakrishnan, G., Guttag, J.: Better aggregation in test-time augmentation. In: Proceedings of the IEEE/CVF International Conference on Computer Vision, pp. 1214–1223 (2021)
32. Simpson, A.L., et al.: A large annotated medical image dataset for the development and evaluation of segmentation algorithms. arXiv preprint arXiv:1902.09063 (2019)
33. Wang, G., Li, W., Aertsen, M., Deprest, J., Ourselin, S., Vercauteren, T.: Aleatoric uncertainty estimation with test-time augmentation for medical image segmentation with convolutional neural networks. Neurocomputing **338**, 34–45 (2019)
34. Wen, Y., Tran, D., Ba, J.: BatchEnsemble: an alternative approach to efficient ensemble and lifelong learning. arXiv preprint arXiv:2002.06715 (2020)
35. Wilson, A.G., Izmailov, P.: Bayesian deep learning and a probabilistic perspective of generalization. In: Advances in Neural Information Processing Systems, vol. 33, pp. 4697–4708 (2020)
36. Zhang, L., Goldstein, M., Ranganath, R.: Understanding failures in out-of-distribution detection with deep generative models. In: International Conference on Machine Learning, pp. 12427–12436. PMLR (2021)

Numerical Uncertainty of Convolutional Neural Networks Inference for Structural Brain MRI Analysis

Inés Gonzalez Pepe[✉], Vinuyan Sivakolunthu, Hae Lang Park, Yohan Chatelain, and Tristan Glatard

Department of Computer Science and Software Engineering, Concordia University, Montreal, Canada
inesgp99@gmail.com

Abstract. This paper investigates the numerical uncertainty of Convolutional Neural Networks (CNNs) inference for structural brain MRI analysis. It applies Random Rounding—a stochastic arithmetic technique— to CNN models employed in non-linear registration (SynthMorph) and whole-brain segmentation (FastSurfer), and compares the resulting numerical uncertainty to the one measured in a reference image-processing pipeline (FreeSurfer recon-all). Results obtained on 32 representative subjects show that CNN predictions are substantially more accurate numerically than traditional image-processing results (non-linear registration: 19 vs 13 significant bits on average; whole-brain segmentation: 0.99 vs 0.92 Sørensen-Dice score on average), which suggests a better reproducibility of CNN results across execution environments.

Keywords: Numerical Stability · Convolutional Neural Networks · Non-Linear Registration · Whole-Brain Segmentation

1 Introduction

A motivating factor to study numerical uncertainty in neuroimaging is to establish measures of reliability in the tools observed, particularly in light of the reproducibility crisis [1–3]. Numerical uncertainty is key to the robustness of neuroimaging analyses. Small computational perturbations introduced in execution environments— including operating systems, hardware architecture, and parallelization—may amplify throughout analytical pipelines and result in substantial differences in the final outcome of analyses [4,5]. Such instabilities have been observed across many different tools and imaging modalities [6,7], and are likely to impact the reproducibility and robustness of analyses.

Convolutional Neural Networks (CNNs) are increasingly adopted for registration [8–10] and segmentation [11–14] of structural MRIs. Once trained, CNNs are orders of magnitude faster than traditional image-processing methods, achieve

---

Supplementary Information The online version contains supplementary material available at https://doi.org/10.1007/978-3-031-44336-7_7.

comparable accuracy, and seem to exhibit better generalizability to image modalities and orientations. However, the numerical uncertainty associated with CNN predictions in neuroimaging remains largely unexplored. While previous works suggested that CNNs might be subject to numerical instability [15–17], it is unclear how such instabilities manifest in specific CNN architectures used in structural brain MRI, and how the resulting numerical uncertainty compares to the one of traditional methods.

This paper measures the numerical uncertainty associated with CNN inference in neuroimaging, focusing specifically on non-linear registration and whole-brain segmentation of structural MRIs. To do so, it applies Random Rounding (RR) [18,19]—a practical stochastic arithmetic technique to estimate numerical uncertainty—to state-of-the-art CNN models SynthMorph [8] and Fast-Surfer [12], and compare their numerical uncertainty to the one measured from the FreeSurfer [20] "recon-all" reference neuroimaging tool.

2   Materials and Methods

We measured the numerical uncertainty of CNN models SynthMorph (non-linear registration) and FastSurfer (whole-brain segmentation) using RR. We applied these models to 35 subjects randomly selected in the CoRR dataset, using the FreeSurfer recon-all pipeline as a baseline for numerical uncertainty comparison.

2.1   Random Rounding

Random Rounding (RR) [18] is a form of Monte-Carlo Arithmetic (MCA) [21] that simulates rounding errors by applying the following perturbation to all floating-point (FP) operations of an application:

$$random\_rounding(x \circ y) = round(inexact(x \circ y))$$

where x and y are FP numbers, $\circ$ is an arithmetic operation, and $inexact$ is a random perturbation defined at a given virtual precision:

$$inexact(x) = x + 2^{e_x - t}\xi$$

where e_x is the exponent in the FP representation of x, t is the virtual precision, and ξ is a random uniform variable of $(-\frac{1}{2}, \frac{1}{2})$. To measure numerical uncertainty, we applied a perturbation of 1 ulp (unit of least precision, a.k.a the spacing between two consecutive FP numbers), which corresponds to a virtual precision of $t = 24$ bits for single-precision and $t = 53$ bits for double-precision.

We applied RR to the CNN models using Verrou [19,22], a tool that implements MCA through dynamic binary instrumentation with Valgrind [23], without needing to modify or recompile the source code. We instrumented the entire executables with RR, additionally using Verrou's custom libmath implementation named Interlibmath to avoid incorrect random perturbations in mathematical functions. We applied RR to FreeSurfer using "fuzzy libmath" [6], a version of the GNU mathematical library instrumented with the Verificarlo [24] compiler following the same principle as Verrou's Interlibmath instrumentation.

2.2   Numerical Uncertainty Metrics

We quantified numerical uncertainty by calculating the number of significant bits across multiple independent RR samples. The number of significant bits is informally defined as the number of bits in common between RR samples for a given FP value. We estimated the number of significant bits using the general non-parametric method described in [25] and implemented in the `significant_digits` package [26]. Given an RR sample X_i ($i \leq n$), this method computes the significance S_i^k of the kth bit in the mantissa of X_i as:

$$S_i^k = \mathbb{1}_{|Z_i| < 2^{-k}}$$

where $Z_i = X_i - x_{\text{IEEE}}$ and x_{IEEE} is the unperturbed result computed with IEEE. The kth bit in the mantissa is considered significant if the absolute value of Z_i is less than 2^{-k}. The number of significant bits across samples, $\hat{s}_b$, is then obtained as the maximal bit index that is significant for all samples:

$$\hat{s}_b = \max \left\{ k \in [\![1, m]\!] \text{ such that } \forall i \in [\![1, n]\!], \ S_i^k = \mathbb{1} \right\}$$

where m is the size of the mantissa, i.e., 53 bits for double precision numbers and 24 bits for single precision numbers. A value of 0 significant bits means that X bears no information while a value of m means that it has maximal information given the FP format used. The difference between the maximal and achieved values quantifies the information loss resulting from numerical uncertainty.

The number of significant bits is a versatile metric that applies to any program that produces results encoded as FP values. This is, however, not the case of segmentation tools that generally produce categorical variables encoded as integers representing segmentation labels despite the use of intermediate FP operations. Therefore, in order to assess the impact of stochastic rounding in these intermediate FP operations we used the minimum Sørensen-Dice scores computed pairwise across RR samples as uncertainty metric for segmentations. In addition, to have a more local uncertainty metric for segmentation results, we defined an entropy metric at each voxel:

$$E = -\sum_{i=1}^{r} p_i \ln p_i \qquad (1)$$

where r is the number of segmented regions, and p_i is the probability of region i at the voxel, computed across n Random Rounding samples. The entropy is 0 when the voxel is labeled with the same region across all RR samples, and it is maximal when the voxel is labeled differently for each RR sample.

2.3   Non-linear Registration

SynthMorph [8] is a 3D convolutional U-Net [27] that performs non-linear image registration robustly across MRI contrasts. The encoding section of the U-Net consists of 4 convolutional blocks, while the decoding section consists of 3 blocks with a skip connection to its respective encoding block. SynthMorph was trained from synthetic label maps created from geometric shapes from which images were generated with various contrasts, deformations, and artifacts. A contrast-invariant loss that measures label overlap was used to optimize model performance. SynthMorph's registration accuracy was shown to outperform state-of-the-art registration methods both within and across contrasts. We applied the SynthMorph "sm-brains" pre-trained model available on GitHub [28] to the linearly registered image produced by FreeSurfer recon-all (output of recon-all's -canorm step), using the MNI305 atlas as reference image. The subject and atlas images were cropped through visual inspection to match the $160 \times 192 \times 224$ dimension required by the model, and intensities were min-max scaled to [0–1]. We applied Verrou directly to the sm-brains model, by instrumenting the entirety of the model and using Verrou's Interlibmath implementation. Synth-Morph takes a couple of minutes to run, but when instrumented with Verrou, the runtime increased to a span of 2–3 days.

FreeSurfer "recon-all" [20] is a widely-used neuroimaging pipeline that implements spatial normalization to a brain template, whole-brain segmentation, and cortical surface extraction. The non-linear registration algorithm (mri_ca_register tool) minimizes through gradient descent an error functional that includes an intensity term, a topology constraining one, a metric preservation term, a smoothness term, and a label term [29]. We first ran recon-all on all the subjects with steps --motioncor --talairach --nuintensitycor --normalization --skullstrip --gcareg --canorm without RR, to obtain the linear registration used as input of SynthMorph. Then we ran the FreeSurfer recon-all step --careg that implements non-linear registration using our FreeSurfer version instrumented with fuzzy libmath. This command typically takes 3 h to run, but when instrumented with fuzzy libmath, the runtime increased to a span of 6 h.

2.4   Whole-Brain Segmentation

FastSurfer [12] is a CNN model that performs whole-brain segmentation, cortical surface reconstruction, fast spherical mapping, and cortical thickness analysis. The FastSurfer CNN is inspired from the QuickNAT model [11], which is composed of three 2D fully convolutional neural networks—each associated with a different 2D slice orientation—that each have the same encoder/decoder U-net architecture with skip connections, unpooling layers and dense connections as QuickNAT. The FastSurfer segmentations were shown to surpass state-of-the-art methods, as well as being generalizable to unseen datasets and having better test-retest reliability. We used the pre-trained model from FastSurfer available on GitHub [30] and we applied Verrou directly to this model, in the same way it was applied to SynthMorph. FastSurfer typically takes 30 min to run, but when instrumented with Verrou, the runtime increased to a span of 16–17 days.

FreeSurfer recon-all also implements whole-brain segmentation [20], through a maximum a-posteriori estimation of the segmentation based on the non-linear registration of the subject image to an atlas. Due to time constraints, only the subcortical structures and brain tissues were segmented by FreeSurfer whereas FastSurfer also segmented cortical structures, therefore a mask was applied to FastSurfer's cortical labels to identify them by the super classes "Left/Right Cerebral Cortex". Only regions common to both were further analysed (see list in Fig. 2a). Similar to FreeSurfer recon-all's non-linear registration, RR was applied to FreeSurfer recon-all's whole brain segmentation through Verificarlo's fuzzy libmath. The FreeSurfer recon-all commands `--motioncor` up to `--calabel`, the command that specifically performs subcortical segmentation were run. Typically, the segmentation takes around 4 h to complete, but with FreeSurfer instrumented with Verificarlo, the runtime increased to 10–12 h.

2.5   Dataset and Processing

We used the Consortium for Reliability and Reproducibility (CoRR) dataset [31], a multi-centric, open resource aimed to evaluate test-retest reliability and reproducibility. We randomly selected 35 T1-weighted MRIs from 35 different subjects, one from each CoRR acquisition site, and accessed them through Datalad [32,33]. The selected images included a range of image dimensions, voxel resolutions and data types (Appendix A (see Supplementary Material)). We excluded 2 subjects that failed linear registration with FreeSurfer recon-all and a third subject that failed segmentation with FastSurfer. Each pipeline or model was run in Singularity containers over 10 RR samples from which we measured numerical uncertainty. Due to long computing times induced by Verrou instrumentation ($\approx$17 days per subject) we were only able to get 4 RR samples for FastSurfer, which we complemented with an IEEE (non-RR) sample conceptually identical to an RR sample.

We processed the data with SynthMorph and FreeSurfer recon-all on the Narval cluster from École de Technologie Supérieure (ETS, Montréal), managed by Calcul Québec and The Digital Alliance of Canada which include AMD Rome 7502, AMD Rome 7532, and AMD Milan 7413 CPUs with 48 to 64 physical cores, 249 GB to 4000 GB of RAM and Linux kernel 3.10. We executed FastSurfer on the slashbin cluster at Concordia University with 8 × compute nodes each with an Intel Xeon Gold 6130 CPU, 250 GB of RAM, and Linux kernel 4.18.0-240.1.1.el8_lustre.x86_64.

We used FreeSurfer v7.3.1, SynthMorph v0.2, FastSurfer v2.1.1, Fuzzy v0.9.1, and Singularity/Apptainer v1.1. Verrou v3.21.0 was used for FastSurfer, while Verrou v3.20.0 with a special fix available on GitHub [34] was used for SynthMorph due to compatibility issues between the model and Verrou's Interlibmath. The scripts and Dockerfiles for this experiment can be found on GitHub [35].

3   Results

The numerical uncertainty measured for the SynthMorph CNN model was lower than for Freesurfer recon-all (Fig. 1a, as measured both in the resampled images

($p < 10^{-6}$, two-tailed paired t-test) and in the warp fields ($p < 10^{-5}$) despite only the libmath libraries in FreeSurfer being instrumented in contrast to the entirety of SynthMorph. The number of significant bits in warp fields was computed as the average number of significant bits across the x, y and z components. On average, out of 24 bits available, the SynthMorph resampled image had 19.56 significant bits while FreeSurfer recon-all's had only 13.43 significant bits; the SynthMorph warp field had 18.55 significant bits while FreeSurfer recon-all's had only 14.12 significant bits. These important differences show a clear superiority of the CNN model compared to FreeSurfer recon-all in terms of numerical uncertainty. Moreover, we also observed a larger variability of the numerical uncertainty across subjects in FreeSurfer recon-all compared to SynthMorph.

The differences in average numerical uncertainty observed between FreeSurfer and SynthMorph were confirmed by visual inspection of the non-linearly registered images and warp fields (Fig. 1b). The numerical uncertainty in registered images was structurally consistent, with higher uncertainty in the gray matter and at the border of the brain than in the white matter, both for SynthMorph and for FreeSurfer recon-all. The numerical uncertainty in warp fields exhibited interesting structural patterns that would benefit from further investigation.

The numerical uncertainty of FastSurfer segmentations was significantly lower than for FreeSurfer recon-all in 31 out of 35 brain regions (Fig. 2a, with

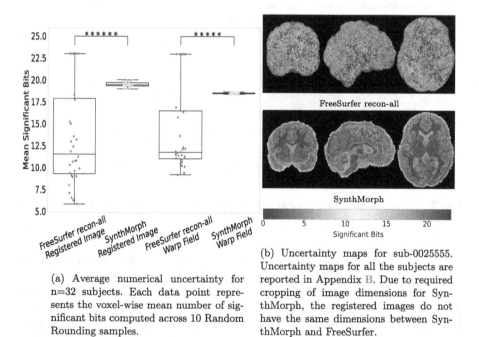

(a) Average numerical uncertainty for n=32 subjects. Each data point represents the voxel-wise mean number of significant bits computed across 10 Random Rounding samples.

(b) Uncertainty maps for sub-0025555. Uncertainty maps for all the subjects are reported in Appendix B. Due to required cropping of image dimensions for SynthMorph, the registered images do not have the same dimensions between SynthMorph and FreeSurfer.

Fig. 1. Numerical uncertainty measured in the non-linearly registered images and warp fields produced by FreeSurfer recon-all and the SynthMorph CNN model.

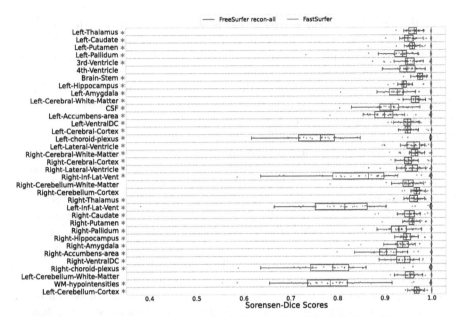

(a) Sørensen-Dice score comparison across FreeSurfer recon-all and FastSurfer for n=33 subjects. Each data point represents the minimum Sørensen-Dice score across all pairs of 5 Random Rounding samples for a given subject. * indicates significant differences between FastSurfer and FreeSurfer recon-all segmentations for the region ($p < 0.001$, two-tailed paired t-test with Bonferroni correction).

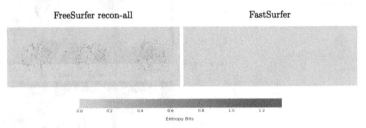

(b) Entropy maps for sub-0027012, computed across r=35 regions and n=5 Random Samples (see Eq. 1). Entropy maps for all the subjects are reported in Appendix C.

Fig. 2. Numerical uncertainty measured in the segmentations produced by FreeSurfer recon-all and the FastSurfer CNN model.

very substantial differences in some regions. Here again, a larger variability was observed in FreeSurfer recon-all segmentations than in FastSurfer segmentations. Overall, FastSurfer averages a Sørensen-Dice score of 0.99 across all regions, while FreeSurfer is at 0.92. The differences in Sørensen-Dice scores observed between FreeSurfer recon-all and FastSurfer were confirmed in local entropy maps (Fig. 2b where we visually noted a substantial discrepancy between both methods. For FreeSurfer recon-all, clusters of non-zero entropy values were observed across the brain, whereas for FastSurfer non-zero entropy values were limited to scattered voxels. The entropy maps, in addition to visual inspection, confirm that, despite the relatively high average Sørensen-Dice scores, FreeSurfer recon-all exhibited variability identifying the edges of subcortical structures, while Fast-Surfer remained certain in its segmentations.

4   Conclusion

The numerical uncertainty measured in CNN models SynthMorph and Fast-Surfer was substantially lower than in FreeSurfer recon-all, amounting to differences in the order of 4 to 6 significant bits in non-linearly registered images, and of up to 0.4 Sørensen-Dice score values in segmentations. We believe that the high numerical uncertainty observed in FreeSurfer recon-all compared to CNN models results from the use of numerical optimization techniques in FreeSurfer recon-all while CNN models only involve low-dimensional convolutions, max-pooling operators, and simple activation functions. The low numerical uncertainty found in CNN models is consistent with previous observations in the very different task of protein function prediction [36]. The numerical uncertainty found in FreeSurfer recon-all is also consistent with previous observations on FreeSurfer recon-all non-linear registration [6] and segmentation [37].

Our results suggest that neuroimaging CNN models are significantly more robust to small numerical perturbations than traditional image processing approaches. Therefore, we expect CNN results to be more reproducible across execution environments than traditional image processing approaches, implying better portability across software and hardware systems.

Our results report on the numerical uncertainty resulting from CNN *inference*, which is a relevant proxy for the uncertainty experienced by model end-users across different execution environments. However, the numerical uncertainty resulting from CNN *training* was not measured in our experiments. We speculate that some of the numerical uncertainty observed in FreeSurfer recon-all results is intrinsic to the problems of subject-to-template non-linear registration and whole-brain segmentation, and should therefore manifest during CNN training. Mathematically, training CNN models involves numerical optimization in high-dimensional spaces, which we expect to be less numerically stable than CNN inference, and comparably stable to FreeSurfer recon-all. Should this assumption be accurate, the numerical uncertainty of predictions made by a sample of CNN models trained with Random Rounding should be substantial, which we plan to leverage in our future work by building efficient ensemble models capturing the numerical variability associated with non-linear registration or segmentation, possibly resulting in improved predictions.

Acknowledgements. Computations were made on the Narval and Béluga super-computers from École de Technologie Supérieure (ETS, Montréal), managed by Calcul Québec and The Digital Alliance of Canada. The operation of these supercomputers are funded by the Canada Foundation for Innovation (CFI), le Ministère de l'Économie, des Sciences et de l'Innovation du Québec (MESI) and le Fonds de recherche du Québec - Nature et technologies (FRQ-NT).

References

1. Botvinik-Nezer, R., et al.: Variability in the analysis of a single neuroimaging dataset by many teams. Nature **582**(7810), 84–88 (2020)
2. Fanelli, D.: Is Science Really facing a reproducibility crisis, and do we need it to? Proc. Nat. Acad. Sci. **115**(11), 2628–2631 (2018). https://www.pnas.org/doi/abs/10.1073/pnas.1708272114
3. Baker, M.: 1,500 scientists lift the lid on reproducibility. Nature **533**(7604), 452–454 (2016)
4. Gronenschild, E.H., et al.: The effects of FreeSurfer version, workstation type, and Macintosh operating system version on anatomical volume and cortical thickness measurements. PLOS ONE **7**(6), e38234 (2012)
5. Glatard, T., et al.: Reproducibility of neuroimaging analyses across operating systems. Front. Neuroinform. **9**, 12 (2015)
6. Salari, A., Chatelain, Y., Kiar, G., Glatard, T.: Accurate simulation of operating system updates in neuroimaging using Monte-Carlo arithmetic. In: Sudre, C.H., et al. (eds.) UNSURE/PIPPI -2021. LNCS, vol. 12959, pp. 14–23. Springer, Cham (2021). https://doi.org/10.1007/978-3-030-87735-4_2
7. Kiar, G., et al.: Numerical uncertainty in analytical pipelines lead to impactful variability in brain networks. PLOS ONE **16**(11), e0250755 (2021)
8. Hoffmann, M., Billot, B., Greve, D.N., Iglesias, J.E., Fischl, B., Dalca, A.V.: SynthMorph: learning contrast-invariant registration without acquired images. IEEE Trans. Med. Imaging **41**(3), 543–558 (2021)
9. Iglesias, J.E.: A ready-to-use machine learning tool for symmetric multi-modality registration of brain MRI. Sci. Rep. **13**(1), 6657 (2023)
10. Balakrishnan, G., Zhao, A., Sabuncu, M., Guttag, J., Dalca, A.V.: VoxelMorph: a learning framework for deformable medical image registration. IEEE TMI Trans. Med. Imaging **38**, 1788–1800 (2019)
11. Roy, A.G., Conjeti, S., Navab, N., Wachinger, C., Initiative, A.D.N., et al.: QuickNAT: a fully convolutional network for quick and accurate segmentation of neuroanatomy. Neuroimage **186**, 713–727 (2019)
12. Henschel, L., Conjeti, S., Estrada, S., Diers, K., Fischl, B., Reuter, M.: FastSurfer - a fast and accurate deep learning based neuroimaging pipeline. Neuroimage **219**, 117012 (2020)
13. Jog, A., Hoopes, A., Greve, D.N., Van Leemput, K., Fischl, B.: PSACNN: pulse sequence adaptive fast whole brain segmentation. Neuroimage **199**, 553–569 (2019)
14. Li, W., Wang, G., Fidon, L., Ourselin, S., Cardoso, M.J., Vercauteren, T.: On the compactness, efficiency, and representation of 3D convolutional networks: brain parcellation as a pretext task. In: Niethammer, M., et al. (eds.) IPMI 2017. LNCS, vol. 10265, pp. 348–360. Springer, Cham (2017). https://doi.org/10.1007/978-3-319-59050-9_28
15. Higham, N.J.: Accuracy and Stability of Numerical Algorithms. SIAM (2002)
16. Kloberdanz, E., Kloberdanz, K.G., Le, W.: DeepStability: a study of unstable numerical methods and their solutions in deep learning. In: Proceedings of the 44th International Conference on Software Engineering, pp. 586–597 (2022)
17. Chakraborty, A., Alam, M., Dey, V., Chattopadhyay, A., Mukhopadhyay, D.: A survey on adversarial attacks and defences. CAAI Trans. Intell. Technol. **6**(1), 25–45 (2021)
18. Forsythe, G.E.: Reprint of a note on rounding-off errors. SIAM Rev. **1**(1), 66 (1959)

19. Févotte, F., Lathuiliere, B.: VERROU: a CESTAC evaluation without recompilation. SCAN **2016**, 47 (2016)
20. Fischl, B., et al.: Whole brain segmentation: automated labeling of neuroanatomical structures in the human brain. Neuron **33**(3), 341–355 (2002)
21. Parker, D.S.: Monte Carlo Arithmetic: Exploiting Randomness in Floating-Point Arithmetic. University of California (Los Angeles). Computer Science Department (1997)
22. Verrou: floating-point error checker. https://github.com/edf-hpc/verrou. Accessed 28 Jun 2023
23. Nethercote, N., Seward, J.: Valgrind: a framework for heavyweight dynamic binary instrumentation. ACM SIGPLAN Not. **42**(6), 89–100 (2007)
24. Denis, C., Castro, P.D.O., Petit, E.: Verificarlo: checking floating point accuracy through Monte Carlo arithmetic. In: 2016 IEEE 23nd Symposium on Computer Arithmetic (ARITH), Los Alamitos, CA, USA, July 2016, pp. 55–62. IEEE Computer Society (2016)
25. Sohier, D., Castro, P.D.O., Févotte, F., Lathuilière, B., Petit, E., Jamond, O.: Confidence intervals for stochastic arithmetic. ACM Trans. Math. Softw. (TOMS) **47**(2), 1–33 (2021)
26. Significant digits package. https://github.com/verificarlo/significantdigits. Accessed 28 Jun 2023
27. Ronneberger, O., Fischer, P., Brox, T.: U-Net: convolutional networks for biomedical image segmentation. In: Navab, N., Hornegger, J., Wells, W.M., Frangi, A.F. (eds.) MICCAI 2015. LNCS, vol. 9351, pp. 234–241. Springer, Cham (2015). https://doi.org/10.1007/978-3-319-24574-4_28
28. Unsupervised learning for image registration. https://github.com/voxelmorph/voxelmorph#SynthMorph. Accessed 28 Jun 2023
29. Fischl, B., et al.: Sequence-independent segmentation of magnetic resonance images. Neuroimage **23**, S69–S84 (2004)
30. PyTorch implementation of FastSurferCNN. https://github.com/Deep-MI/FastSurfer. Accessed 28 Jun 2023
31. Zuo, X.-N., et al.: An open science resource for establishing reliability and reproducibility in functional connectomics. Sci. Data **1**(1), 1–13 (2014)
32. Halchenko, Y., et al.: DataLad: distributed system for joint management of code, data, and their relationship. J. Open Source Softw. **6**(63), 3262 (2021)
33. Corr DataLad dataset. http://datasets.datalad.org/?dir=/corr/RawDataBIDS. Accessed 28 Jun 2023
34. Verrou fix for SynthMorph. https://github.com/yohanchatelain/verrou/tree/synchroLib-v2.4.0. Accessed 28 Jun 2023
35. Scripts used in the experiments. https://github.com/InesGP/structural_mri_uncertainty/tree/main. Accessed 28 Jun 2023
36. Pepe, I.G., Chatelain, Y., Kiar, G., Glatard, T.: Numerical stability of DeepGOPlus inference. arXiv preprint arXiv:2212.06361 (2022)
37. Salari, A., Kiar, G., Lewis, L., Evans, A.C., Glatard, T.: File-based localization of numerical perturbations in data analysis pipelines. GigaScience **9**(12), giaa106 (2020)

How Inter-rater Variability Relates to Aleatoric and Epistemic Uncertainty: A Case Study with Deep Learning-Based Paraspinal Muscle Segmentation

Parinaz Roshanzamir[1]([envelope]), Hassan Rivaz[1], Joshua Ahn[2], Hamza Mirza[2], Neda Naghdi[3], Meagan Anstruther[3], Michele C. Battié[4], Maryse Fortin[3], and Yiming Xiao[5]

[1] Department of Electrical and Computer Engineering, Concordia University, Montreal, Canada
parinaz.roshanzamir@concordia.ca
[2] Faculty of Health Sciences, Western University, London, Canada
[3] Health, Kinesiology, and Applied Physiology, Concordia University, Montreal, Canada
[4] School of Physical Therapy and Western's Bone and Joint Institute, Western University, London, Canada
[5] Department of Computer Science and Software Engineering, Concordia University, Montreal, Canada

Abstract. Recent developments in deep learning (DL) techniques have led to great performance improvement in medical image segmentation tasks, especially with the latest Transformer model and its variants. While labels from fusing multi-rater manual segmentations are often employed as ideal ground truths in DL model training, inter-rater variability due to factors such as training bias, image noise, and extreme anatomical variability can still affect the performance and uncertainty of the resulting algorithms. Knowledge regarding how inter-rater variability affects the reliability of the resulting DL algorithms, a key element in clinical deployment, can help inform better training data construction and DL models, but has not been explored extensively. In this paper, we measure aleatoric and epistemic uncertainties using test-time augmentation (TTA), test-time dropout (TTD), and deep ensemble to explore their relationship with inter-rater variability. Furthermore, we compare UNet and TransUNet to study the impacts of Transformers on model uncertainty with two label fusion strategies. We conduct a case study using multi-class paraspinal muscle segmentation from T2w MRIs. Our study reveals the interplay between inter-rater variability and uncertainties, affected by choices of label fusion strategies and DL models.

Keywords: Inter-rater variability · Uncertainty · TransUNet · Segmentation

1 Introduction

In recent years, deep learning (DL) techniques have shown remarkable success in various fields, including medical domains. However, using DL models in safety-critical applications, such as medical diagnosis and treatment, requires not only high accuracy but also a proper understanding of the model's uncertainty, which is crucial for the safety and adaptability of medical DL algorithms. In general, a DL model's uncertainty can be classified into two main categories: epistemic and aleatoric [4]. Epistemic uncertainty is related to the model's lack of knowledge about the data and can be reduced by collecting more data or optimizing the model's architecture and training process. On the other hand, aleatoric uncertainty is related to inherent factors of the data (e.g., noise) and cannot be reduced. Additionally, in image segmentation tasks, where supervised learning is widely used, another important factor that can affect uncertainty is inter-rater variability. Supervised segmentation algorithms require training data with well-annotated ground truth (GT) masks. While GT masks obtained by fusing annotations of multiple experts are commonly recommended, it is still costly and the best practice to combine different annotations is still being explored. Various factors can affect inter-rater variability in manual medical image segmentation, including differences in expertise, rater style [18], image noise, extreme anatomical variations among individuals, and so on. In turn, inter-rater variability propagates the influences of these factors to the resulting DL models through training as uncertainties of the algorithms. For example, image noise and measurement errors (e.g., due to partial volume effects) can result in aleatoric uncertainty while extreme individual anatomical variations, which may not be sufficiently represented in the data, can contribute to epistemic uncertainty. Therefore, knowledge regarding the relationship of inter-rater variability with aleatoric and epistemic uncertainties in DL models can help better understand their performance and reliability and inform the dataset design and learning strategies to improve them.

To date, various methods have been proposed to measure aleatoric and epistemic uncertainties of DL models. In terms of epistemic uncertainty, Bayesian DL estimates a distribution for each weight in the network and uses these distributions to measure epistemic uncertainty [10, 20]. As Bayesian networks can bear high computational costs, more efficient approaches have been reported for uncertainty estimation. Gal and Ghahramani [6] proposed dropout at test-time to approximate Bayesian neural networks for uncertainty estimation while deep ensemble trained multiple versions of the same DL model to derive epistemic uncertainty [11]. Finally, variational inference [9] has also been used but limits the types of DL models in application. Different approaches have been reported ever since to improve the quality of the uncertainties obtained from these methods [12]. Another important aspect in accurate uncertainty quantification is the metric. Camarasa et al. [1] performed an extensive study on different metrics for measuring epistemic uncertainty using test-time dropout (TTD). They concluded that the measure of entropy produces uncertainty maps that are in correspondence with the misclassification in the model. Utilizing a sampling strategy similar to TTD, Wang et al. [19] proposed test-time augmentation (TTA) for aleatoric uncertainty assessment, which samples from the data distribution by using input data augmentation at inference time.

In training data, inter-rater variability can be measured as the entropy of the rater annotations. Lemay et al. [13] showed the superiority of random sampling and STAPLE in inter-rater variability preservation and image segmentation accuracy with a UNet. Jensen et al. [8] discovered that random sampling leads to higher classification accuracy and better-calibrated results. Vincent et al. [18] characterized rater style in terms of bias and variance of raters' annotations and explored the relationship between rater bias and data uncertainty. Nichyporuk et al. [15] proposed a segmentation model that can learn the bias in the annotations for better results. However, previous studies haven't explored the impact of label fusion methods on aleatoric and epistemic uncertainties, or the potential relationship between inter-rater variability and these uncertainties. In addition, most of them only used a conventional UNet as the base model. In recent years, Transformers that better model long-range dependencies via self-attention have gained popularity in vision tasks [5], and the hybrid Transformer-convolutional neural network (CNN) models that complement their merits, such as TransUNet [2], have shown better segmentation accuracy [16]. With a different mechanism, the addition of Transformers can have potential effects on the uncertainty of a segmentation model, which has not been investigated, but can be highly valuable.

To address the aforementioned knowledge gaps, In this study, we investigate inter-rater variability in relation to DL model uncertainties using commonly employed TTA, TTD, and deep ensemble techniques for MRI-based paraspinal muscle segmentation, with a comparison of UNet and TransUNet. Our work has three main novel contributions: First, we are the first to compare Transformers and CNNs for their impacts on model uncertainties and the encoding of inter-rater variability, especially in a multi-class segmentation setting. Second, we explore the effect of label fusion methods during network training on DL model uncertainty (aleatoric and epistemic) for the first time. Lastly and most importantly, we explore the relationship between inter-rater variability and aleatoric/epistemic uncertainties, which has not been done so far. We hope the article will offer instrumental insights to facilitate the design and selection of DL datasets, training strategies, and model architectures.

2 Materials and Methodology

2.1 Inter-rater Variability

To measure inter-rater variability, we use the entropy of the average GT annotations for each image [13]. The pixel-wise entropy is calculated as:

$$H(y_i) = -\sum_{c=1}^{C} P(y_i = c)\log(P(y_i))$$ (1)

where C is the number of classes, and y_i is the GT annotation at voxel i, obtained by simply averaging the one-hot GT masks from all raters. Similarly, the entropy of the model predictions can be calculated as the entropy of the softmax layer outputs before binarization. This entropy can be considered as the prediction inter-rater variability. *An ideal model should preserve the inter-rater variability during inference and produce prediction entropies similar to the GT entropy.* To quantify the perseverance of inter-rater variability in a model, we calculated the class-wise Brier score [13] as:

$$Brier\ Score = \frac{1}{N_{image}}\sum_{k=1}^{N_{image}} \left(\frac{1}{N_{voxel}} \sum_{i=1}^{N_{voxel}} (y_{i,k} - \widehat{y_{i,k}})^2 \right)$$ (2)

where N_{image} is the total number of images in the test set, N_{voxel} is the number of voxels in each image, $y_{i,k}$ is the average GT, and $\widehat{y_{i,k}}$ is the prediction for voxel i of image k (the softmax probability). A Brier score close to zero indicates perfect preservation of inter-rater variability in model predictions [13].

2.2 Aleatoric and Epistemic Uncertainty Assessment

In this study, we compare TTD and deep ensemble for epistemic uncertainty assessment, and use TTA for measuring aleatoric uncertainty for both the UNet and TransUNet. In each experiment, we acquire 10 samples. In TTA and TTD, these samples are obtained through 10 forward passes through the model for each image, and in deep ensembles, each image is fed to 10 independently trained models of the same architecture. The obtained samples are then averaged to produce a final prediction for each image. This prediction is then used to calculate the entropy based on Eq. 1. To compare the quality of the resulting uncertainty maps of TTD and deep ensembles, we measure the association between uncertainties and misclassifications, using the framework provided by Mobiny et al. [14]. Conventionally, in a confusion matrix the term "positive" is used for "capturing a target label/class", but here, we define it as "capture a high uncertainty". An ideal model should be uncertain only when making a wrong prediction. Thus, a "false positive" means that the model is highly uncertain about a correct classification. Identifying a voxel as "uncertain" requires thresholding an uncertainty map. We perform the operation at multiple values, calculate the corresponding precision and recall metrics, and finally use the area under the precision-recall curve (AUC-PR) as an indicator of the quality of an uncertainty map.

2.3 Network Architectures and Label Fusion

Lemay et al. [13] showed that the method used for label fusion in a multi-rater dataset can affect the model calibration and how well it preserves inter-rater variability. In this study, we used two different methods for integrating multi-rater annotations into our training framework: 1) The majority vote of all raters is used as the GT for each image; 2) The annotation of one rater is randomly selected at each epoch during training (refer to as random sampling). In order to explore the impact of self-attention modules on uncertainty, we train two sets of models, using TransUNet and UNet as the base model architectures. The TransUNet model has four upsampling layers with two convolution blocks at each layer. For a fair comparison, we used a UNet model with the same number of layers as the TransUNet (4 layers). With these two architectures and two label fusion methods, we trained four models for TTA and TTD-related analysis. To achieve deep ensembles for measuring epistemic uncertainty, we also trained a set of 10 UNets and a set of 10 TransUNets with majority vote GT.

2.4 Dataset

Our dataset consists of a total of 673 lumbosacral T2-weighted (T2w) MR images of 119 patients (59 male, age = 30 59y) from the European research consortium project, Genodisc, on commonly diagnosed lumbar pathologies. The subjects were selected with the factors of sex and age roughly equally distributed. Our study was approved by local research ethics board. The MRI scans are from 6 different disc levels. However, due to imaging artifacts and cropping, not all patients have usable axial slices at all spinal levels. All axial MR images were processed with non-local means denoising [3] and N4 inhomogeneity correction [17] to improve image quality. Then, the left and right multifidus (MF) and erector spinae (ES) muscles were manually segmented for all patients independently by three different raters to study low back pain [21], resulting in four segmentation classes for each image (see Fig. 1). All raters had two training sessions to ensure the quality and consistent protocol of the segmentation.

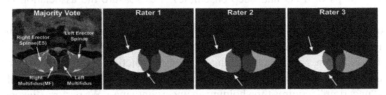

Fig. 1. Left to right: axial MRI of paraspinal muscles, along with the majority vote label and the individual rater annotations. The arrows indicate the differences among rater annotations.

3 Experiments and Results

3.1 Experimental Set-Up and Implementation Details

Each model is trained to segment four paraspinal muscles. We divide the dataset subject-wise into training, validation, and test sets with respect to age group and sex. Specifically, 24 subjects are selected for testing, 76 for training, and 19 for validation. For TTD, we add a dropout layer to each of the convolution blocks in the upsampling layers of UNet and TransUNet, resulting in the addition of a total of 8 dropouts in each model. Both models are trained for 250 epochs with early stopping applied to avoid overfitting. We applied random rotation, translation, intensity shift, and Gaussian noise during the training and applied the same augmentations at test time for TTA [19]. As mentioned in the previous section, we use entropy for measuring uncertainties in this study (Eq. 1). In order to explore the correlation between aleatoric and epistemic uncertainties with inter-rater variability, we calculate the Pearson correlation coefficients and conduct a variance partitioning analysis to verify the percentage of variance explained by the uncertainties for inter-rater variability (i.e., GT entropy).

3.2 Results

The Brier scores for inter-rater variability preservation assessment are listed in Table 1 for all the models and all segmented muscle groups. Additionally, we also plotted the prediction entropy against GT entropy with the associated correlations in Fig. 2(a). These results indicate that compared with UNet, TransUNet better preserves inter-rater variability with lower Brier scores and higher "prediction entropy vs. GT entropy" correlations. Also, we observe that training with random sampling results in lower Brier scores than using majority vote for the same models. To evaluate the quality of epistemic uncertainty estimation, the AUC-PR results are detailed in Table 2, where TransUNet outperforms its UNet counterpart in both TTD and deep ensemble approaches. Here, random sampling, TTD, and deep ensemble show similar performance so for the rest of the experiments to compare random sampling and majority vote, we only trained the deep ensemble model with majority vote GT. Table 3 contains the correlations of inter-rater variability with aleatoric and epistemic uncertainties, and the evidence shows that in our case study, inter-rater variability is more strongly associated with epistemic uncertainty than the aleatoric one, and the phenomenon is stronger for TransUNet. The superiority of TransUNet is further demonstrated in Table 4, where the models' performance is evaluated with Dice score. According to the scatter plots of Fig. 2(b), we also see that higher correlation is produced with random sampling training, and the UNet model contains higher epistemic uncertainties. Finally, from the variance partitioning analysis (see Table 5), we observe that epistemic uncertainty accounts for ~35% of the GT entropy variance with TransUNet and ~12% with UNet. Additionally, we observe that aleatoric uncertainty only explains a very small portion of the variance.

Table 1. Quantitative assessment of inter-rater variability preservation in the trained models.

	Average Brier Score ($\times 10^{-3}$)			
	Right MF	Left MF	Right ES	Left ES
TransUNet (majority vote)	1.324	1.209	1.936	1.890
UNet (majority vote)	2.071	1.973	3.286	3.146
TransUNet (random sampling)	1.179	1.103	1.742	1.758
UNet (random sampling)	1.769	1.670	2.866	2.912

Table 2. AUC-PR for epistemic uncertainty. Each column shows a method for measuring the uncertainty and the training method, while the rows indicate the utilized models.

	AUC-PR		
	TTD-majority vote	TTD-random sampling	Deep Ensemble
TransUNet	0.3753	0.3737	0.3831
UNet	0.3387	0.3337	0.3265

Table 3. Correlation of epistemic and aleatoric uncertainties with inter-rater variability. Majority vote is shown as "Maj" while random sampling is shown as "Rand".

	Pearson Correlation Coefficient				
	TTD - Maj	TTD - Rand	Deep Ensemble	TTA - Maj	TTA -Rand
TransUNet	0.5874	0.6165	0.5985	0.0500	0.1028
UNet	0.3380	0.3635	0.3574	0.0719	0.0163

4 Discussion

With the experiments, the results of the Brier scores and "prediction entropy vs. GT entropy" correlations indicate that both the TransUNet architecture and random sampling have positive impacts on preserving inter-rater variability. Furthermore, as Fig. 2(b) shows, TransUNet produces lower epistemic uncertainty with tighter distribution. Our results confirm the conclusion of Lemay et al. [13] on the benefit of random sampling in preserving inter-rater variability. Furthermore, we observe that it also results in higher prediction entropies (Fig. 2(a)) with more uncertain results. When assessing AUC-PR, TransUNet offers a better quality of epistemic uncertainty estimation while the advantages of different estimation techniques and training strategies are not clear. When comparing the correlations of inter-rater variability (i.e., GT entropy) with aleatoric and epistemic uncertainties, the results in Table 3 demonstrate that epistemic uncertainty has a stronger association in our segmentation task and database while no significant correlations with aleatoric uncertainties were found, regardless of the DL model choice. This may be partially explained by the fact that manual segmentations were performed based on pre-processed images with similar noise levels, reducing the chance of inter-rater variability being affected by image noise. Future studies to explore the impact of image noise levels and artifacts (e.g., bias fields) can further verify this hypothesis, but require a more extensive and costly experimental set-up with human raters. In addition, there is also a higher correlation between inter-rater variability and epistemic uncertainty with TransUNet and random sampling as shown in Table 3, proving that model uncertainty can be network-dependent and better preservation of inter-rater variability leads to a stronger link to the model uncertainty. Although better "epistemic uncertainty vs. inter-rater variability" correlation and preservation of inter-rater variability are desirable as they can result in more effective reduction of uncertainty through lowering inter-rater variability, the overall higher prediction entropy and epistemic uncertainty may be a price to pay in the case of random sampling compared to majority vote. As a final evaluation, we used variance partitioning (Table 5) to quantify the contributions of aleatoric and epistemic uncertainties toward inter-rater variability. This way, we leverage the DL models to understand the source of inter-rater variability, which is difficult to quantify from human raters [7]. The results indicate a partial influence of epistemic uncertainty that may be due to the factors of anatomical variability (common in pathological paraspinal muscles) and difference in visual perception, and minimum contribution from aleatoric uncertainty. This suggests the benefit of preprocessing and systematic training for expert labeling. For all experiments, the incorporation of Transformers has positive impacts in lowering the uncertainty and encoding inter-rater variability, potentially leading to better segmentation accuracy. Their ability to encode long-range content over the image may play a key role in the observed behaviors.

Table 4. Model performance measured by Dice Score. The superior performance of TransUNet compared to the UNet counterpart is indicated by **($p < 0.01$) and *($p < 0.05$).

	Average Dice Score (%)			
	Right MF	Left MF	Right ES	Left ES
TransUNet (majority vote-TTD)	**94.36 ± 2.74	**94.77 ± 2.37	**94.29 ± 3.35	**94.18 ± 3.77
UNet (majority vote-TTD)	92.41 ± 8.9	92.77 ± 8.52	92.21 ± 9.52	92.06 ± 9.31
TransUNet (random sampling-TTD)	94.15 ± 3.14	94.44 ± 2.53	*94.08 ± 3.38	*93.87 ± 3.94
UNet (random sampling-TTD)	92.76 ± 8.86	93.07 ± 8.67	92.49 ± 9.06	91.92 ± 10.04
TransUNet (ensemble)	*94.72 ± 2.38	*94.80 ± 2.49	**94.75 ± 3.26	**94.50 ± 3.18
UNet (ensemble)	92.83 ± 8.73	93.23 ± 8.56	92.79 ± 8.96	92.05 ± 10.12

Table 5. Variance partitioning analysis for inter-rater variability. The values show the percentage of inter-rater variability variation related to the epistemic and aleatoric uncertainties.

		Epistemic (%)	Aleatoric (%)	Joint (%)
TransUNet	TTA + TTD(majority vote)	34.506	0.251	34.896
	TTA + TTD(random sampling)	38.007	0.251	38.360
	TTA + Ensemble	35.803	0.251	35.986
UNet	TTA + TTD(majority vote)	11.422	0.517	11.517
	TTA + TTD(random sampling)	12.772	0.517	12.919
	TTA + Ensemble	13.215	0.517	13.385

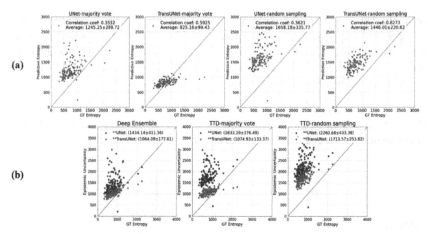

Fig. 2. (a) Assessment of preservation of inter-rater variability, along with the average entropy and Pearson correlation coefficient shown in the graphs. (b) Comparison of epistemic uncertainty with inter-rater variability, along the average uncertainties shown in the graphs. Significant correlation is denoted by **(p < 0.01).

5 Conclusion

In this paper, we explored the relationship of inter-rater variability with aleatoric and epistemic uncertainties, using two DL models and two label fusion methods. Our case study indicated that inter-rater variability has a high correlation with epistemic uncertainty and no significant correlation with aleatoric uncertainty. Moreover, we showed that TransUNet better preserves inter-rater variability and its correlation with epistemic uncertainty, and it also has lower epistemic uncertainty and prediction entropy than UNet, potentially explaining its segmentation accuracy. Finally, our results showed that the label fusion method not only affects the preservation of inter-rater variability but it also affects epistemic uncertainty as well.

Acknowledgment. We acknowledge the support of the Natural Sciences and Engineering Research Council of Canada (NSERC) and NVIDIA for donation of the GPU.

References

1. Camarasa, R., et al.: A quantitative comparison of epistemic uncertainty maps applied to multi-class segmentation. Mach. Learn. Biomed. Imaging **1**, 1–39 (2021)
2. Chen, J., et al.: Transunet: transformers make strong encoders for medical image segmentation. arXiv preprint arXiv:2102.04306 (2021)
3. Coupe, P., Yger, P., Prima, S., Hellier, P., Kervrann, C., Barillot, C.: An optimized block-wise nonlocal means denoising filter for 3-D magnetic resonance images. IEEE Trans. Med. Imaging **27**(4), 425–441 (2008). https://doi.org/10.1109/TMI.2007.906087.PMID:18390341;PMCID:PMC2881565

4. Der Kiureghian, A., Ditlevsen, O.D.: Aleatoric or epistemic? Does it matter? Struct. Saf. **31**(2), 105–112 (2009). https://doi.org/10.1016/j.strusafe.2008.06.020

5. Dosovitskiy, A., et al.: An image is worth 16x16 words: transformers for image recognition at scale. arXiv preprint arXiv:2010.11929 (2020)

6. Gal, Y., Ghahramani, Z.: Dropout as a Bayesian approximation: representing model uncertainty in deep learning. In: Proceedings of the 33rd International Conference on Machine Learning, pp. 1050–1059. PMLR (2016)

7. Ghandeharioun, A., Eoff, B., Jou, B., Picard, R.: Characterizing sources of uncertainty to proxy calibration and disambiguate annotator and data bias. In: IEEE/CVF International Conference on Computer Vision Workshop (ICCVW), pp. 4202–4206 (2019)

8. Jensen, M.H., Jørgensen, D.R., Jalaboi, R., Hansen, M.E., Olsen, M.A.: Improving uncertainty estimation in convolutional neural networks using inter-rater agreement. In: Shen, D., et al. (eds.) MICCAI 2019. LNCS, vol. 11767, pp. 540–548. Springer, Cham (2019). https://doi.org/10.1007/978-3-030-32251-9_59

9. Jones, C.K., Wang, G., Yedavalli, V., Sair, H.: Direct quantification of epistemic and aleatoric uncertainty in 3D U-net segmentation. J. Med. Imaging (Bellingham) **9**(3), 034002 (2022). https://doi.org/10.1117/1.JMI.9.3.034002. Epub 2022 Jun 8. PMID: 35692283; PMCID: PMC9174341

10. Kendall, A., Gal, Y.: What uncertainties do we need in bayesian deep learning for computer vision? Adv. Neural Inf. Process. Syst. **30** (2017)

11. Lakshminarayanan, B., Pritzel, A., Blundell, C.: Simple and scalable predictive uncertainty estimation using deep ensembles. Adv. Neural Inf. Process. Syst. **30** (2017)

12. Laves, M.H., Ihler, S., Fast, J., Kahrs, L., Ortmaier, T.: Recalibration of aleatoric and epistemic regression uncertainty in medical imaging. Mach. Learn. Biomed. Imaging **1**, 1–26 (2021)

13. Lemay, A., Gros, C., Naga Karthik, E., Cohen-Adad, J.: Label fusion and training methods for reliable representation of inter-rater uncertainty. Mach. Learn. Biomed. Imaging **1**, 1–27 (2022)

14. Mobiny, A., Yuan, P., Moulik, S.K., Garg, N., Wu, C.C., Van Nguyen, H.: Dropconnect is effective in modeling uncertainty of bayesian deep networks. Sci. Rep. **11**(1), 1–14 (2021)

15. Nichyporuk, B., et al.: Rethinking generalization: the impact of annotation style on medical image segmentation. Mach. Learn. Biomed. Imaging **1**, 1–37 (2022)

16. Roshanzamir, P., et al.: Joint paraspinal muscle segmentation and inter-rater labeling variability prediction with multi-task TransUNet. In: International Workshop on Uncertainty for Safe Utilization of Machine Learning in Medical Imaging, 14 September 2022, pp. 125–134. Springer, Cham (2022). https://doi.org/10.1007/978-3-031-16749-2_12

17. Tustison, N.J., et al.: N4ITK: improved N3 bias correction. IEEE Trans. Med. Imaging **29**(6), 1310 (2010)

18. Vincent, O., Gros, C., Cohen-Adad, J.: Impact of individual rater style on deep learning uncertainty in medical imaging segmentation. arXiv preprint arXiv:2105.02197 (2021)

19. Wang, G., Li, W., Aertsen, M., Deprest, J., Ourselin, S., Vercauteren, T.: Aleatoric uncertainty estimation with test-time augmentation for medical image segmentation with convolutional neural networks. Neurocomputing **338**, 34–45 (2019)

20. Wilson, A.G., Izmailov, P.: Bayesian deep learning and a probabilistic perspective of generalization. Adv. Neural. Inf. Process. Syst. **33**, 4697–4708 (2020)

21. Xiao, Y., Fortin, M., Ahn, J., Rivaz, H., Peters, T.M., Battie, M.C.: Statistical morphological analysis reveals characteristic paraspinal muscle asymmetry in unilateral lumbar disc herniation. Sci. Rep. **11**, 15576 (2021). https://doi.org/10.1038/s41598-021-95149-6

Uncertainty Estimation and Propagation in Accelerated MRI Reconstruction

Paul Fischer[1(✉)], K. Thomas[2], and Christian F. Baumgartner[1]

[1] Cluster of Excellence – Machine Learning for Science, University of Tübingen,
Tübingen, Germany
paul.fischer@uni-tuebingen.de
[2] Medical Image and Data Analysis Lab, University Hospital of Tübingen,
Tübingen, Germany

Abstract. MRI reconstruction techniques based on deep learning have led to unprecedented reconstruction quality especially in highly accelerated settings. However, deep learning techniques are also known to fail unexpectedly and hallucinate structures. This is particularly problematic if reconstructions are directly used for downstream tasks such as real-time treatment guidance or automated extraction of clinical parameters (e.g. via segmentation). Well-calibrated uncertainty quantification will be a key ingredient for safe use of this technology in clinical practice. In this paper we propose a novel probabilistic reconstruction technique (PHiRec) building on the idea of conditional hierarchical variational autoencoders. We demonstrate that our proposed method produces high-quality reconstructions as well as uncertainty quantification that is substantially better calibrated than several strong baselines. We furthermore demonstrate how uncertainties arising in the MR reconstruction can be propagated to a downstream segmentation task, and show that PHiRec also allows well-calibrated estimation of segmentation uncertainties that originated in the MR reconstruction process.

1 Introduction

Fast magnetic resonance imaging (MRI) techniques play a vital role in clinical practice, allowing to scan an increased number of patients while alleviating patient discomfort caused by prolonged acquisition times. Highly accelerated MR acquisitions also hold the key unlocking novel applications such as real-time MR-guided radiation therapy [31], or shortened scans for directly estimating clinical parameters via segmentations potentially without human oversight [4, 26, 30].

In recent years, MRI reconstruction techniques relying on deep learning (DL) have gained substantial interest due to their excellent performance at very high acceleration rates [11, 12, 20] and ability to provide real-time reconstructions [8, 35]. Although DL-based reconstructions often appear realistic and of high quality, they have also been shown to fail unexpectedly [7], and hallucinate structural details [18]. Crucially, they lack the ability to indicate regions

---

Supplementary Information The online version contains supplementary material available at https://doi.org/10.1007/978-3-031-44336-7_9.

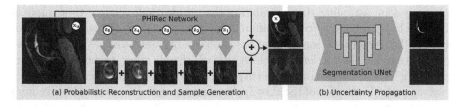

Fig. 1. (a) In our proposed Probabilistic Hierarchical Reconstruction (PHiRec) model, five latent variables z_l generate residual changes at different resolution scales. These residual changes are added to the undersampled input image x_u to generate the final output x. The model can be used to sample likely reconstructions and to obtain reliable uncertainty estimates. (b) These samples can then be propagated to a subsequent segmentation network allowing to estimate the resulting segmentation uncertainty.

in the reconstructed images that are uncertain. This problem is exacerbated in scenarios where reconstructed images are used directly for downstream tasks, such as real-time treatment guidance [31], or extraction of clinical parameters via segmentation [30].

The reconstruction process inherently contains *aleotoric*, or irreducible, uncertainty due to the fact that a single undersampled acquisition can correspond to an infinite number of potential reconstructions with varying likelihoods [33]. Moreover, *epistemic* uncertainty may arise when the reconstruction model is applied outside the domain on which it was trained. Developing DL-based reconstruction techniques that are able to reflect those uncertainties is crucial, especially in applications without human oversight.

Several approaches have been proposed to model uncertainty of DL-based MRI reconstruction techniques. Schlemper et al. [25] proposed to estimate epistemic and aleotoric uncertainty using MC dropout and a heteroscedastic variance term, respectively. Hepp et al. [9] presented promising preliminary results for estimating epistemic uncertainty using an ensemble of networks. However, the approach does not scale well since the number of samples that can be generated is equal to the number of networks in the ensemble. Narnhofer et al. [19] modelled epistemic uncertainty by combining the previously proposed Total Deep Variation approach [14] with the Bayes-by-Backprop technique, which models every network weight as a Gaussian with individual mean and variance [3]. We note that this approach has heavy GPU-memory requirements and limits the complexity of the network architecture that can be used. Tezcan et al. [29] have proposed learning the prior distribution of MR images using a variational autoencoder (VAE) and using Markov-Chain Monte-Carlo (MCMC) to sample possible reconstructions. However, this approach is severely limited by the sampling times and is not suitable for real-time applications. Angelopoulos et al. [1] proposed an uncertainty quantification method based on conformal prediction, which offers a straightforward implementation and comes with mathematical guarantees. However, this method does not allow generating samples which could be used to explore potential reconstructions or propagate uncertainty to subsequent tasks. Recently diffusion models have demonstrated exceptional reconstruction performance [5,11,22,32]. While uncertainty quantification is feasible in those models, it is currently hindered by extremely long sampling times rendering them unsuitable for real-time applications. In closely related work on a different imaging modality, Zhang et al. [34] proposed a PET reconstruction method based on conditional VAEs (cVAE) [27]. The approach employed a bottleneck architecture which only allows to model the uncertainty at a low spatial resolution and is prone to producing blurry reconstructions. Lastly, a major limitation of the existing literature is that none of the above studies present a quantitative evaluation of uncertainty quantification or a thorough comparison with baseline methods, instead relying solely on qualitative interpretation of the uncertainty maps.

In this paper, we propose a novel approach for estimating aleotoric uncertainty based on a hierarchical conditional VAE [27]. Hierarchical cVAEs have been shown to perform exceptionally well for estimating aleotoric uncertainty in segmentation tasks [2,15]. Specifically, they address two issues encountered in non-hierarchical cVAEs: blurry samples and limited expressivity to model high-dimensional spatial probability distributions [16,34]. However, despite their promise, hierarchical cVAEs remain unexplored in the context of MRI reconstruction. Here, we build on the Probabilistic Hierarchical Segmentation (PHiSeg) model by Baumgartner et al. [2], which was originally proposed for segmentation to create a novel *P*robabilistic *Hi*erarchical *R*econstruction technique which we coin PHiRec[1]. Our contributions are as follows:

- We propose PHiRec and show that it outperforms several strong baselines in terms of calibration of its uncertainty quantification.
- We demonstrate that the uncertainties originating in the MR reconstruction can be *propagated* to a downstream segmentation task in order to estimate the resulting segmentation uncertainties. This is, to the best of our knowledge, the first work to explore the propagation of uncertainties arising in DL-based MRI reconstruction to a downstream task.
- We present the first comprehensive *quantitative* evaluation of uncertainty quantification for MRI reconstruction contrasting several baselines.

2   Methods

We denote a fully-sampled MR image as $\mathbf{x} \in \mathbb{C}^N$ where N is the number of pixels. In a multi-coil MR acquisition, the acquired k-space data can be modelled as $\mathbf{y} = \mathcal{MFS}\mathbf{x} + \eta$, where $\mathcal{M}$ is an undersampling operator, $\mathcal{F}$ is the Fourier operator, $\mathcal{S}$ is an operator encoding the spatial sensitivity of each coil, and η is used to model thermal scanner noise. The goal of MRI reconstruction is to estimate the maximimum a-posteriori of the distribution $p(\mathbf{x}|\mathbf{y})$. For uncertainty estimation we are additionally interested in the spread of this distribution.

We pose the reconstruction as a de-aliasing problem by modelling the distribution $p(\mathbf{x}|\mathbf{x}_u)$, where the undersampled image $\mathbf{x}_u$ is obtained by applying the inverse Fourier operator to the zero-filled measurement data $\mathbf{y}$. In the following, we show how a hierarchical cVAE approach can be employed to model the distribution $p(\mathbf{x}|\mathbf{x}_u)$. As shown in Fig. 1, we model the distribution using a cVAE

---

[1] The code for PHiRec is available at https://github.com/paulkogni/MR-Recon-UQ.

that has $L = 5$ separate latent variables $\mathbf{z}_l$ each operating on a different resolution scale. For instance, $\mathbf{z}_1$ operates at the original image resolution, while $\mathbf{z}_5$ operates at a resolution that was four times downpooled by a factor of 2. Each resolution level is responsible for probabilistically generating residual changes that are added to the input image $\mathbf{x}_u$ in order to remove undersampling artifacts and obtain the reconstructed image $\mathbf{x}$. Our modelling assumption includes that the distribution of each $\mathbf{z}_l$ depends on the input image $\mathbf{x}_u$ as well as the latent variable of the resolution level below $\mathbf{z}_{l+1}$. This allows higher resolution levels to have a notion of what changes were already performed in the resolution level below. As was previously shown, this hierarchical approach is a very expressive model for capturing high-dimensional probability distributions [2,15]. Note that in contrast to the hierarchical cVAE methods developed in the context of segmentation [2,15], our proposed PHiRec model contains a skip connection from the input to the output which we found to facilitate the de-aliasing problem. This is reflected by the dependence of the likelihood $p(\mathbf{x}|\mathbf{z}_{1:L}, \mathbf{x}_u)$ on $\mathbf{x}_u$ in the equations below.

Using the above modelling assumptions $p(\mathbf{x}|\mathbf{x}_u)$ can be written as

$$p(\mathbf{x}|\mathbf{x}_u) = \int p(\mathbf{x}|\mathbf{z}_{1:L}, \mathbf{x}_u)p(\mathbf{z}_1|\mathbf{z}_2, \mathbf{x}_u)\ldots p(\mathbf{z}_{L-1}|\mathbf{z}_L, \mathbf{x}_u)p(\mathbf{z}_L|\mathbf{x}_u)d\mathbf{z}_{1:L}.$$

Following the standard variational approach we maximise the evidence lower bound, $\mathrm{ELBO}(\mathbf{x}|\mathbf{x}_u) := \log p(\mathbf{x}|\mathbf{x}_u) - KL(q(\mathbf{z}_{1:L}|\mathbf{x}, \mathbf{x}_u)||(p(\mathbf{z}_{1:L}|\mathbf{x}, \mathbf{x}_u))$, which is a lower bound on the true log likelihood. Using our model assumptions, and following the derivation in Baumgartner et al. [2], we can write the ELBO as

$$\mathrm{ELBO}(\mathbf{x}|\mathbf{x}_u) = \mathbb{E}_{q(\mathbf{z}_{1:L}|\mathbf{x}_u,\mathbf{x})} \left[\log p(\mathbf{x}|\mathbf{z}_{1:L}, \mathbf{x}_u)\right] - \alpha_L KL \left[q(\mathbf{z}_L|\mathbf{x}, \mathbf{x}_u)||p(\mathbf{z}_L|\mathbf{x}_u)\right]$$

$$- \sum_{l=1}^{L} \alpha_l \mathbb{E}_{q(\mathbf{z}_{l+1}|\mathbf{x}_u,\mathbf{x})} \left[KL \left[q(\mathbf{z}_l|\mathbf{z}_{l+1}, \mathbf{x}, \mathbf{x}_u)||p(\mathbf{z}_l|\mathbf{z}_{l+1}, \mathbf{x}_u)\right]\right],$$

where $\alpha_l := 4^{(l-1)}$ are heuristic weight terms to equalize the magnitude of the KL-terms of the different resolution levels. The prior and posterior distributions are modelled using axis-aligned Normal distributions

$$p(\mathbf{z}_l|\mathbf{z}_{l+1}, \mathbf{x}_u) = \mathcal{N}\left(\mathbf{z}_l|\Phi_l^{(\mu)}(\mathbf{z}_{l+1}, \mathbf{x}_u), \Phi_l^{(\sigma)}(\mathbf{z}_{l+1}, \mathbf{x}_u)\right)$$

$$q(\mathbf{z}_l|\mathbf{z}_{l+1}, \mathbf{x}, \mathbf{x}_u) = \mathcal{N}\left(\mathbf{z}_l|\Theta_l^{(\mu)}(\mathbf{z}_{l+1}, \mathbf{x}, \mathbf{x}_u), \Theta_l^{(\sigma)}(\mathbf{z}_{l+1}, \mathbf{x}, \mathbf{x}_u)\right),$$

where $\Phi_l^{(\mu)}$, $\Phi_l^{(\sigma)}$, $\Theta_l^{(\mu)}, \Theta_l^{(\sigma)}$ are neural network functions that estimate each distribution's mean and variance. The likelihood of the final de-aliased reconstruction $p(\mathbf{x}|\mathbf{z}_{1:L}, \mathbf{x}_u)$ is also modelled as a Normal distribution with a fixed variance and a mean that is estimated using another neural network. While in principle a mathematically valid model could be implemented using any neural network architecture the method lends itself to implementation as a U-Net-like architecture with the prior and posteriors implemented as U-Net encoders, and the likelihood as a decoder. For simplicity here we use the architecture proposed by Baumgartner et al. [2] with the aforementioned addition of a skip connection from input to output (see Fig. 1). A schematic of this architecture is shown in the supplementary materials.

We train the entire architecture end-to-end with pairs of undersampled images $\mathbf{x}_u$ and ground truth reconstructions $\mathbf{x}$ using the ELBO defined above as objective. After training the posterior network is no longer required. The prior network can be used to predict the means and standard deviations of the $\mathbf{z}_l$ variables. Given these values an arbitrary number of latent variable samples can be generated, and decoded using the likelihood network, to obtain final reconstruction samples. The mean prediction as well as the spread of the distribution $p(\mathbf{x}|\mathbf{x}_u)$ can then be calculated from these samples $\{\mathbf{x}_i\}$.

Uncertainty Propagation. Given a separately trained deterministic segmentation network $f : \mathbf{x} \mapsto \mathbf{s}$, we can furthermore estimate the distribution of the segmentations $\mathbf{s}$ given the undersampled image $\mathbf{x}_u$, $p(\mathbf{s}|\mathbf{x}_u)$, using the Monte Carlo method. Specifically, we can segment each of our reconstruction samples $\{\mathbf{x}_i\}$ using f and analyse the resulting distribution of segmentations empirically.

3   Experiments and Results

Baselines. We compared our proposed PHiRec technique to several baseline strategies for estimating aleotoric and epistemic uncertainty. Firstly, we compared with Schlemper et al.'s [25] approach for which we separately evaluated the epistemic uncertainty quantification based on MC Dropout, the aleatoric uncertainty estimation rooted in a heteroscedastic variance term, as well as the combination of the two approaches as originally described. Furthermore, we compared to the ensemble based approach for estimating epistemic uncertainty initially demonstrated by Hepp et al. [9]. Specifically, we created an ensemble of 20 separately trained reconstruction networks. Lastly, we extended the probabilistic U-Net [16] to MRI reconstruction using the same strategy as for PHiRec to allow a comparison to another cVAE-based method. In order to focus the evaluation on the uncertainty quantification mechanism rather than on architectural details, all baseline methods were implemented using U-Nets, or U-Net-like architectures in the case of the probabilistic U-Net and our PHiRec. Furthermore, to ensure a fair comparison to our proposed approach, we implemented a skip connection from input to output for all baselines. We used the mean and standard deviation calculated using 20 samples for all methods and in all experiments to obtain the final prediction and spread of the distribution, respectively.

Data. All experiments were performed on the Stanford Knee MRI Multi-Task Evaluation (SKM-TEA) dataset [6], which comprises raw multi-coil k-space data of knee scans, along with segmentations for six anatomical structures. We employed the supplied undersampling masks, which were designed with a Poisson-Disc pattern. The provided coil sensitivities were used in a SENSE reconstruction [23] to obtain the fully-sampled ground truth reconstruction $\mathbf{x}$ as well as the undersampled network inputs $\mathbf{x}_u$. We divided the dataset into a training, validation, and test set using the official splits.

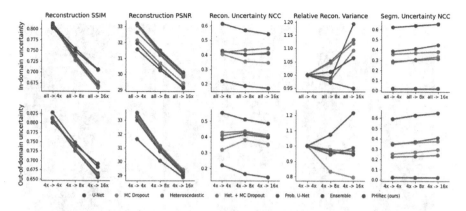

Fig. 2. Quantitative results for the ID (top row), and OOD (bottom row) settings.

Experiment Settings. All experiments were performed in two distinct experimental settings: *in-domain (ID)* and *out-of-domain (OOD)*. In the ID setting, we simultaneously trained and also evaluated on images with acceleration rates 4x, 8x, and 16x. Since all acceleration factors have been seen during training, this setting is dominated by aleotoric uncertainty, that stems from the fact that there are multiple plausible solutions for each undersampled image. In the OOD setting, we trained only on images that have been accelerated 4x, but again tested on images with 4x, 8x, and 16x acceleration. In this setting, for 8x and 16x, there is an additional component of epistemic uncertainty in addition to the aleotoric uncertainty as the testing data moves away from the data that the model has seen during training.

Training Details. All models were implemented in PyTorch [21] and were trained with the Adam optimizer [13] with a learning rate of 10^{-4} using a batch size of 6. The models were trained on NVIDIA RTX 2080 GPUs except the heteroschedastic models and PHiRec which were trained on an NVIDIA Tesla V100 GPU due to increased GPU memory demands. We trained all models for 10 days and model selection was performed based on structural similarity index (SSIM) of the reconstructions on a held-out validation set.

Evaluation of Reconstruction Quality. For both the ID and OOD setting, we evaluated the reconstruction quality in terms of SSIM and peak signal to noise ratio (PSNR). Here, we additionally compared against a standard reconstruction U-Net without uncertainty quantification [10] to ensure the uncertainty quantification does not lead to a general performance degradation. The results are shown in the first two columns of Fig. 2. We observed that, as expected, the performance of all methods degraded with increasing acceleration rates for both settings. This can also be visually confirmed by the squared error maps in Fig. 3 for the OOD setting. Similar effects were observed for the ID setting (see results in supplementary materials). We further observed that all methods performed similarly in terms of pure reconstruction quality. However, PHiRec slightly underperformed in terms of PSNR, but slightly outperformed the other

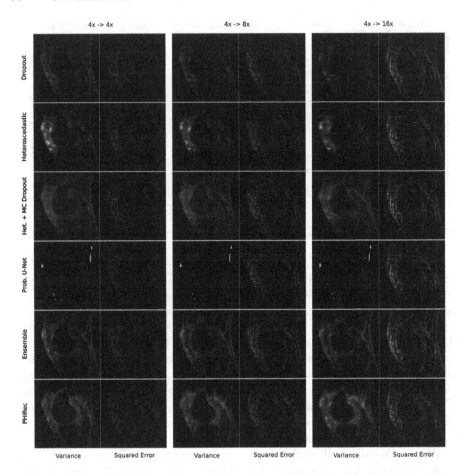

Fig. 3. Variance maps and reconstruction squared error maps in the OOD setting where the column labels have the format "train acceleration" → "test acceleration".

methods in terms of SSIM. This is consistent with the qualitative observation that, while PHiRec reproduced the structural properties exceptionally well, it had a slightly blurry quality. Example reconstructions for all methods are shown in the supplementary materials.

Evaluation of Reconstruction Uncertainty. A crucial quality for a robust uncertainty quantification method is that the model is *calibrated*, i.e. that the uncertainty correlates with the model error [17]. To assess calibration, we computed the average normalised cross correlation (NCC) between the reconstruction uncertainty and the reconstruction squared error for all test images. The results in the third column of Fig. 2 show that PHiRec is substantially better calibrated than the baselines in all settings. It is followed by the MC Dropout + Heteroscedastic Variance approach by Schlemper et al. [25]. The probabilistic U-Net [16], which was originally proposed for segmentation in a multi-annotator regime, performed the worst in this category due to its poor sample diversity. These results can also be visually confirmed by comparing the uncertainty maps and corresponding error maps in Fig. 3. It is surprising that PHiRec, which is designed to model aleotoric uncertainties, also performed best in the OOD setting. We believe this might be due to the fact that differing acceleration factors do not constitute a large enough domain shift to add significant epistemic uncertainty.

In addition to calibration, we also measured the intuition that the uncertainty should monotonically *increase* with increasing acceleration rates. To this end, we calculated the relative change of the cumulative variance of all image pixels of the 8x and 16x settings with respect to the 4x setting. The results are shown in column four ("Relative Recon. Variance") of Fig. 2. Surprisingly, PHiRec is the only model for which the uncertainty consistently increases for higher acceleration rates. Instead, we found the uncertainty unexpectedly *decreased* for most models between 4x and 8x acceleration. This can be visually confirmed for the OOD setting in the example image shown in Fig. 3.

Evaluation Uncertainty Propagation. Lastly, we investigated propagating the uncertainty to a downstream segmentation task. To this end, we trained a standard deterministic segmentation U-Net with pairs of ground truth images $\mathbf{x}$ and corresponding segmentation masks $\mathbf{s}$ from the SKM-TEA training set. As before we generated a set of 20 reconstruction samples $\{\mathbf{x}_i\}$ for our accelerated test images using all investigated techniques and obtained the corresponding segmentation $\{\mathbf{s}_i\}$ using the segmentation net. We calculated the spread of the segmentation distribution using γ-maps which were defined by Baumgartner et al. [2] as $\gamma(\{\mathbf{s}_i\}) = \mathbb{E}[CE(\bar{\mathbf{s}}, \mathbf{s}_i)]$, where CE denotes the cross-entropy and $\bar{\mathbf{s}}$ is the mean segmentation. Figure 4 shows pairs of γ-maps and segmentation error maps for an example image in the OOD setting with 16x acceleration. The scaling of the color maps is shared for all images. Qualitatively samples generated by PHiRec exhibited an excellent correlation between the error and the variance outperforming the baselines. We also computed the NCC between the error maps and the segmentation variance (i.e. γ-maps) to measure the calibration of the segmentation uncertainty. The results are shown in column five of Fig. 2. Again, PHiRec clearly outperformed the baseline methods.

4 Discussion

Well-calibrated uncertainty estimation is a crucial component for safely applying DL-based techniques to MRI reconstruction. In this paper, we described PHiRec, a novel reconstruction approach based on hierarchical conditional VAEs, which produces uncertainty estimates substantially better calibrated than several strong baselines. We further demonstrated, how uncertainties originating in the reconstruction process can be propagated to the downstream task of segmentation. In addition to our methodological contributions, we also present the, to our knowledge, first thorough quantitative comparison of different methods for uncertainty quantification in MRI reconstruction.

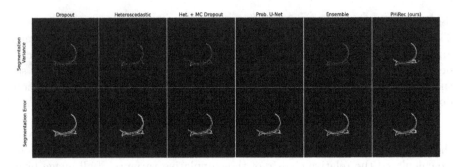

Fig. 4. Segmentation variance maps (measured by γ-maps) and segmentation error maps in the OOD setting with 16x acceleration.

Propagation of uncertainty to downstream tasks may allow to build fail-safe mechanisms to identify when uncertainties are too large to safely make a clinical decision or to guide a treatment. While our study used the simple U-Net as a base architecture and did not enforce data consistency with the measured k-space data, in future work we aim to combine our findings with state-of-the-art methods that are using multiple prediction and data consistency stages (e.g. [14, 24, 28]). Future work will also focus on investigating the interplay of aleotoric and epistemic uncertainty for larger domain shifts such as changes in anatomy.

Acknowledgments. Funded by the Deutsche Forschungsgemeinschaft (DFG, German Research Foundation) under Germany's Excellence Strategy - EXC number 2064/1 - Project number 390727645. The authors thank the International Max Planck Research School for Intelligent Systems (IMPRS-IS) for supporting Paul Fischer.

References

1. Angelopoulos, A.N., et al.: Image-to-image regression with distribution-free uncertainty quantification and applications in imaging, February 2022. arXiv arXiv:2202.05265 [cs, eess, q-bio, stat]
2. Baumgartner, C.F., et al.: Phiseg: Capturing uncertainty in medical image segmentation (2019). https://doi.org/10.48550/ARXIV.1906.04045, arXiv:1906.04045
3. Blundell, C., Cornebise, J., Kavukcuoglu, K., Wierstra, D.: Weight uncertainty in neural network. In: International Conference on Machine Learning, pp. 1613–1622. PMLR (2015)
4. Calivá, F., et al.: Breaking speed limits with simultaneous ultra-fast MRI reconstruction and tissue segmentation. In: Medical Imaging with Deep Learning, pp. 94–110. PMLR (2020)
5. Chung, H., Ye, J.C.: Score-based diffusion models for accelerated MRI. Med. Image Anal. **80**, 102479 (2022)
6. Desai, A.D., et al.: SKM-TEA: a dataset for accelerated MRI reconstruction with dense image labels for quantitative clinical evaluation (2022)
7. Gottschling, N.M., Antun, V., Adcock, B., Hansen, A.C.: The troublesome kernel: why deep learning for inverse problems is typically unstable. arXiv preprint arXiv:2001.01258 (2020)

8. Hauptmann, A., Arridge, S., Lucka, F., Muthurangu, V., Steeden, J.A.: Real-time cardiovascular MR with spatio-temporal artifact suppression using deep learning-proof of concept in congenital heart disease. Magn. Reson. Med. **81**(2), 1143–1156 (2019)

9. Hepp, T., Gatidis, S., Hammernik, K., Küstner, T.: Uncertainty estimation via ensembling for deep learning-based MR image reconstruction. In: ISMRM, vol. 685 (2022)

10. Hyun, C.M., Kim, H.P., Lee, S.M., Lee, S., Seo, J.K.: Deep learning for undersampled MRI reconstruction. Phys. Med. Biol. **63**(13), 135007 (2018)

11. Jalal, A., Arvinte, M., Daras, G., Price, E., Dimakis, A.G., Tamir, J.I.: Robust compressed sensing MRI with deep generative priors, December 2021. arXiv arXiv:2108.01368 [cs, math, stat]

12. Jin, K.H., McCann, M.T., Froustey, E., Unser, M.: Deep convolutional neural network for inverse problems in imaging. IEEE Trans. Image Process. **26**(9), 4509–4522 (2017). https://doi.org/10.1109/TIP.2017.2713099, http://ieeexplore. ieee.org/document/7949028/

13. Kingma, D.P., Ba, J.: Adam: a method for stochastic optimization (2017)

14. Kobler, E., Effland, A., Kunisch, K., Pock, T.: Total deep variation for linear inverse problems. In: Proceedings of the IEEE/CVF Conference on Computer Vision and Pattern Recognition, pp. 7549–7558 (2020)

15. Kohl, S.A.A., et al.: A hierarchical probabilistic u-net for modeling multi-scale ambiguities (2019)

16. Kohl, S.A.A., et al.: A probabilistic u-net for segmentation of ambiguous images (2018). https://doi.org/10.48550/ARXIV.1806.05034, https://arxiv.org/abs/1806. 05034

17. Laves, M.H., Ihler, S., Fast, J.F., Kahrs, L.A., Ortmaier, T.: Recalibration of aleatoric and epistemic regression uncertainty in medical imaging. arXiv preprint arXiv:2104.12376 (2021)

18. Morshuis, J.N., Gatidis, S., Hein, M., Baumgartner, C.F.: Adversarial robustness of MR image reconstruction under realistic perturbations. In: Haq, N., Johnson, P., Maier, A., Qin, C., Würfl, T., Yoo, J. (eds.) Machine Learning for Medical Image Reconstruction, vol. 13587, pp. 24–33. Springer, Cham (2022). https://doi. org/10.1007/978-3-031-17247-2_3

19. Narnhofer, D., Effland, A., Kobler, E., Hammernik, K., Knoll, F., Pock, T.: Bayesian uncertainty estimation of learned variational MRI reconstruction. IEEE Trans. Med. Imaging **41**(2), 279–291 (2022). https://doi.org/10.1109/TMI.2021. 3112040

20. Ongie, G., Jalal, A., Metzler, C.A., Baraniuk, R.G., Dimakis, A.G., Willett, R.: Deep learning techniques for inverse problems in imaging, May 2020. arXiv arXiv:2005.06001 [cs, eess, stat]

21. Paszke, A., et al.: An imperative style, high-performance deep learning library. In: Advances in Neural Information Processing Systems, vol. 32, pp. 8024–8035. Curran Associates, Inc. (2019). http://papers.neurips.cc/paper/9015-pytorch-an-imperative-style-high-performance-deep-learning-library.pdf

22. Peng, C., Guo, P., Zhou, S.K., Patel, V., Chellappa, R.: Towards performant and reliable undersampled MR reconstruction via diffusion model sampling (2022). https://doi.org/10.48550/ARXIV.2203.04292, arXiv:2203.04292

23. Pruessmann, K.P., Weiger, M., Scheidegger, M.B., Boesiger, P.: SENSE: sensitivity encoding for fast MRI. Magn. Reson. Med. Off. J. Int. Soci. Magn. Reson. Med. **42**(5), 952–962 (1999)

24. Schlemper, J., Caballero, J., Hajnal, J.V., Price, A.N., Rueckert, D.: A deep cascade of convolutional neural networks for dynamic MR image reconstruction. IEEE Trans. Med. Imaging **37**(2), 491–503 (2017)

25. Schlemper, J., et al.: Bayesian deep learning for accelerated MR image reconstruction. In: Knoll, F., Maier, A., Rueckert, D. (eds.) MLMIR 2018. LNCS, vol. 11074, pp. 64–71. Springer, Cham (2018). https://doi.org/10.1007/978-3-030-00129-2_8

26. Schlemper, J., et al.: Cardiac MR segmentation from undersampled k-space using deep latent representation learning. In: Frangi, A.F., Schnabel, J.A., Davatzikos, C., Alberola-López, C., Fichtinger, G. (eds.) MICCAI 2018. LNCS, vol. 11070, pp. 259–267. Springer, Cham (2018). https://doi.org/10.1007/978-3-030-00928-1_30

27. Sohn, K., Lee, H., Yan, X.: Learning structured output representation using deep conditional generative models. In: Advances in Neural Information Processing Systems, vol. 28 (2015)

28. Sriram, A., et al.: End-to-end variational networks for accelerated MRI reconstruction. In: Martel, A.L., et al. (eds.) MICCAI 2020. LNCS, vol. 12262, pp. 64–73. Springer, Cham (2020). https://doi.org/10.1007/978-3-030-59713-9_7

29. Tezcan, K.C., Karani, N., Baumgartner, C.F., Konukoglu, E.: Sampling possible reconstructions of undersampled acquisitions in MR imaging with a deep learned prior. IEEE Trans. Med. Imaging **41**(7), 1885–1896 (2022)

30. Tolpadi, A.A., et al.: K2S challenge: from undersampled k-space to automatic segmentation. Bioengineering **10**(2), 267 (2023)

31. Waddington, D.E.J., et al.: On real-time image reconstruction with neural networks for MRI-guided radiotherapy, May 2022. arXiv:2202.05267 [physics]

32. Xie, Y., Li, Q.: Measurement-conditioned denoising diffusion probabilistic model for under-sampled medical image reconstruction. In: Wang, L., Dou, Q., Fletcher, P.T., Speidel, S., Li, S. (eds.) Medical Image Computing and Computer Assisted Intervention, vol. 13436, pp. 655–664. Springer, Cham (2022). https://doi.org/10.1007/978-3-031-16446-0_62

33. Zeng, G., et al.: A review on deep learning MRI reconstruction without fully sampled k-space. BMC Med. Imaging **21**(1), 195 (2021). https://doi.org/10.1186/s12880-021-00727-9

34. Zhang, C., Barbano, R., Jin, B.: Conditional variational autoencoder for learned image reconstruction. Comput. **9**(11), 114 (2021)

35. Zhou, Z., et al.: Parallel imaging and convolutional neural network combined fast MR image reconstruction: applications in low-latency accelerated real-time imaging. Med. Phys. **46**(8), 3399–3413 (2019)

Uncertainty-Based Quality Assurance of Carotid Artery Wall Segmentation in Black-Blood MRI

Elina Thibeau-Sutre[(✉)], Dieuwertje Alblas, Sophie Buurman, Christoph Brune, and Jelmer M. Wolterink

Mathematics of Imaging and AI, Department of Applied Mathematics, Technical Medical Centre, University of Twente, Enschede, The Netherlands
{e.thibeau-sutre,j.m.wolterink}@utwente.nl

Abstract. The application of deep learning models to large-scale data sets requires means for automatic quality assurance. We have previously developed a fully automatic algorithm for carotid artery wall segmentation in black-blood MRI that we aim to apply to large-scale data sets. This method identifies nested artery walls in 3D patches centered on the carotid artery. In this study, we investigate to what extent the uncertainty in the model predictions for the contour location can serve as a surrogate for error detection and, consequently, automatic quality assurance. We express the quality of automatic segmentations using the Dice similarity coefficient. The uncertainty in the model's prediction is estimated using either Monte Carlo dropout or test-time data augmentation. We found that (1) including uncertainty measurements did not degrade the quality of the segmentations, (2) uncertainty metrics provide a good proxy of the quality of our contours if the center found during the first step is enclosed in the lumen of the carotid artery and (3) they could be used to detect low-quality segmentations at the participant level. This automatic quality assurance tool might enable the application of our model in large-scale data sets.

Keywords: Uncertainty estimation · Quality assurance · Deep learning · Carotid artery · Segmentation

1 Introduction

Ischemic stroke refers to a neurological deficit due to insufficient blood flow to the brain and may lead to long-term disability [8]. Its prevalence is expected to rise in the coming years in the European population, leading to the need for improved prevention of this medical condition [12]. Imaging of the head and neck can provide information on vascular biomarkers, such as the geometry and anatomy of the carotid arteries, which provide the brain with blood [3]. For example, it has been shown the thickness of the carotid artery wall and its geometry are risk factors for stroke independently from traditional risk factors such as hypertension [4,10].

Supplementary Information The online version contains supplementary material available at https://doi.org/10.1007/978-3-031-44336-7_10.

C. H. Sudre et al. (Eds.): UNSURE 2023, LNCS 14291, pp. 95–103, 2023.
https://doi.org/10.1007/978-3-031-44336-7_10

Unraveling the relationship between vascular biomarkers and stroke requires large-scale imaging studies, in which accurate manual segmentation of relevant structures is a tedious task. To alleviate this problem, there have been efforts to develop deep learning algorithms for carotid artery segmentation in MRI [6,14, 17]. One of these methods included an uncertainty regularisation component in their loss and used uncertainty to interpret their network [9]. Likewise, we have developed a deep learning-based algorithm for carotid artery inner and outer wall segmentation that exploits symmetry and anatomical priors and achieved top-ranking quantitative and qualitative results in the MICCAI & SMRA 2021 Carotid Artery Vessel Wall Segmentation Challenge [1].

While our method achieved excellent results on a curated challenge dataset, it is likely to make errors when applied to large-scale data sets. Automatic identification of such errors using a quality assurance mechanism would have major practical value. Here, we study the feasibility of developing such a system by investigating the use of uncertainty quantification of the algorithm as a proxy for the quality of the segmentations it produces. We distinguish two types of uncertainty used in Bayesian modelling: the *aleatoric uncertainty* that can be attributed to noise in the data, and the *epistemic uncertainty*, which represents the limitation of the model and its ability to capture the underlying distribution of the data [7]. Correlations between these different types of uncertainties and the quality of deep learning predictions were previously found in medical image analysis [11,13]. We here study this relation in the context of carotid artery segmentation in black-blood MRI where we focus on two potential sources of error: variations in image quality, and variations in the quality of a pre-processing step that is essential to our algorithm.

2   Methods

2.1   Data Set

Experiments were conducted using the black-blood MRI training set of the MICCAI & SMRA 2021 Carotid Artery Vessel Wall Segmentation Challenge [15]. This data set is a subset of the larger CARE-II data set, acquired from 13 different hospitals and medical centers throughout China [16]. In the training subset, images were acquired according to two different protocols, leading to two different distributions (20 patients in the first distribution and three in the second one). Only one black-blood MRI image is available per participant. Manual annotations of the contour of the lumen and outer wall of the common, internal, and external carotid artery were provided by the challenge organizers in a subset of axial image slices, for both the left and the right carotid arteries. We preprocessed each image volume by rescaling its intensities between 0 and 1 according to its 5th and 95th intensity percentiles. All volumes were oriented according to the RAS coordinate system (Fig.1).

2.2   Segmentation Method

We previously developed a deep learning-based algorithm for the segmentation of carotid black-blood MRI images [1]. This method consists of two steps. In the

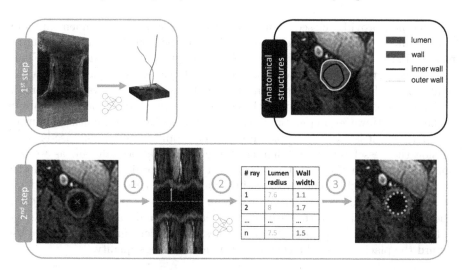

Fig. 1. Illustration of our previously developed automatic segmentation pipeline. The first step consists of finding the centerlines of the internal (red) and external (green) carotid arteries. The second step consists of (1) a polar coordinate transformation, (2) regression of the lumen radii (light blue) and wall widths (dark blue), and (3) inversion of the polar transform [1] (Color figure online)

first step, the centerlines of the left and right common, internal, and external carotid arteries are detected. For each artery centerline, a 3D U-Net predicts a proximity map, which is subsequently used for centerline extraction using Dijkstra's algorithm. For both the internal and the external carotid artery, we find a centerline that includes the common carotid artery. Hence, for each 3D volume, we find four centerlines.

In the second step, contours for the inner and outer wall are detected for each centerline point. We exploit rotation equivariance in the data by transforming our Cartesian images to a polar coordinate system centered at the centerline point, in three steps:

1. **Polar transform**: We cast 31 equiangular rays of length 127 pixels from the center in the axial plane. This is also done for the three adjacent slices in both directions so that we obtain a cylindrical volume of $31 \times 127 \times 7$ voxels.
2. **Regression of radii and widths**: For each of the rays in the center slice, and hence for each angle, a translation equivariant 3D CNN estimates the radius of the lumen wall and the nonzero offset between the lumen wall and the outer wall. By adding this offset to the lumen wall radius, we obtain the outer wall radius for each angle, resulting in a 31×2 matrix of predictions.
3. **Polar transform inversion**: We transform the detected contours back to the original Cartesian space and obtain a ring-shaped segmentation of the vessel wall.

This method provides closed, non-intersecting contours for the lumen wall and outer wall for each centerline point, which can be combined into watertight meshes. In the MICCAI & SMRA 2021 Carotid Artery Wall Segmentation Challenge, this led to results that were both quantitatively and qualitatively superior to all other submissions. An implementation of this method is available online[1].

The true center corresponds to the center of the manually annotated contour of the lumen. However, in practice as the center is estimated automatically during the first step, it is not always perfectly centered, and in the worst case located outside the vessel lumen. In that case, the segmentation will fail, as we are unable to perform the transformation to a polar coordinate system, and the assumption that the lumen wall radius and offset to the outer wall add up no longer holds. Moreover, image quality in black-blood MRI can vary widely, leading to uncertainty in the estimated lumen radius and wall thickness. Hence, in this study, we aim to assess the robustness and uncertainty of the procedure toward the placement of the center, as well as the image quality.

2.3   Simulation of Inputs

To simulate what our model might encounter in large-scale datasets, we simulate two types of data using the original data set described in Sect. 2.1. First, we reduce the image quality by linearly adding Gaussian noise to the original image $\alpha * noise + (1 - \alpha) * image$, where α is a noise level.

Second, we simulate the effect of poor-quality centerline extraction in the first step of our algorithm. To reproduce this issue, centers with different spatial offsets were generated. Based on the manual contour annotations in training samples, we define the true center of the artery in a cross-sectional image. The point on the inner wall contour with the largest distance to the true center is taken to find the direction along which new centers are sampled. The spatial offset corresponds to the distance to the true center normalised by the radius. Consequently, a spatial offset of 0 corresponds to the true center, an offset between 0 and 1 to a center inside the lumen, and an offset above 1 to a center outside the lumen. This last option corresponds to the scenario in which an improper centerline was found in the first step of the algorithm.

2.4   Training and Evaluation of the Networks

The CNNs assessing the lumen radii and wall widths were trained using the open-source implementation of our method. The CNNs have eight convolutional layers, between which Dropout layers with a rate of 0.2 are included. The training loss is the mean squared error on the lumen radii and wall widths. The model was trained for 50 epochs, and the final version corresponds to the one which obtained the best validation loss during training at the end of an epoch during training.

---

[1] https://github.com/MIAGroupUT/carotid-segmentation.

2.5 Uncertainty Quantification and Quality Assessment

In this study, we aim to investigate the correlation between segmentation quality and uncertainty estimation. The quality of the segmentations is assessed using the Dice similarity coefficient between the manually annotated and automatically computed contours. To estimate the uncertainty of the model, two different methods were implemented:

1. *dropout* corresponds to Monte Carlo Dropout, in which we keep the Dropout layers active during inference and estimate the contours 20 times. This procedure was introduced to approximate Bayesian inference and computes an estimation of epistemic uncertainty [5].
2. *centers* computes contours based on polar transformed images acquired using the eight neighboring pixels of the original centers. This can be seen as a form of test-time augmentation, a procedure for improved aleatoric uncertainty estimation [2].

Subsequently, the variability on the result is estimated using two different methods:

1. *mean* computes for each ray the mean value and the standard deviation of the distances, corresponding to an output distance and its uncertainty, respectively.
2. *polar* computes the polar coordinates of all the points of the set of contours and fits a degree 2 polynomial model between the sine and cosine of the angle and the distance. The output distance corresponding to an angle θ is computed using this model, and the uncertainty corresponds to the distance to the model of all the points in $[\theta - \frac{1}{32}\pi; \theta + \frac{1}{32}\pi]$ (see supplementary Fig. 1).

The *polar* method was developed to estimate the final contours and uncertainties using the *centers* variability, and it can also be used with *dropout*. In both cases, the result is normalised by the output distance, as we observed that this led to better results.

The correlation between the uncertainty and the Dice score was assessed using linear regression and quantified using the coefficient of determination R^2. This correlation was computed at three different levels. At the contour level, the uncertainties of the 31 points of a contour were averaged and correlated to the Dice score of the corresponding contour. At the vessel or participant level, the uncertainties of the points of all annotated contours were averaged and compared to the average Dice score of all contours of one vessel or one participant, respectively. The lumen and wall contours were considered separately to compute the correlation strengths. Illustrations are given in Appendix A1 (Fig. 2).

3 Results

The three images acquired with a different protocol were put in the test set to assess if the correlation between uncertainty estimation and image quality holds on a distribution never seen by the network. Among the other 20 images, ten were put on the test set and ten were in the training/validation set of the networks. This last set is split into the training (eight images) and validation (two images) sets.

The Dice scores obtained without uncertainty estimation (0.78 ± 0.18) were similar to or less than those obtained with the different uncertainty estimations: $dropout_{mean}$ (0.82 ± 0.12), $dropout_{polar}$ (0.82 ± 0.12), $centers_{polar}$ (0.78 ± 0.18). To note, the three participants with different acquisition parameters obtained similar Dice scores as the others.

Image Quality. Figure 2a shows that the quality of segmentations decreases as the level of noise increases. We observe a strong correlation between the quality of the image and the uncertainty of the segmentations at the participant level but not at the contour or vessel levels (Table 1). The strongest correlations are obtained with $dropout_{polar}$. Note that the segmentation quality remains relatively high (mean Dice > 0.6), as the true center is used to create the polar transformed images, and any correctly centered contour with reasonable radius estimates is bound to have a decent overlap with the annotation.

Table 1. Values of the coefficient of determination R^2 of the correlation of the uncertainty and quality of the segmentations obtained with different levels of noise different centers in the lumen.

Experiment	Correlation level	Structure	$dropout_{polar}$	$dropout_{mean}$	$centers_{polar}$
Image quality	contour	lumen	**0.33**	0.31	0.24
		wall	**0.38**	0.30	0.24
	vessel	lumen	**0.59**	0.56	0.29
		wall	**0.67**	0.56	0.30
	participant	lumen	0.85	**0.87**	0.77
		wall	**0.88**	0.83	0.72
Center quality	contour	lumen	**0.56**	0.50	0.54
		wall	**0.53**	0.24	0.42
	vessel	lumen	**0.81**	0.75	0.80
		wall	**0.85**	0.73	0.64
	participant	lumen	0.93	0.89	**0.96**
		wall	**0.95**	0.86	0.90

Center Quality. Figure 2b shows that the uncertainty of the segmentation model increases while the Dice score decreases until a spatial offset of 1.3 is reached. After that, the uncertainty decreases again though the quality is still decreasing. We assessed the correlation between uncertainty and quality for spatial offsets < 1, which corresponds to centers in the lumen. We observe a strong correlation between the quality of the segmentations and the uncertainty of the model at the participant and vessel levels, but still not at the contour level (Table 1), obtained with $dropout_{polar}$.

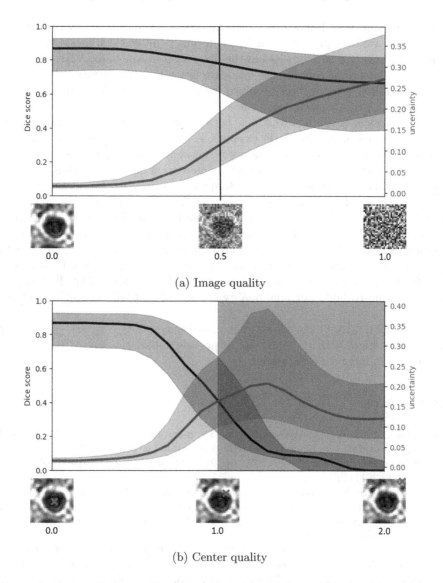

(a) Image quality

(b) Center quality

Fig. 2. Evolution of the quality (black) and the uncertainty (blue) while degrading the image quality (a) or the center quality (b). The colored space around the lines correspond to the inter-quartile range. The red region corresponds to centers which are outside the lumen. (Color figure online)

4   Discussion and Conclusion

We find that across different potential sources of error in our segmentations, the estimated uncertainty in the model's predictions is a good proxy of the quality of the segmentation obtained. This correlation is particularly present at the participant level. Interestingly, we found that for shifting artery centers, the correlation was only present when the centerline point was still inside the artery. This is the case for 95% of slices in the data set (see Appendix A2).

Depending on the context, the best correlation between segmentation quality and uncertainty estimate was obtained with a different method. In most cases, $dropout_{polar}$ performs best, and the second best is $centers_{polar}$ to assess the center quality, whereas $dropout_{mean}$ better estimates the image quality. This confirms the use of Monte Carlo Dropout as a robust uncertainty estimator. In practice, a combination of uncertainty estimation methods could be considered to improve further the correlation with segmentation quality, and thus the value of uncertainty estimation as a means to quality assurance.

A limitation of this study is the set of contours that were manually annotated: the bifurcation between the external and internal carotids, which is the most difficult region to segment for our algorithm, was only scarcely annotated by the organisers of the challenge. Annotations that we will collect in new data sets to assess the performance of our algorithm should focus on this region. Future work will further focus on the automatic assessment of the quality of the first step in our algorithm to build our final quality check tool that will be applied to large data sets.

In conclusion, we have shown that model uncertainty can serve as a proxy for segmentation, with the potential to provide automatic quality assurance of our model in large-scale data sets.

References

1. Alblas, D., Brune, C., Wolterink, J.M.: Deep-learning-based carotid artery vessel wall segmentation in black-blood MRI using anatomical priors. In: Medical Imaging 2022: Image Processing, vol. 12032, pp. 237–244. SPIE (2022). https://doi.org/10.1117/12.2611112
2. Ayhan, M.S., Kühlewein, L., Aliyeva, G., Inhoffen, W., Ziemssen, F., Berens, P.: Expert-validated estimation of diagnostic uncertainty for deep neural networks in diabetic retinopathy detection. Med. Image Anal. **64**, 101724 (2020). https://doi.org/10.1016/j.media.2020.101724
3. Balu, N., Yarnykh, V.L., Chu, B., Wang, J., Hatsukami, T., Yuan, C.: Carotid plaque assessment using fast 3D isotropic resolution black-blood MRI. Magn. Reson. Med. **65**(3), 627–637 (2011). https://doi.org/10.1002/mrm.22642
4. Chambless, L.E., et al.: Carotid wall thickness is predictive of incident clinical stroke: the atherosclerosis risk in communities (ARIC) study. Am. J. Epidemiol. **151**(5), 478–487 (2000). https://doi.org/10.1093/oxfordjournals.aje.a010233
5. Gal, Y., Ghahramani, Z.: Bayesian convolutional neural networks with Bernoulli approximate variational inference (2016). Comment: 12 pages, 3 figures, ICLR format, updated with reviewer comments. https://doi.org/10.48550/arXiv.1506.02158
6. Huang, X., Wang, J., Li, Z.: 3D carotid artery segmentation using shape-constrained active contours. Comput. Biol. Med. **153**, 106530 (2023). https://doi.org/10.1016/j.compbiomed.2022.106530

7. Kendall, A., Gal, Y.: What uncertainties do we need in Bayesian deep learning for computer vision? In: Proceedings of the 31st International Conference on Neural Information Processing Systems, NIPS 2017, pp. 5580–5590. Curran Associates Inc., Red Hook, NY, USA (2017)

8. Lai, S.M., Studenski, S., Duncan, P.W., Perera, S.: Persisting consequences of stroke measured by the stroke impact scale. Stroke **33**(7), 1840–1844 (2002). https://doi.org/10.1161/01.STR.0000019289.15440.F2

9. Lavrova, E., et al.: UR-CarA-Net: a cascaded framework with uncertainty regularization for automated segmentation of carotid arteries on black blood MR images. IEEE Access **11**, 26637–26651 (2023). https://doi.org/10.1109/ACCESS.2023.3258408

10. Phan, T.G., et al.: Carotid artery anatomy and geometry as risk factors for carotid atherosclerotic disease. Stroke **43**(6), 1596–1601 (2012). https://doi.org/10.1161/STROKEAHA.111.645499

11. Roy, A.G., Conjeti, S., Navab, N., Wachinger, C.: Bayesian QuickNAT: model uncertainty in deep whole-brain segmentation for structure-wise quality control. Neuroimage **195**, 11–22 (2019). https://doi.org/10.1016/j.neuroimage.2019.03.042

12. Wafa, H.A., Wolfe, C.D.A., Emmett, E., Roth, G.A., Johnson, C.O., Wang, Y.: Burden of stroke in Europe. Stroke **51**(8), 2418–2427 (2020). https://doi.org/10.1161/STROKEAHA.120.029606

13. Wang, G., Li, W., Aertsen, M., Deprest, J., Ourselin, S., Vercauteren, T.: Aleatoric uncertainty estimation with test-time augmentation for medical image segmentation with convolutional neural networks. Neurocomputing **338**, 34–45 (2019). https://doi.org/10.1016/j.neucom.2019.01.103

14. Wang, Y., Yao, Y.: Application of artificial intelligence methods in carotid artery segmentation: a review. IEEE Access **11**, 13846–13858 (2023). https://doi.org/10.1109/ACCESS.2023.3243162

15. Yuan, C., et al.: Carotid vessel wall segmentation challenge (2021). https://doi.org/10.5281/zenodo.4575301

16. Zhao, X., Li, R., Hippe, D.S., Hatsukami, T.S., Yuan, C., CARE-II Investigators: Chinese atherosclerosis risk evaluation (CARE II) study: a novel cross-sectional, multicentre study of the prevalence of high-risk atherosclerotic carotid plaque in Chinese patients with ischaemic cerebrovascular events—design and rationale. Stroke Vasc. Neurol. **2**(1), 15–20 (2017). https://doi.org/10.1136/svn-2016-000053

17. Ziegler, M., et al.: Automated segmentation of the individual branches of the carotid arteries in contrast-enhanced MR angiography using DeepMedic. BMC Med. Imaging **21**(1), 38 (2021). https://doi.org/10.1186/s12880-021-00568-6

Multi-layer Aggregation as a Key to Feature-Based OOD Detection

Benjamin Lambert[1,2,3(✉)], Florence Forbes[4], Senan Doyle[3], and Michel Dojat[1,2]

[1] University Grenoble Alpes, U1216 Inserm, France
[2] Grenoble Institut Neurosciences, Grenoble 38000, FR, France
[3] Pixyl, Research and Development Laboratory, 38000 Grenoble, FR, France
benjamin.lambert@univ-grenoble-alpes.fr
[4] University Grenoble Alpes, Inria, CNRS, Grenoble INP, LJK, 38000 Grenoble, FR, France

Abstract. Deep Learning models are easily disturbed by variations in the input images that were not observed during the training stage, resulting in unpredictable predictions. Detecting such Out-of-Distribution (OOD) images is particularly crucial in the context of medical image analysis, where the range of possible abnormalities is extremely wide. Recently, a new category of methods has emerged, based on the analysis of the intermediate features of a trained model. These methods can be divided into 2 groups: *single-layer* methods that consider the feature map obtained at a fixed, carefully chosen layer, and *multi-layer* methods that consider the ensemble of the feature maps generated by the model. While promising, a proper comparison of these algorithms is still lacking. In this work, we compared various feature-based OOD detection methods on a large spectra of OOD (20 types), representing approximately 7800 3D MRIs. Our experiments shed the light on two phenomenons. First, *multi-layer* methods consistently outperform *single-layer* approaches, which tend to have inconsistent behaviour depending on the type of anomaly. Second, the OOD detection performance is variable depending on the architecture of the underlying neural network. We provide our implementation of the feature-based OOD detectors at https://github.com/benolmbrt/MedicOOD.

Keywords: Uncertainty · Deep learning · Anomaly Detection · Medical images analysis

1 Introduction

Out-of-distribution (OOD) images correspond to samples that are significantly different from the ones observed during training. Deep Learning (DL) models tend to behave inconsistently for this type of inputs, making OOD image detection crucial to avoid hidden model deficiencies [28]. It is especially required in real-world automated pipelines, where input images may not be visually

Supplementary Information The online version contains supplementary material available at https://doi.org/10.1007/978-3-031-44336-7_11.

inspected before running the analysis. In the context of medical-images analysis, a large variety of phenomenons in the input images can impact a model and lead to unpredictable responses: noise, artifacts, variations in the imaging acquisition protocol and device, or pathological cases that were not included in the initial training dataset. Various methods were proposed for their detection, which can roughly be divided into two different categories [3]: methods that build a model specifically dedicated to OOD detection and methods that rely on the uncertainty or intermediate activations of a task-specific model (e.g. image segmentation) to detect abnormal inputs.

Within the first category, the most straightforward approach is to build a classifier to directly detect OOD images. For this, a Convolutional Neural Network (CNN) can be trained in a supervised manner, thus requiring the construction of an annotated dataset containing various types of real-world OOD [4]. On the contrary, Unsupervised Anomaly Detection (UAD) proposes to detect abnormal inputs without explicit labels for OOD samples, by learning to model the appearance of normal images. Popular approaches include reconstruction-based methods [10], self-supervision [32] or memory-bank-based models [30].

Among the second category, uncertainty-based methods propose to detect OOD inputs directly from the outputs of an existing neural network. They rely on the hypothesis that the uncertainty of the deployed model should be high in the presence of a train-test mismatch, allowing its detection. A standard method consists of producing a set of diverse and plausible predictions for the same input image, with MC dropout [9] and Deep Ensemble [21] being popular approaches. Uncertainty can then be estimated by computing the variance among the predictions. Alternatively, feature-based methods propose to analyse the intermediate activations of an existing model to detect OOD inputs [29]. It is based on the assumption that the hidden activations of the model should be different for an ID image compared to an OOD image. A taxonomy of these feature-based methods is possible based on the number of layers used for OOD detection. *Single-layer* methods only target one specific convolutional layer. In the context of medical image segmentation, popular choices are the end of the encoder [11] or the penultimate convolutional layer [7,16]. *Multi-layer* methods are an extension of the former that consider the entire set of convolutional layers in the trained model for OOD detection [5]. Although gaining popularity, a proper comparison of these algorithms is still lacking. The contributions of our work are as follows:

– We develop a large MRI segmentation benchmark comprising 20 different OOD datasets of various types and strengths, representing 7796 3D MRI volumes. We use this benchmark to compare 5 different feature-based OOD detectors.
– We adapt single-layer methods to a multi-layer fashion to demonstrate the potential performance gain that can be obtained with this enhancement.

2   Compared Methods

2.1   Feature-Based Methods

Feature-based methods rely on a trained segmentation model and follow the same principle. First, a set of feature maps $F_i \in \mathbb{R}^{N_i \times H_i \times W_i \times D_i}$ is collected from a

ID dataset for one convolution layer i (single-layer methods) or all convolution layers (multi-layer methods). Here, N_i correponds to the number of convolutional filters in the i-th layer, and $H_i \times W_i \times D_i$ to the spatial dimensions of the feature map. Second, at inference time, a metric is computed to estimate the distance between the test features and the ID features to detect OOD samples.

Spectral Signatures [16] was proposed as a single-layer method focusing on the features obtained at the penultimate convolutional layer. Features are flattened to a 2D matrix $F_{2D} \in \mathbb{R}^{N \times HWD}$, and its singular values S are calculated. The spectral signature is then taken as $\phi = \frac{log(S)}{\|log(S)\|_2}$. To detect OOD at test time, the distances d_j between the signature of the test image ϕ^i_{test} and the signatures of a set of ID samples ϕ^j_{ID} is obtained by using the Euclidean distance. The final proposed OOD score corresponds to the minimum of the d_j distances.

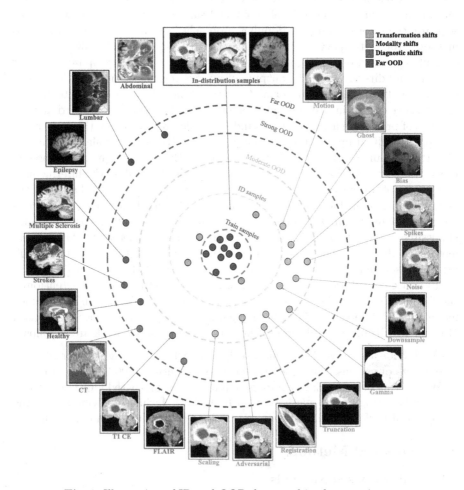

Fig. 1. Illustration of ID and OOD data used in the experiments.

Prototypes [7] is a single-layer method that operates from the penultimate layer features and the segmentation masks predicted by the segmentation network. To obtain a prototype for a specific class and input image, features are multiplied with the binarized class mask, and average pooling is applied on the masked features. This yields to prototypes $P \in \mathbb{R}^{N \times C}$, C being the number of segmented classes. An average ID prototype P_{ID} is finally obtained by averaging the prototypes collected on the ID dataset. At test time, the OOD score is taken as the cosine dissimilarity between P_{ID} and the test image prototype P_j.

The Mahalanobis Distance (MD) was recently investigated in 2 distinct studies for OOD detection in 3D medical images. In [11], authors focus on the features from the end of the encoder part of the network. They apply consecutive average pooling until the number of elements M in the feature maps falls below a defined threshold of $1e4$, and then flatten it to obtain 1D vectors z_i $\in \mathbb{R}^M$, for each ID image i. From these vectors, they compute the parameters of a multivariate Gaussian: the mean $\mu \in \mathbb{R}^M$ and covariance $\Sigma \in \mathbb{R}^{M \times M}$. At test time, the MD is computed given the fitted Gaussian and the test image feature representation. We refer to this single-layer method as *MD Pool*. A similar approach is implemented in the multi-layer Free Rejection of Out-of-Distribution (FRODO) approach [5]. This work differs in two ways: first, they directly compute the average of the feature map over the spatial dimensions ($H \times W \times D$) instead of applying average poolings. Second, they fit a multivariate Gaussian independently for each convolutional layer and compute the final OOD score as the average of each layer score.

One-Class SVM. (OCSVM) is an unsupervised algorithm for OOD detection that can be trained using only ID samples. It aims at finding the optimal boundary around the expected (ID) data. At test time, the distance to the boundary can be used as an OOD score, with ID sample being attributed with negative distances, and OOD samples with positive distances. Following [35], we fit a OCSVM per convolution based on the averaged layer activations obtained from the ID images. At test time, each OCSVM produces a score, and the final OOD score is taken as the maximum of these scores.

2.2   Adapting Single-Layer Methods to Multi-layer Methods

To assess the contribution of multi-layer aggregation to OOD detection, we propose to adapt single-layer methods (Spectrum, Prototypes and MD Pool) to multi-layer style. To achieve this, we replicate the OOD score computation step for each of the K convolutional layers of the model independently, yielding to *layer-wise* scores l_i. As in FRODO, the final multi-layer score L_{multi} is taken as the average of the scores of the individual layers:

$$L_{multi} = \frac{1}{K} \sum_{i=1}^{K} l_i \tag{1}$$

3   Material and Method

3.1   In-Distribution Datasets

Our work relies on the open-source BraTS 2021 dataset [2] containing 1251 patients. The dataset initially includes four MRI sequences for each patient with four ground truth segmentation masks: the background, the necrotic tumor core, the edematous and the GD-enhancing tumor. We choose to focus on T1w sequences as this sequence is common and sufficient for experiment with multiple OOD settings. We also simplify the prediction task by focusing on the segmentation of the *whole tumor core*, concatenation of all tumors sub-classes. The dataset is randomly split into a training fold (651), a calibration fold (200) used to fit the OOD detectors and a testing fold (400) (referred to as *Test ID* in the following). Additionally, we propose to include *control* samples in our protocol, representing images that share the same properties than the training samples (same modality, organ and pathology), but that were acquired in a different imaging center. An effective model *should* be able to generalize to these images and thus, the OOD detector should identify them as ID samples to prevent false alarms. We thus propose to use the LUMIERE glioblastoma dataset [31] as a *Control* dataset, from which we select 74 T1-w pre-operative brain MRI. Figure 1 illustrates the data used in the different experiments.

3.2   Out-of-distribution Datasets

Following the categorization of [11], we propose to investigate *Transformation*, *Diagnosis* and *Far* OODs, as well as a new proposed setting, *Modality* shifts.

Transformation Shifts. Finding real images with a controlled amount of artifacts to allow evaluation of OOD detection methods is difficult. We therefore generate realistic synthetic artifacted images from the set of *Test ID* images [8,11]. We used the TorchIO Data Augmentation library [19] to generate *Bias*, *Motion*, *Ghost*, *Spikes*, *Downsample*, *Noise*, and *Scaling* artifacts. We add a set of novel transformations: the *Registration* that applies noise to the registration matrix to simulate an erroneous registration, the *Gamma* that applies extreme gamma modification to the image to mimick errors in the intensity normalization step, and the *Truncation* that crops half of the brain. Finally, we also implement *Adversarial* attacks, using the popular Fast Gradient Sign Method (FGSM) [12].

Diagnosis Shifts. DL segmentation models are usually trained with images showing a single pathology (e.g. brain tumor or strokes). However, once deployed, the model can be confronted with images exhibiting unseen anomalies, which can lead to incorrect predictions. To test OOD detection methods on this scenario, we use T1w brain MRI with various diseases: 170 subjects from the White Matter Hyperintensities (WMH) 2017 challenge [20], 655 subjects from the ATLAS-2 brain stroke dataset [22] and 162 subjects from the EPISURG dataset [27] containing epileptic subjects who underwent resective brain surgery. We also use 582 T1-w MRIs from healthy and young subjects from the IXI dataset [1].

Modality shifts. Medical images are usually stored in DICOM formats, whose meta-data (headers) may be incorrectly filled [13]. As a result, mismatches between the expected input modality (e.g. T1w) and the test image modality (e.g. CT or T2w) may be undetected. We construct 3 different *Modality* shift OOD datasets. First, we use the FLAIR and T1ce sequences corresponding to the 400 test subjects. Second, we extract 437 brain CT-scans from the CQ500 dataset, exhibiting intracranial hemorrhage or cranial fractures.

Far OOD. corresponds to images that show little to no similarity with the ID samples. We use 2 non-brain T1w MRI datasets, respectively 80 abdominal MRI from the CHAOS dataset [17] and 515 images from the Lumbar Spine MRI dataset [25], as far OOD samples.

3.3   Influence of the Segmentation Model Architecture

Feature-based OOD detection methods rely on the hypothesis that the activations of the trained segmentation models are representative of the conformity of the input sample. To verify if this holds true for any segmentation model, we use the MONAI library [6] to train 6 different segmentation models: an Attention UNet (AttUNet) [26], a Residual UNet (ResUNet) [18], a Dynamic UNet (DynUNet) [15], a UNet++ [36], a VNet [24] and a Transformer-based model, namely the UneTR [14]. All models are trained with the Dice loss [24], instance normalization [33], a 3D dropout rate of 20% and a batch size of 1, using the ADAM optimizer [19] with a learning rate of $2e^{-4}$.

3.4   Evaluation Setting

We cast OOD detection as a binary classification problem, where ID samples correspond to the positive class and OOD samples to the negative class. Each method produces a score for each OOD sample, which is compared with the scores obtained on the ID data in order to compute classification scores. We carry our evaluation using the Area Under the ROC curve (AUROC) and provide a similar analysis using the Area Under the Precision-Recall curve (AUPR) in Supplementary Material (SM). The segmentation performance on Test ID is assessed using the Dice score.

4   Results and Discussion

Fig. 2 presents the OOD detection scores (AUROC) of each feature-based method, averaged across the 6 segmentation backbones, for each OOD dataset. All OOD detectors achieve high detection accuracy on *Far OOD* with mixed performances on other OOD types, showing that restricting to extreme OOD examples is insufficient to robustly validate a method. The best performer is FRODO, achieving a perfect detection of non-conform inputs (AUROC=1.00) in 12 out of 20 settings, followed by the multi-layer implementation of Spectrum, and OCSVM. Overall, multi-layer methods outperform their single-layer version, with an average increase of the AUROC score of 11.9% for Spectrum, 14.8% for MD Pool and 7.58% for Prototypes. Single-layer methods exhibit more variable performances depending on the OOD type, in accord with observations on 2D image classification [35].

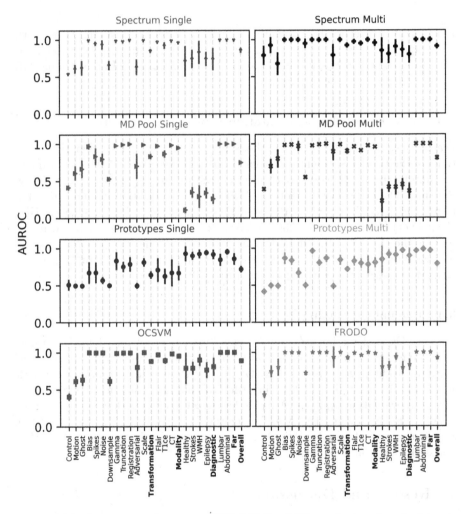

Fig. 2. OOD detection performance (AUROC) for OOD method and each dataset. Results are averaged across the six segmentation models and presented along their standard deviation.

The magnitude of standard deviation in Fig. 2 provides insights about the stability of the OOD detector with respect to the underlying segmentation model.

First, the instability increases with the difficulty of the OOD detection setting. For instance, the AUROC scores fluctuate significantly for the *Adversarial* and *Healthy* datasets, while they are extremely stable for the far-OOD settings which are associated with higher AUROC scores. Second, the stability is not uniform depending on the OOD method, with FRODO being the most stable, while Spectrum Single and Multi exhibit larger standard deviations. This occasional instability may be related to the *feature collapse* phenomenon that can occur in certain neural architectures [34], causing OOD images to be mapped to ID feature representations, lowering the performance of feature-based OOD detectors. In Fig. 3 we investigate this phenomenon in further details by considering the *Overall* AUROC performance of FRODO for each of the 6 segmentation architectures, with respect to their respective segmentation performance (Dice on Test ID dataset). The higher OOD detection performances are achieved with Unet++, DynUnet and AttUnet, which are also the three most accurate segmentation models in terms of Dice scores. This suggests a link between the performance of the model with respect to the target task (e.g. segmentation of brain tumor) and the performance of feature-based OOD detection. Similar results shown in Fig. 2 and Fig. 3 are observed using AUPR (see SM).

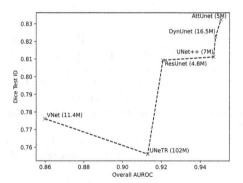

Fig. 3. Average Dice on the Test ID dataset with respect to the *Overall* OOD detection score (AUROC) for the FRODO approach. The number of parameters of each model is indicated in millions (M).

Note that several strategies have been proposed in the context of 2D image classification to alleviate the issue of feature collapse, such as adding Gradient Penalty [34], Lipschitz constraints [23], or a reconstruction term in the loss [29]. These methods aim at enforcing a discriminative feature space for OOD detection, requiring changes in the training paradigm of the model, possibly resulting in sub-optimal predictive performances. To summarize, our main findings are:

- Feature-based methods monitoring the activation of *all* convolution layers are more performant and robust than methods only targeting a single layer, whose performance is highly variable depending on the type of OOD.

– The performance of these methods is dependent on the underlying segmentation architecture, with may be linked to feature collapse in certain neural architectures, undermining the sensibility of OOD detection.

References

1. The IXI brain dataset. https://brain-development.org/ixi-dataset/
2. Baid, U., Ghodasara, S., et al.: The rsna-asnr-miccai brats 2021 benchmark on brain tumor segmentation and radiogenomic classification. arXiv preprint arXiv:2107.02314 (2021)
3. Berger, C., et al.: Confidence-based out-of-distribution detection: a comparative study and analysis. Unsure **2021**, 122–132 (2021)
4. Bottani, S., et al.: Automatic quality control of brain t1-weighted magnetic resonance images for a clinical data warehouse. Med. Image Anal. **75**, 102219 (2022)
5. Çallı, E., Van Ginneken, B., et al.: Frodo: an in-depth analysis of a system to reject outlier samples from a trained neural network. IEEE Trans. Med. Imaging **42**(4), 971–981 (2022)
6. Cardoso, M.J., Li, W., et al.: MONAI: an open-source framework for deep learning in healthcare. arXiv preprint arXiv:2211.02701 (2022)
7. Diao, Z., et al.: A unified uncertainty network for tumor segmentation using uncertainty cross entropy loss and prototype similarity. Knowl. Based Syst. **246**, 108739 (2022)
8. Fuchs, M., Gonzalez, C., Mukhopadhyay, A.: Practical uncertainty quantification for brain tumor segmentation. Med. Imaging Deep Learn. (MIDL) (2021)
9. Gal, Y., Ghahramani, Z.: Dropout as a Bayesian approximation: representing model uncertainty in deep learning. ICML **48**, 1050–1059 (2016)
10. Gong, D., Liu, L., et al.: Memorizing normality to detect anomaly: memory-augmented deep autoencoder for unsupervised anomaly detection. In: ICCV, pp. 1705–1714 (2019)
11. González, C., Gotkowski, K., et al.: Distance-based detection of out-of-distribution silent failures for COVID-19 lung lesion segmentation. Med. Image Anal. **82**, 102596 (2022)
12. Goodfellow, I.J., Shlens, J., Szegedy, C.: Explaining and harnessing adversarial examples. In: 3rd International Conference on Learning Representations, ICLR 2015 (2015)
13. Gueld, M.O., Kohnen, M., et al.: Quality of DICOM header information for image categorization. Medical imaging 2002: PACS and integrated medical information systems: design and evaluation **4685**, 280–287 (2002)
14. Hatamizadeh, A., et al.: Unetr: Transformers for 3d medical image segmentation. In: Proceedings of the IEEE/CVF Winter Conference on Applications of Computer Vision, pp. 574–584 (2022)
15. Isensee, F., Jaeger, P.F., et al.: nnU-Net: a self-configuring method for deep learning-based biomedical image segmentation. Nat. Methods **18**(2), 203–211 (2021)
16. Karimi, D., Gholipour, A.: Improving calibration and out-of-distribution detection in deep models for medical image segmentation. IEEE Trans. Artif. Intell. **4**(2), 383–397 (2023). https://doi.org/10.1109/TAI.2022.3159510
17. Kavur, A.E., et al.: Chaos challenge-combined (CT-MR) healthy abdominal organ segmentation. Med. Image Anal. **69**, 101950 (2021)

18. Kerfoot, E., Clough, J., et al.: Left-ventricle quantification using residual u-net. Statistical Atlases and Computational Models of the Heart. Atrial Segmentation and LV Quantification Challenges Workshop, Held in Conjunction with MICCAI 2018, pp. 371–380 (2019)
19. Kingma, D.P., Ba, J.: Adam: A method for stochastic optimization. arXiv preprint arXiv:1412.6980 (2014)
20. Kuijf, H.J., et al.: Standardized assessment of automatic segmentation of white matter hyperintensities and results of the WMH segmentation challenge. IEEE Trans. Med. Imaging **38**(11), 2556–2568 (2019)
21. Lakshminarayanan, B., Pritzel, A., Blundell, C.: Simple and scalable predictive uncertainty estimation using deep ensembles. Adv. Neural. Inf. Process. Syst. **30**, 6402–6413 (2017)
22. Liew, S.L., Lo, B.P., et al.: A large, curated, open-source stroke neuroimaging dataset to improve lesion segmentation algorithms. Sci. Data **9**(1), 320 (2022)
23. Liu, J., Lin, Z., Padhy, S., et al.: Simple and principled uncertainty estimation with deterministic deep learning via distance awareness. Adv. Neural. Inf. Process. Syst. **33**, 7498–7512 (2020)
24. Milletari, F., Navab, N., Ahmadi, S.A.: V-net: Fully convolutional neural networks for volumetric medical image segmentation. In: 2016 Fourth International Conference on 3D vision (3DV), pp. 565–571 (2016)
25. Natalia, F., Meidia, H., et al.: Development of ground truth data for automatic lumbar spine MRI image segmentation. HPCC/SmartCity/DSS **2018**, 1449–1454 (2018)
26. Oktay, O., Schlemper, J., et al.: Attention u-net: Learning where to look for the pancreas. Med. Imaging with Deep Learn. (MIDL) (2018)
27. Pérez-García, F., Rodionov, R., Alim-Marvasti, A., Sparks, R., Duncan, J.S., Ourselin, S.: Simulation of brain resection for cavity segmentation using self-supervised and semi-supervised learning. In: Martel, A.L., et al. (eds.) Medical Image Computing and Computer Assisted Intervention – MICCAI 2020: 23rd International Conference, Lima, Peru, October 4–8, 2020, Proceedings, Part III, pp. 115–125. Springer, Cham (2020). https://doi.org/10.1007/978-3-030-59716-0_12
28. Pooch, E.H.P., Ballester, P., Barros, R.C.: Can we trust deep learning based diagnosis? the impact of domain shift in chest radiograph classification. In: Petersen, J., et al. (eds.) Thoracic Image Analysis: Second International Workshop, TIA 2020, Held in Conjunction with MICCAI 2020, Lima, Peru, October 8, 2020, Proceedings, pp. 74–83. Springer, Cham (2020). https://doi.org/10.1007/978-3-030-62469-9_7
29. Postels, J., et al.: On the practicality of deterministic epistemic uncertainty. ICML **162**, 17870–17909 (2022)
30. Roth, K., Pemula, L., Zepeda, J., Schölkopf, B., Brox, T., Gehler, P.: Towards total recall in industrial anomaly detection. In: Proceedings of the IEEE/CVF Conference on Computer Vision and Pattern Recognition, pp. 14318–14328 (2022)
31. Suter, Y., Knecht, U., et al.: The LUMIERE dataset: longitudinal glioblastoma MRI with expert RANO evaluation. Sci. data **9**(1), 768 (2022)
32. Tan, J., Hou, B., Day, T., Simpson, J., Rueckert, D., Kainz, B.: Detecting outliers with poisson image interpolation. In: de Bruijne, M., et al. (eds.) MICCAI 2021. LNCS, vol. 12905, pp. 581–591. Springer, Cham (2021). https://doi.org/10.1007/978-3-030-87240-3_56
33. Ulyanov, D., Vedaldi, A., Lempitsky, V.: Instance normalization: The missing ingredient for fast stylization. arXiv preprint arXiv:1607.08022 (2016)

34. Van Amersfoort, J., et al.: Uncertainty estimation using a single deep deterministic neural network. In: International Conference on Machine Learning, pp. 9690–9700 (2020)
35. Wang, H., Zhao, C., et al.: Layer adaptive deep neural networks for out-of-distribution detection. In: Advances in Knowledge Discovery and Data Mining: 26th Pacific-Asia Conference, pp. 526–538 (2022). https://doi.org/10.1007/978-3-031-05936-0_41
36. Zhou, Z., Rahman Siddiquee, M.M., Tajbakhsh, N., Liang, J.: UNet++: a nested U-Net architecture for medical image segmentation. In: Stoyanov, D., et al. (eds.) DLMIA/ML-CDS -2018. LNCS, vol. 11045, pp. 3–11. Springer, Cham (2018). https://doi.org/10.1007/978-3-030-00889-5_1

Feature-Based Pipeline for Improving Unsupervised Anomaly Segmentation on Medical Images

Daria Frolova[1,2]([✉]), Aleksandr Katrutsa[1,2], and Ivan Oseledets[1,2]

[1] Skolkovo Institute of Science and Technology, Moscow, Russia
Daria.Frolova@skoltech.ru
[2] AIRI, Moscow, Russia

Abstract. Unsupervised methods for anomaly segmentation are promising for computer-aided diagnosis since they can increase the robustness of medical systems and do not require large annotated datasets. In this work, we propose a simple yet effective two-stage pipeline for improving the performance of existing anomaly segmentation methods. The first stage is used for better anomaly localization and false positive rate reduction. For this stage, we propose the PatchCore3D method, which is based on the PatchCore algorithm and a backbone, pre-trained on 3D medical images. Any existing anomaly segmentation method can be used at the second stage for the precise anomaly segmentation in the region suggested by PatchCore3D. We evaluate PatchCore3D and the proposed pipelines in combination with six top-performing anomaly segmentation methods of different types. We use brain MRI datasets, testing healthy subjects against subjects with brain tumors. Using PatchCore3D pipeline with every considered anomaly segmentation method increases segmentation AUROC almost twice by better anomaly localization.

Keywords: Anomaly segmentation · Anomaly detection · Brain MRI

1 Introduction

Deep learning models have shown a big potential in medical imaging, helping to speed up and automate the work of experts [8]. Although traditional supervised methods have achieved great performance, the lack of labeled data and the high cost of its annotation limit their usage. Therefore, unsupervised approaches are promising to process large amounts of available unlabelled data. In solving the problems of detection and segmentation of anomalies, unsupervised methods can improve automated pathology detection. Therefore, we focus on such methods. In this study we primarily focus on the anomaly segmentation task and consider methods that were initially designed to segment anomalies. However, we also report the sample-level anomaly detection performance.

Most approaches for unsupervised anomaly segmentation problems for 3D medical data (e.g. MRI or CT data) are reconstruction-based or restoration-based [4]. Reconstruction-based methods compute an anomaly segmentation

C. H. Sudre et al. (Eds.): UNSURE 2023, LNCS 14291, pp. 115–125, 2023.
https://doi.org/10.1007/978-3-031-44336-7_12

map as the difference between an original image and its feed-forward reconstruction, while restoration-based methods vary the latent until the input image's normal counterpart from the normal training distribution is found. Again, the pixelwise discrepancy between the image and its restoration is used as an anomaly map. Thus, during inference, a model can reconstruct a normal image and fails to reconstruct an anomalous region. These methods use variational autoencoders (VAE) [6,14,23,27,31], generative adversarial networks (GAN) [7,22,24], decoder-only networks for implicit field learning (**IF 3D**) [17]. Silva-Rodríguez et al. [23] proposed anomaly segmentation method **AMCons** which uses 2D VAE and optimization with constraints on attention maps. Recently, diffusion models were applied to medical anomaly segmentation [11,26]. **AnoDDPM** [26] use 2D diffusion with multi-scale simplex noise, while **mDDPM** [11] apply masked image modeling and masked frequency modeling to a 2D denoising diffusion probabilistic model (DDPM).

Despite the prevalence of generative models, Meissen et al. [15] noticed that reconstruction-based methods have proven to be "white object detection" methods. In particular, histogram equalization (**HistEq**) of an image highlights the brightest voxels labeled as anomalies. This approach works better than most of the latter approaches. Initially, HistEq was applied to FLAIR modality, but it surpasses other methods even in T2. However, this naive method assumes that anomalies are white and is not applicable in the general case.

To solve the anomaly segmentation task, self-supervised methods are also developed [13,25,30]. They generate artificial anomalies and are trained to solve the segmentation task in a supervised manner. As an example of such methods, we consider **CGV**[1] method, which is the top-performing in the pixel-level task of Medical Out-of-Distribution (MOOD) Challenge 2022 [32] and uses a 3D segmentation network. However, the prior knowledge about the source of anomalies limits the performance of CGV and leads to a performance drop with the change of the source of anomalies (see Sect. 3.2).

The majority of anomaly segmentation methods use 2D networks on image slices, thus losing the spatial context of a volumetric image. According to the studies [6,24], the use of 3D networks is beneficial over 2D networks in anomaly segmentation. Moreover, in other domains of computer vision, anomaly segmentation methods go beyond reconstruction-based approaches. One of the current top-performing anomaly segmentation methods is PatchCore [19]. It combines features extracted from a pre-trained model with the k-nearest neighbor anomaly detector. The studies [7,20] applied PatchCore or a similar approach to data from the medical imaging domain without any adaptation, e.g. taking the backbone pre-trained on the ImageNet for feature extraction, and did not show superior performance. Therefore, we take the basic PatchCore method, modify it for the medical imaging domain and use it in the first stage of our pipeline. At the same time, we observe that using the result of the proposed PatchCore3D method as input to the existing medical image anomaly segmentation methods algorithm

---

[1] https://github.com/2na-97/CGV_MOOD2022/.

can improve the segmentation performance. Therefore, we combine them in a pipeline that is evaluated in this study.

Our contributions are as follows.

1. We propose the PatchCore3D method to solve the anomaly segmentation task. To preserve the spatial information and improve the segmentation quality, PatchCore3D uses a 3D backbone pre-trained on the medical data.
2. We propose a novel two-stage pipeline for improving the performance of existing anomaly segmentation methods. It firstly uses PatchCore3D for improved anomaly localization and false positives reduction, and then applies any anomaly segmentation method in the previously defined region.
3. We evaluate PatchCore3D and pipelines in combination with various top-performing anomaly segmentation methods of different types. The evaluation is done on brain MRI datasets with both healthy subjects and patients with brain tumors. Building PatchCore3D pipeline upon every anomaly segmentation method boosts its performance by better anomaly localization.
4. We demonstrate the robustness of the proposed method to the reduction of the memory bank size if the elements of the memory bank were sampled according to the coreset subsampling procedure.

2   Pipeline

In this section, we propose a fully unsupervised pipeline for anomaly segmentation and detection. We describe two stages of the pipeline, discuss the features of 3D medical images and propose the PatchCore3D method for the first stage.

2.1   Basic PatchCore Method

Assume we have a pre-trained model, train and test sets. PatchCore [19] method takes the train images, constructs specific features for them from the pre-trained model, and uses these features to identify abnormal image regions in the inference stage via nearest neighbor search. If any region of a test image is sufficiently far from the nearest neighbor, then this region is labeled as abnormal. A more detailed description of PatchCore is the following. Firstly, it extracts features from the second and the third block of a WideResNet50 network [28] pre-trained on the ImageNet dataset and concatenates them for images from the train set. Since every block of WideResNet50 consists of convolution operations, the extracted features correspond to a region of a training image which is further referred to as a patch. Each patch feature is locally aware, so anomalies in extracted features are related to anomalies in original patches. Secondly, to reduce the inference cost, PatchCore selects a maximally representative subset $\widehat{\mathcal{M}} \subset \mathcal{M}$ with the coreset subsampling procedure [1]. We will further denote the composing of the effective memory bank $\widehat{\mathcal{M}}$ as a training stage although no parameters are updated. In the inference stage, one passes a test image through the pre-trained model and extracts the corresponding test patch features. Finally, to compute the patch-level anomaly score, Patch-Core uses the distance from the test patch features to the nearest neighbor [12] from $\widehat{\mathcal{M}}$. After computing anomaly scores for each patch, the resulting anomaly map is interpolated to the original test image resolution. We label the test image as abnormal if at least one patch is abnormal, so the sample-level anomaly score is the maximum among patch scores. Since the PatchCore method uses a network pre-trained on the ImageNet, we have to consider changing the domain and replacing the backbone, respectively.

2.2   Data

There is no established benchmark for evaluating anomaly segmentation and detection methods on medical data. Multiple studies [4, 6, 15, 23, 27, 31] use different versions of BraTS dataset [16] as a source of anomalies. They test healthy subjects against subjects with glioma and use tumor annotation as an anomaly segmentation mask. In [27, 31], publicly available datasets with brain MRIs of healthy people are suggested for this task. However, these datasets contain images acquired from only one scanner, thus introducing an easy-to-detect bias between normal and anomalous data on the sample level. So we take IXI[2] dataset with 577 T2 MR images of healthy subjects, acquired from three different hospitals. We use 80% of this dataset as a train set and 20% of the dataset as a part of the test set. As a source of anomalous data for the test set, we take a train set of BraTS 2021 [2, 3, 16] dataset. It has 1251 MR images and corresponding glioma subregions ("enhancing tumor", "tumor core", and "whole tumor") masks. Since the tumor core and the whole tumor are better visible on T2 scans, we use T2 scans in our experiments.

2.3   The Proposed PatchCore3D Method

In order to apply basic PatchCore to the considered dataset, we need to replace a model, pre-trained on ImageNet, with a model pre-trained on medical images. We call the result method PatchCore3D. The proper model is any convolutional neural network for classification or segmentation tasks such that there is an intermediate layer where the spatial resolution and the number of channels are sufficiently large. The large spatial resolution is needed for accurate interpolation of anomaly map to the original image spatial resolution. Also, a number of channels should be selected as a trade-off between detection performance based on nearest neighbor search and computational costs. If the number of channels is low, then the nearest neighbor search may give an irrelevant patch from the train set, and a detection error occurs. Since only healthy samples are in the train set, the test image is labeled as abnormal if the distance of its embedding to the assigned embedding is larger than the pre-defined threshold.

There is no widely used pre-trained model for medical images due to a large number of imaging modalities and a lack of annotated data. However, recent progress of self-supervised methods in pretraining networks on medical images

---

[2] http://brain-development.org/ixi-dataset/.

helped to outperform transfer learning [29]. This fact signals that such a network can be a good base for the PatchCore3D method. Thus we use a publicly available[3] 3D adaptation of DenseNet121 model [10] pre-trained with contrastive learning on 10^4 healthy brain T1 MR images, taken from multiple hospitals [9].

2.4 The Proposed Pipeline

We have noticed that PatchCore3D is sufficiently good at the localization of tumors while it gives coarse segmentation masks due to the low spatial resolution of a feature map. At the same time, existing methods for anomaly segmentation produce segmentation maps with high spatial resolution but with high false positive segmentation rates. To tackle this issue, we propose a two-stage pipeline that takes the best from both sides. Firstly, we predict continuous anomaly maps with PatchCore3D and any other anomaly segmentation method, e.g. AMCons. Then to improve the anomaly segmentation given by the latter method, we perform the elementwise multiplication of anomaly maps given by PathCore3D and the other method.

3   Results and Discussion

3.1   Experimental Setup

Implementation Details. The effect of using PatchCore3D as the first stage of the pipeline is tested in combination with reconstruction-based AMCons [23], restoration-based IF 3D [17], classification-based CGV, diffusion-based AnoD-DPM [26] and mDDPM [11], and naive HistEq [15], as they were reported to show high anomaly segmentation performance and belong to different types of methods. We take the default hyperparameters of AMCons, CGV, AnoDDPM, and mDDPM methods, because they were trained on the same task and domain as ours: healthy brain MRIs; mDDPM was even trained on IXI dataset.

We use 3D DenseNet121 as a pre-trained backbone in the PatchCore3D method. Both train and test parts of IXI dataset were preprocessed in the same way as BraTS: co-registration to the same anatomical template SRI24 [18], resampling to a uniform isotropic resolution with CaPTk toolkit and skull-stripping with HD-BET [21]. For all images voxel intensities are clipped to $[1, 99]$-percentiles and finally scaled to $[0, 1]$ interval. Although 3D DenseNet121 was trained on images with $1.5 \times 1.5 \times 1.5$ mm spacing, the original 1 mm isotropic spacing gives much better results because of the increased resolution in anomaly maps. This model has four dense blocks, and we take features from the third dense block, as it gives the best performance. Finally, we reduce the dimension of the obtained patch feature vectors from 1024 to 128 using adaptive average pooling. To reproduce the presented results, we release the source code https://github.com/DFrolova/PatchCore3D.

---

[3] https://github.com/Duplums/yAwareContrastiveLearning/.

Table 1. Comparison of the existing anomaly segmentation methods with their Patch-Core3D pipelines. Inference time is given per image. *AnoDDPM has very slow inference, so we evaluate it on 44 random images from our test set.

Method	Segmentation ↑				Detection				Time	
	⌈Dice_WT⌉	⌈Dice_TC⌉	⌈Dice_ET⌉	AUPRC	AUROC ↑	FPR ↓	FNR ↓	Train, m	Infer., s
PatchCore3D	0.324	0.195	0.109	0.212	0.965	0.026	0.237	4.4	1.057
PatchCore3D-10%	0.322	0.193	0.107	0.210	0.967	0.009	0.491	75.4	1.021
PatchCore3D-1%	0.317	0.190	0.105	0.207	0.970	0.009	0.484	11.5	1.021
AMCons	0.234	0.166	0.073	0.162	0.759	1.	0.	350.9	6.967
PatchCore3D + AMCons	**0.448**	**0.306**	**0.170**	**0.381**	0.965	0.043	0.206	355.3	8.024
IF 3D	0.204	0.135	0.087	0.138	**0.999**	0.	0.001	419.2	101.70
PatchCore3D + IF 3D	**0.341**	**0.222**	**0.129**	**0.265**	0.965	0.	0.115	423.6	102.08
AnoDDPM*	0.065	0.026	0.017	0.029	0.944	1.	0.	2093	8940
PatchCore3D + AnoDDPM*	**0.146**	**0.076**	**0.052**	**0.082**	1.	1.	0.	2097	8941
mDDPM	0.137	0.113	0.032	0.069	0.171	1.	0.	3714	27.85
PatchCore3D + mDDPM	**0.265**	**0.228**	**0.096**	**0.186**	0.965	0.112	0.073	3718	28.91
HistEq	0.309	0.168	0.085	0.197	0.682	1.	0.	0	0.325
PatchCore3D + HistEq	**0.467**	**0.298**	**0.168**	**0.384**	0.965	0.026	0.245	4.4	1.382
CGV	0.088	0.034	0.021	0.037	0.497	1.	0.	932.1	0.946
PatchCore3D + CGV	**0.158**	**0.101**	**0.068**	**0.092**	0.965	0.078	0.213	936.5	2.003

Metrics. To measure anomaly detection performance, we use the area under the receiver operating characteristic curve (AUROC). We report PatchCore3D detection scores for the pipeline, although one may still use initial method scores, e.g. for IF 3D. For the anomaly segmentation task, we follow [4] and use the area under the precision-recall curve (AUPRC) and highest possible dice score (⌈Dice⌉) obtained with the optimal threshold τ_{opt}. Dices are computed for the enhancing tumor (ET), the tumor core (TC), and the whole tumor (WT) subregions, but we primarily focus on the WT as the entire tumor, since it is a natural source of anomalies in our setup. Thus, AUPRC is reported for WT subregion. Following [13,19], both metrics for the segmentation task are computed on a dataset-level, i.e. across all voxels of all test images. Since computing voxel-level metrics on a large dataset is computationally expensive, we interpolate predicted anomaly masks together with ground truths to a shape of $(70, 70, 45)$, which is a common approach [4,5,13,24]. Also, we measure the fraction of normal images with false positive and false negative anomaly segmentations (FPR and FNR, respectively) produced with τ_{opt}.

3.2 Results

The results of the comparison of existing anomaly detection and segmentation methods with their PatchCore3D pipelines are presented in Table 1. We also report PatchCore3D performance using both complete memory bank $\mathcal{M}$ and coreset-subsampled memory bank $\widehat{\mathcal{M}}$, e.g. PatchCore3D-10%. From this Table follows that the addition of PatchCore3D as the first stage of the pipeline to any of the considered anomaly segmentation methods improves their anomaly segmentation performance: the pipeline results are uniformly better for all tumor subregions. Building pipeline improves over the standard method at least by

94% in AUPRC in our experiments. Moreover, even the proposed PatchCore3D method itself outperforms the considered competitors in anomaly segmentation. PatchCore3D is almost perfect in terms of sample-level anomaly detection, while many methods are much worse. Thus, with the pipeline, one can increase also anomaly detection performance of weak methods by taking PatchCore3D predictions for anomaly detection.

Additionally, we perform an analysis of the considered methods using the FPR and FNR metrics. In our experiments, all considered methods (except IF 3D) produce false anomaly segmentations on each normal image from the test set. HistEq shows poor FPR by design since each predicted anomaly map contains a voxel with a value of 1, resulting in anomaly detection in every image. At the same time, PatchCore3D performs almost perfectly on normal images and does not produce false positive predictions, while the false negative rate is high. Hence, the proposed pipeline gives the FPR close to the original PatchCore3D and FNR smaller than the original PatchCore3D.

Training and Inference Time. We perform a comparison of the inference and training runtime of the considered methods (Table 1). During the training stage, PatchCore3D needs only to extract embeddings from the training data and optionally perform coreset subsampling. So, it is much faster than training a network for AMCons or CGV. Moreover, combining PatchCore3D with any considered method in a pipeline adds negligible computational overhead compared to the original method. Also, coreset subsampling in PatchCore3D reduces inference time but adds computational overhead for the training stage. The smaller the size of the coreset is, the smaller the corresponding overhead is.

Restoration-based IF 3D and diffusion-based methods have very slow inference, which makes them hardly applicable in real-world scenarios. AnoDDPM requires more than two hours to produce an anomaly segmentation map for a single image, so we evaluated it on 44 random images from our test set. All models were evaluated on Nvidia Tesla V100 GPU.

Visual Quality of Segmentation. In addition to the aforementioned metrics comparison, we provide a set of samples and compare the considered methods visually. Figure 1 shows anomaly maps predicted with various methods for different scans. HistEq and AMCons are top-performing methods, and they are visually better than PatchCore3D in predicting exact tumor shapes but have noisy anomaly maps. AnoDDPM gives extremely noisy anomaly maps because it was trained on image slices that do not coincide with slices plotted in Fig. 1. PatchCore3D does not produce detailed contours of a tumor, but it successfully localizes the anomalous region with a small false positive rate. PatchCore3D produces coarse anomaly maps since they are interpolated from the spatial resolution of a feature map to the resolution of the original image. In our case, the spatial resolution of the feature map is $(15, 15, 9)$ and the resolution of the original image is $(240, 240, 155)$. Building the PatchCore3D pipeline upon a method, for example, AMCons, takes the best from both methods and provides precise anomaly localization and more detailed segmentations.

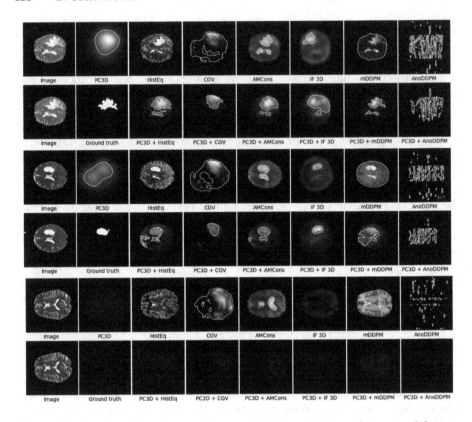

Fig. 1. Visualization of the whole tumor anomaly segmentation performance of the considered methods and the proposed PatchCore3D (PC3D) pipeline. Contoured regions represent anomalies obtained with the optimal binarisation threshold τ_{opt}.

Robustness to the Memory Bank Size. The natural idea to speed up the inference of PatchCore3D is to reduce the number of embeddings in the memory bank. One can take a random subset of a training set or use a greedy coreset subsampling procedure [1], as in the original PatchCore method. The segmentation AUROC degrades by 10% with random subsampling to 1% of the memory bank $\mathcal{M}$, while using the coreset subsampling to 1% of $\mathcal{M}$, the performance of PatchCore3D remains the same compared to using the whole memory bank.

In case of increasing the train set size or using feature extractors with higher spatial resolution, the memory bank size will grow, thus slowing down the nearest neighbor search and inference, respectively. In this case, coreset subsampling may highly speed up the inference since the number of candidates to be the nearest neighbors decreases. In our experiments, this approach does not speed up inference much (see Table 1), which indicates that the size of the train set is not large and the nearest neighbor search with highly optimized `faiss` library [12] does not induce a significant overhead.

4   Conclusion

In this paper, we present a two-stage unsupervised pipeline for solving anomaly segmentation and detection problems in medical imaging, which improves the performance of existing anomaly segmentation methods. The first stage is used for better anomaly localization and reduction of false positive segmentation rates, while the second stage performs precise segmentation in the suggested region. For the first stage, we propose a feature-based method PatchCore3D, whose main ingredients are the backbone, pre-trained on the 3D medical data and anomaly decision rule based on the nearest neighbor search. Any anomaly segmentation method can be used in the second stage. We evaluate the proposed pipeline in the combination with six top-performing anomaly segmentation methods of different types, and show a significant quality improvement provided with the pipeline for each of the methods.

References

1. Agarwal, P.K., Har-Peled, S., Varadarajan, K.R., et al.: Geometric approximation via coresets. Comb. Comput. Geom. **52**(1), 1–30 (2005)
2. Baid, U., et al.: The rsna-asnr-miccai brats 2021 benchmark on brain tumor segmentation and radiogenomic classification. arXiv preprint arXiv:2107.02314 (2021)
3. Bakas, S., et al.: Advancing the cancer genome atlas glioma MRI collections with expert segmentation labels and radiomic features. Sci. Data **4**(1), 1–13 (2017)
4. Baur, C., Denner, S., Wiestler, B., Navab, N., Albarqouni, S.: Autoencoders for unsupervised anomaly segmentation in brain MR images: a comparative study. Med. Image Anal. **69**, 101952 (2021)
5. Behrendt, F., Bengs, M., Rogge, F., Krüger, J., Opfer, R., Schlaefer, A.: Unsupervised Anomaly Detection in 3D Brain MRI using Deep Learning with impured training data. In: 2022 IEEE 19th International Symposium on Biomedical Imaging (ISBI). pp. 1–4. IEEE (2022)
6. Bengs, M., Behrendt, F., Krüger, J., Opfer, R., Schlaefer, A.: 3-Dimensional deep learning with spatial erasing for unsupervised anomaly segmentation in brain MRI. arXiv preprint arXiv:2109.06540 (2021)
7. Bercea, C.I., Wiestler, B., Rueckert, D., Schnabel, J.A.: Reversing the abnormal: Pseudo-healthy generative networks for anomaly detection. arXiv preprint arXiv:2303.08452 (2023)
8. Chan, H.P., Hadjiiski, L.M., Samala, R.K.: Computer-aided diagnosis in the era of deep learning. Med. Phys. **47**(5), e218–e227 (2020)
9. Dufumier, B., et al.: Contrastive learning with continuous proxy meta-data for 3D MRI classification. In: de Bruijne, M., et al. (eds.) MICCAI 2021. LNCS, vol. 12902, pp. 58–68. Springer, Cham (2021). https://doi.org/10.1007/978-3-030-87196-3_6
10. Huang, G., Liu, Z., Van Der Maaten, L., Weinberger, K.Q.: Densely connected convolutional networks. In: Proceedings of the IEEE conference on computer vision and pattern recognition, pp. 4700–4708 (2017)
11. Iqbal, H., Khalid, U., Hua, J., Chen, C.: Unsupervised anomaly detection in medical images using masked diffusion model. arXiv preprint arXiv:2305.19867 (2023)
12. Johnson, J., Douze, M., Jégou, H.: Billion-scale similarity search with gpus. IEEE Trans. Big Data **7**(3), 535–547 (2019)

13. Kascenas, A., Young, R., Jensen, B.S., Pugeault, N., O'Neil, A.Q.: Anomaly Detection via Context and Local Feature Matching. In: 2022 IEEE 19th International Symposium on Biomedical Imaging (ISBI), pp. 1–5. IEEE (2022)
14. Marimont, S.N., Tarroni, G.: Anomaly detection through latent space restoration using vector quantized variational autoencoders. In: 2021 IEEE 18th International Symposium on Biomedical Imaging (ISBI), pp. 1764–1767. IEEE (2021)
15. Meissen, F., Kaissis, G., Rueckert, D.: Challenging current semi-supervised anomaly segmentation methods for brain MRI. In: International MICCAI brainlesion workshop, pp. 63–74. Springer (2022). https://doi.org/10.1007/978-3-031-08999-2_5
16. Menze, B.H., et al.: The multimodal brain tumor image segmentation benchmark (BRATS). IEEE Trans. Med. Imaging **34**(10), 1993–2024 (2014)
17. Naval Marimont, S., Tarroni, G.: Implicit Field Learning for Unsupervised Anomaly Detection in Medical Images. In: de Bruijne, M., et al. (eds.) MICCAI 2021. LNCS, vol. 12902, pp. 189–198. Springer, Cham (2021). https://doi.org/10.1007/978-3-030-87196-3_18
18. Rohlfing, T., Zahr, N.M., Sullivan, E.V., Pfefferbaum, A.: The SRI24 multichannel atlas of normal adult human brain structure. Hum. Brain Mapping **31**(5), 798–819 (2010)
19. Roth, K., Pemula, L., Zepeda, J., Schölkopf, B., Brox, T., Gehler, P.: Towards total recall in industrial anomaly detection. In: Proceedings of the IEEE/CVF Conference on Computer Vision and Pattern Recognition, pp. 14318–14328 (2022)
20. Salehi, M., Sadjadi, N., Baselizadeh, S., Rohban, M.H., Rabiee, H.R.: Multiresolution knowledge distillation for anomaly detection. In: Proceedings of the IEEE/CVF conference on computer vision and pattern recognition, pp. 14902–14912 (2021)
21. Schell, M., et al.: Automated brain extraction of multi-sequence MRI using artificial neural networks. European Congress of Radiology-ECR 2019 (2019)
22. Schlegl, T., Seeböck, P., Waldstein, S.M., Langs, G., Schmidt-Erfurth, U.: f-AnoGAN: fast unsupervised anomaly detection with generative adversarial networks. Med. Image Anal. **54**, 30–44 (2019)
23. Silva-Rodríguez, J., Naranjo, V., Dolz, J.: Constrained unsupervised anomaly segmentation. arXiv preprint arXiv:2203.01671 (2022)
24. Simarro Viana, J., de la Rosa, E., Vande Vyvere, T., Robben, D., Sima, D.M., et al.: Unsupervised 3d brain anomaly detection. In: International MICCAI Brainlesion Workshop, pp. 133–142. Springer (2020)
25. Tan, J., Hou, B., Batten, J., Qiu, H., Kainz, B.: Detecting outliers with foreign patch interpolation. arXiv preprint arXiv:2011.04197 (2020)
26. Wyatt, J., Leach, A., Schmon, S.M., Willcocks, C.G.: Anoddpm: Anomaly detection with denoising diffusion probabilistic models using simplex noise. In: Proceedings of the IEEE/CVF Conference on Computer Vision and Pattern Recognition, pp. 650–656 (2022)
27. You, S., Tezcan, K.C., Chen, X., Konukoglu, E.: Unsupervised lesion detection via image restoration with a normative prior. In: International Conference on Medical Imaging with Deep Learning, pp. 540–556. PMLR (2019)
28. Zagoruyko, S., Komodakis, N.: Wide residual networks. arXiv preprint arXiv:1605.07146 (2016)
29. Zhou, Z., Sodha, V., Pang, J., Gotway, M.B., Liang, J.: Models genesis. Med. Image Anal. **67**, 101840 (2021)

30. Zimmerer, D., et al.: Mood 2020: a public benchmark for out-of-distribution detection and localization on medical images. IEEE Trans. Med. Imaging **41**(10), 2728–2738 (2022)
31. Zimmerer, D., Isensee, F., Petersen, J., Kohl, S., Maier-Hein, K.: Unsupervised Anomaly Localization Using Variational Auto-Encoders. In: Shen, D., et al. (eds.) MICCAI 2019. LNCS, vol. 11767, pp. 289–297. Springer, Cham (2019). https://doi.org/10.1007/978-3-030-32251-9_32
32. Zimmerer, D., et al.: Medical out-of-distribution analysis challenge (2022). https://doi.org/10.5281/zenodo.6362313

Redesigning Out-of-Distribution Detection on 3D Medical Images

Anton Vasiliuk[1,2(✉)], Daria Frolova[1,3], Mikhail Belyaev[1,3], and Boris Shirokikh[1,3]

[1] Artificial Intelligence Research Institute (AIRI), Moscow, Russia
[2] Moscow Institute of Physics and Technology, Moscow, Russia
vasilyuk@phystech.edu
[3] Skolkovo Institute of Science and Technology, Moscow, Russia
boris.shirokikh@skoltech.ru

Abstract. Detecting out-of-distribution (OOD) samples for trusted medical image segmentation remains a significant challenge. The critical issue here is the lack of a strict definition of abnormal data, which often results in artificial problem settings without measurable clinical impact. In this paper, we redesign the OOD detection problem according to the specifics of volumetric medical imaging and related downstream tasks (e.g., segmentation). We propose using the downstream model's performance as a pseudometric between images to define abnormal samples. This approach enables us to weigh different samples based on their performance impact without an explicit ID/OOD distinction. We incorporate this weighting in a new metric called Expected Performance Drop (EPD). EPD is our core contribution to the new problem design, allowing us to rank methods based on their clinical impact. We demonstrate the effectiveness of EPD-based evaluation in 11 CT and MRI OOD detection challenges.

Keywords: CT · MRI · Out-of-Distribution Detection · Anomaly Detection · Segmentation

1 Introduction

To apply a machine learning (ML) model in clinical practice, one needs to ensure that it can be trusted when faced with new types of samples [14]. Unfortunately, the current methodology for evaluating the model's robustness does not fully address the challenges posed by volumetric medical imaging. Out-of-distribution (OOD) detection is primarily designed for the classification problem [20], where classification is not defined on novel classes and thus cannot be scored on the abnormal samples. Contrary, the predictions of segmentation models, the most prevalent task in medical imaging [17], can be scored for abnormal images. The definition of the *background* class is often indistinguishable from the *absence of labeled target diseases* class. So any novel occurrences can be attributed to the background, allowing us to measure segmentation quality on such samples.

Additionally, the existing OOD detection application is complicated by the continuous nature of the problem. To assess a segmentation model's reliability, two continuous aspects are addressed in a binary manner. Firstly, the segmentation quality is measured on a gradual scale, meaning that a single prediction can be partially correct rather than simply classified as either correct or incorrect. Secondly, the difference between the distribution of the data used for training the model and the distribution of novel data can also be continuous. For example, when a new location that is different from the locations in the training set is tackled as an OOD problem [5], the transition is gradual rather than abrupt.

When studying these challenges using a discrete approach, where only binary classification is considered, it becomes necessary to manually select thresholds for decision-making. This approach does not allow for a proper estimation of potential errors or losses that may occur on novel data, hindering our understanding of the model's performance in such scenarios.

To address the continuous nature of novel data distributions, we can use the distance in the image space. However, the image distribution is too complex to be traceable. To overcome this challenge, we propose projecting the image distribution into a one-dimensional distribution of the model's performance scores. By doing this, any difference between the performance scores can be used as an indicator of dissimilarity in the image space. As a result, we can establish a pseudometric in the image space based on the observed variations in performance scores. Consequently, a sample is classified as abnormal if and only if it has a discernible impact on the segmentation performance.

The proposed projection provides an immediate benefit, allowing us to weigh samples based on their performance impact. We incorporate this weighting in a novel metric called Expected Performance Drop (EPD). Instead of artificial ID/OOD classification, as in previous studies, EPD measures the actual impact of an OOD detection method on the segmentation model scores. Moreover, one can train a more robust segmentation model which provides correct predictions on noisy data instead of rejecting them as abnormal. While the standard metrics indicate this case as a detection mistake, our metric reveals actually improved performance. So EPD explicitly addresses the question of how much performance can be maintained by applying OOD detection methods.

Overall, our contribution may be described as follows:

1. We redesign the OOD detection problem into a Performance-OOD (POOD) one based on medical image segmentation specifics. POOD exploits the actual decline in the downstream performance and provides a justification for such pipeline application.
2. We propose a new metric called EPD, which accounts for the continuous OOD nature. We evaluate the performance of the existing methods using EPD with experiments conducted in 11 OOD detection setups.

2 Background

2.1 Problem Setting

In the field of medical imaging various anomaly sources are examined under OOD detection framework. These anomalies can arise from continuous changes in factors such as the age of the subject [13,18], image acquisition parameters [13,16], or the presence of synthesized noises [4,16]. Although it is crucial to detect these anomalies, they do not fit neatly into the classification-based OOD framework, as the prediction classes remain the same. While these changes could be considered within the framework of Anomaly Detection (AD), their significance is supported by a decline in the performance of downstream models. In other words, the impact of these anomaly sources becomes evident when we observe a drop in the performance of models that rely on the anomaly-free input.

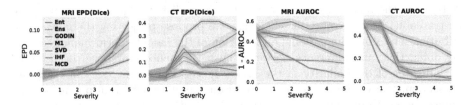

Fig. 1. Comparison of (1-AUROC) and EPD on synthetic datasets, lower values are preferable. The data is obtained by corrupting ID data with augmentations of different severity, where severity 0 represents the original data. AUROC scores indicate that the least distorted samples are the hardest to detect, while EPD scores indicate that the most distorted samples are the most important to detect.

Other studies have also emphasized the continuous nature of occuring anomalies. In a review of similar works [20], the AD definition by Grubbs (1969) is cited as finding "samples that appear to deviate markedly from other members of the sample in which it occurs." As the authors note, this definition is ambiguous without a distance measure between distributions and a defined threshold. To resolve this ambiguity, we therefore suggest using a downstream model, which can induce a pseudometric in the image space. Application of the downstream model allows to assess the performance impact of the distinct anomaly samples.

Moreover, ensuring model reliability does not solely rely on rejecting certain samples. In fact, a comprehensive study was conducted by [4] to investigate the methods robustness on abnormal samples. The authors' objective was to minimize the difference in segmentation performance between synthesized anomaly sources and the performance achieved on in-distribution (ID) samples. However, a unified framework is desired, which would enable the evaluation of model trustworthiness through both model robustness and anomaly rejection. This framework design should not be limited to specific methods and should be capable of assessing the practical impact of OOD pipelines in medical segmentation.

The estimation of performance, considering the ability to reject samples, is closely connected to the Selective Prediction (SP) framework. SP enables us to retain a subset of data samples to gain performance on the remaining samples [9]. However, it's important to note that the SP framework assumes the evaluation on in-distribution data. Consequently, this methodology is not suitable for estimating performance on anomalous data, making it challenging to scale its application for OOD performance estimation.

The frameworks mentioned above have shown effectiveness in enhancing the robustness of ML models. However, they are specific to certain contexts and lack the capability to assess the potential harm caused by anomalous samples. To address this limitation, we propose a Performance-OOD detection that extends the existing methodologies. This framework aims to tackle the challenge of improving model reliability while also providing an evaluation of its practical impact. By adopting the POOD, we can generalize and expand upon the existing approaches, enabling a comprehensive assessment of model robustness as the consequences of encountering anomalous samples.

2.2   OOD Detection Metrics

Classification metrics are conventionally used to measure the OOD detection performance. We discuss the most commonly used ones below.

AUROC provides a holistic view of classifier performance across many thresholds [10]. But in practice, any algorithm works only at a specified one [20]. We believe that the issue in applying AUROC to OOD detection is averaging scores across many *irrelevant* thresholds. In OOD detection, the rate of outliers is expected to be orders of magnitude lower than the ID data rate. However, AUROC mainly scores at thresholds, where it does not preserve the majority of ID samples (e.g., < 0.95 true positive rate). Thus, a large part of the AUROC score is attributed to the performance in irrelevant scenarios.

AUPR is another classification metric that is frequently used to assess OOD detection [10]. Besides the same issue of averaging across irrelevant thresholds, as in AUROC, the AUPR value also depends on the unknown ratio between positive and negative classes.

FPR@TPR=N is a metric that quantifies the percent of misclassified abnormal samples at a threshold where $N\%$ of ID samples is preserved [3]. Most importantly, this metric reflects the OOD detection performance focusing on maintaining the ID data, when N values are close to 100. We further build our metric upon FPR@TPR=N due to its clear interpretation. Besides, one can use a robust version, FPR@TPR=$N+$, which averages over thresholds $\geq N$, or vary the value of N, depending on the task at hands. The proposed metric adjusts the same way FPR does when changing N or $N+$.

All described metrics use the underlying assumption of the binary nature of the OOD detection task. They a priori discard the intuitive observation that abnormal samples can impact the downstream model's performance differently. Contrary, our redesigned setup considers the varying impact of these samples.

3   Expected Performance Drop

The impact of various anomalies on a segmentation model is not uniform. Thus, we develop a metric that assesses methods based on the downstream prediction performance. Firstly, we establish a threshold on the test ID set, aiming to retain $N\%$ of the ID data; $N = 95$ by default. Threshold selection follows the motivation behind the FPR@TPR=95 metric: abnormal events are assumed to be rare, and most of the ID data should be preserved. On the occurring data, we then reject (classify as OOD) all samples above the selected threshold. We evaluate the drop in segmentation performance on the remaining data compared to the expected ID performance. Hence, achieving a zero drop is possible either through accurate OOD detection or by avoiding erroneous predictions. Mathematically, the Expected Performance Drop (EPD) metric is defined as follows:

$$\text{EPD} = \mathop{\mathbb{E}}_{(x,y)\sim X_{ood}} (S_0 - S(x,y))\mathbb{1}[\text{id}(x) = 1], \qquad (1)$$

where X_{ood} is the test OOD data, x - image, y - segmentation, $\text{id}(x)$ - prediction of whether x is ID, $S(x,y)$ - segmentation model's score. $S_0 = \mathbb{E}_{(x,y)\sim X_{id}} S(x,y)$ is the expected score on the test ID set X_{id}. Lower EPD values are better[1].

Choosing Segmentation Metric. The EPD metric depends on but is not restricted to any segmentation metric in particular. When dataset has nontrivial segmentation masks, we employ the Dice similarity coefficient (DSC). For instance, even though anomalies like noise or changes in acquisition protocols differ semantically, we can still acquire ground truth masks to evaluate the performance decline, as in [4]. However, in scenarios where the downstream problem is absent, such as different scanning locations, the average number of false positive predictions (AvgFP) may provide more informative results.

Modifying Segmentation Model. Changing the model changes the scores $S(x,y)$ in Eq. 1. Thus, any quality improvements from methods, such as Ensemble, as well as possible losses due to the model modifications are taken into account. Alternative modification can be made independently of any OOD detection method also, aiming at improving the model's robustness. For example, one can train the same model with the extended data augmentations and potentially increase the scores $S(x,y)$ instead of improving the OOD detection method.

---

[1] A reader might suspect that EPD has a failure case, a trivial detection method that labels everything as OOD ($\text{id}(x) = 0$ $\forall x$), providing EPD $= 0$. Here, we note that any method is required to retain at least 95% TPR on the test ID set by the problem design. So the trivial detector, which outputs the same score for every image, thus the same label, is forced to label every image as ID, resulting in a valid EPD $= \mathbb{E}_{(x,y)\sim X_{ood}}(S_0 - S(x,y))$.

4 Experiments and Results

4.1 Datasets and Methods

Among the proposed OOD detection benchmarks on 3D medical images, we find [24] to be the most diverse in terms of public datasets and compared methods. The authors also link their setup to the downstream segmentation tasks. This allows us to fully re-evaluate the benchmark from the POOD perspective.

Datasets. Following their setup, we train lung nodules (CT) [1] and vestibular schwannoma (MRI) [21] segmentation models based on 3D U-Net [6]. The CT OOD datasets include Cancer500 [19], CT-ICH [11], LiTS [2], Medseg9[2], and MIDRC [23]. The MRI OOD datasets are CC359 [22], CrossMoDA [7], and EGD [25]. In all splits, data preprocessing, and synthetic setups we follow the instructions provided in [24].

OOD Detection Methods. Similarly, we explore the same set of OOD detection methods: entropy of predicted probability (Entropy) [10], Monte-Carlo Dropout (MCD) [8], ensemble of models (Ensemble) [15], generalized ODIN (G-ODIN) [12], and singular value decomposition (SVD) [13]. Most of them are considered either baselines or state-of-the-art in the field. We also explore two AD methods evaluated in [24]: intensity histogram features (IHF) and MOOD-1, an implementation of the MOOD 2022 [26] winner's solution (team CitAI).

Contrary to previous studies, operating in the POOD framework allows us to compare OOD detection methods to using segmentation model on abnormal data as is, without samples rejection. We call the latter approach *no-ood*.

Table 1. Comparison of EPD and AUROC across the studied shifts. Methods are ranked by their mean performance. Smaller EPD (DSC) values are better.

Lung Cancer (CT)	EPD (DSC)							AUROC							
	M1	SVD	IHF	MCD	GODIN	Ens	Ent	no-ood	IHF	SVD	GODIN	MCD	Ens	M1	Ent
Scanner	**.23**	.28	.27	.29	.29	.29	.25	.32	**.73**	.58	.72	.58	.55	.51	.65
Synthetic (Elastic)	**.01**	.07	**.01**	.09	.18	.07	.29	.35	**.97**	.86	.85	.84	.85	.78	.65
Location (Head)	.01	**.00**	**.00**	.05	.11	.10	.09	.29	**1.0**	**1.0**	.83	.85	.79	.83	.62
Location (Liver)	.27	**.06**	.25	.42	.27	.44	.38	.47	.89	**.97**	.88	.42	.45	.61	.67
Population (COVID-19)	**.26**	.38	.27	.29	.29	.30	.45	.50	**.88**	.74	.86	.79	.80	.66	.72
meanCT	**.15**	.16	.16	.23	.23	.24	.29	.38	**.89**	.83	.83	.69	.69	.68	.66

Vestibular Schwannoma (MRI)	EPD (DSC)							AUROC							
	Ent	SVD	IHF	Ens	M1	no-ood	GODIN	MCD	IHF	SVD	GODIN	M1	MCD	Ens	Ent
Population (Glioblastoma)	**−.07**	.00	.00	.02	.01	.06	.14	.14	**1.0**	**1.0**	.96	.87	.44	.41	.14
Population (Healthy)	**−.06**	.00	.00	−.04	.03	.07	.00	.13	**1.0**	**1.0**	**1.0**	.86	.44	.16	.15
Scanner	.01	.00	.00	.01	.01	.03	.00	.02	**1.0**	**1.0**	**1.0**	.83	.70	.74	.59
Synthetic (K-space noise)	**.00**	.00	.00	.02	.09	.08	.06	.02	**1.0**	.86	.81	.24	.56	.63	.66
Synthetic (Anisotropy)	.03	.00	.01	.04	.03	.06	.11	.05	**.98**	.94	.81	.57	.63	.63	.71
Synthetic (Motion)	.01	.00	.00	.01	.01	.01	.06	.01	**.99**	.75	.78	.48	.57	.54	.57
meanMRI	**−.01**	.00	.00	.01	.03	.05	.06	.06	**1.0**	.93	.89	.64	.56	.52	.47

---

[2] https://radiopaedia.org/articles/covid-19-3.

Experimental Setup. Given the OOD and segmentation scores calculated following [24], we compute EPD coupled with the DSC and AvgFP metrics using Eq. 1.

To address reliability enhancement through training modification, we design a second setup that differs in addition of training augmentations (random slice drop, Gaussian noise, gamma correction, and flip). As such training affect ID segmentation performance, the EPD is scored against the baseline model segmentation performance. This alternative training setup is called U-Net+augm.

4.2   Results and Discussion

Firstly, we compare EPD scores against the standard AUROC metric in Table 1. EPD reflects the actual influence of the OOD detection integration into a segmentation pipeline. For lung cancer segmentation, all reviewed methods establish a considerable reliability improvement. While for vestibular schwannoma segmentation, G-ODIN performance degrades despite its high AUROC scores.

Further, the Entropy performed the poorest according to AUROC. In MRI setup this is partially due to lower OOD scores in Population shifts than on the ID set, resulting in AUROC lower 0.5. However, the EPD effectively captures the ability of the segmentation model to correctly perform under these Population shifts. This results in the lowest rejection rate, thus a better average DSC compared to the ID test set. Consequently, we demonstrate that the IHF method's AUROC score of 1.0 can be further improved if the implemented method filters out erroneous data only.

Secondly, EPD provides us with a comprehensive framework to investigate OOD detection using any relevant metric. For example, if the selection of a model is influenced by the number of false positive (FP) predictions, EPD produces a different ranking, as shown in Table 2. These results highlight the effectiveness of the *Ensemble*, *G-ODIN*, and *MCD* methods in reducing the number of FP predictions. Therefore, these methods should be preferred when minimizing FP detections is the primary criterion. None of these observations can be inferred from the AUROC metric as well as the other classification metrics.

Table 2. Influence of the training pipeline on the *minus* AvgFP on the CT datasets. The values are averaged across all CT shifts. Since AvgFP behaves inversely to DSC (lower is better), we negate it to preserve the same EPD relation, lower *EPD (-AvgFP)* is better.

	EPD (-AvgFP)								AUROC						
	Ens	GODIN	MCD	SVD	IHF	M1	no-ood	Ent	IHF	SVD	GODIN	MCD	Ens	M1	Ent
Unet	**-4.71**	-4.57	-4.42	-3.05	-2.95	1.22	1.53	2.33	**.89**	.83	.83	.69	.69	.68	.66
Unet+augm	-5.19	-6.39	-5.45	-2.79	-2.94	-2.90	**-7.04**	-6.11	**.89**	.86	.77	.66	.56	.68	.61

Furthermore, EPD metric enables joint optimisation of the OOD methods and a downstream model's robustness. In Table 2, we demonstrate how EPD

	Dice							Dice			-Avg. FP					
	Pop. (Glioma)	Pop. (Healthy)	Scanner	MRI ID	Syn. (K-space)	Syn. (Anisotropy)	Syn. (Motion)	Scanner	CT ID	Syn. (Elastic)	Scanner	CT ID	Syn. (Elastic)	Loc. (Head)	Loc. (Liver)	Pop. (COVID19)
Ent	1	1	0.8	0.8	0.9	0	0	0.5	0	0.3	-0.2	0	-0.2	0	-0.3	0
Ens	0.3	0.2	0	0	0.2	0	0	0	0	0.5	0	0	-0.5	0	0	0
MCD	0	0	0	0	0	0	0	0	0	0.4	0	0	-0.4	0	0	0
GODIN	0	0.3	0.6	0	0	0.4	0.4	0	0	-0.3	0	0	0.3	0	0	0
SVD	0	0.3	0.4	0	0.4	0.6	0.3	0	0	0.5	0	0	-0.5	0	0	0
IHF	0	-0.3		0	0.5	0	0.3	0.2	0	0.5	-0.2	0	-0.5	0	0	0
M1	0	0	0	0	-0.3	0	-0.2	0	0	0.5	0	0	0	0	0	0

Fig. 2. Spearman correlation values between OOD and performance scores. Correlations with p-value $> 10^{-4}$ are indicated by 0.

advances the utilization of training augmentations to improve model reliability. Specifically, Unet+augm model without OOD rejection (no-ood) produces the lowest number of FP detection across studied methods. Additionally, further application of OOD pipelines adversely affects this performance. In contrast, the AUROC metric exhibits similar scores for both methods and cannot represent the difference of various performance quantification.

Finally, EPD excludes the criteria of whether data is abnormal. As shown in Fig. 1, AUROC gives $0.5 - 0.6$ score for data with minor variations. This may lead to inadequate conclusions, such as "further research is needed to detect close-OOD samples." In practice, such samples do not impact segmentation performance and can be safely ignored by the OOD detection method. And EPD indicates this safe behavior with close to 0 values at Severity ≤ 1. Therefore only such samples that influence model performance are considered abnormal.

A side benefit of the EPD metric is its ability to capture inherent correlations between the OOD score and prediction quality. As we show in Fig. 2, such correlations exist for certain datasets and methods, thus rejecting samples affects performance on the remaining data. EPD captures this correlation by design, resulting in accurate produced scores.

5   Conclusion

In this study, we reviewed the OOD detection problem, with a focus on the downstream performance drop on new data. By studying a segmentation model with the ability to reject samples, we provided a versatile perspective on the model's reliability regarding any chosen ID quality measure. Our approach enabled the analysis of arbitrary distant distributions without a requirement to define a threshold between ID and OOD. Through the application of the proposed Expected Performance Drop metric in 11 OOD detection challenges, we obtained detailed insights into the performance of segmentation models using Dice and Avg. FP scores on anomaly data. Additionally, we demonstrated that the proposed POOD framework facilitates the improvement of model reliability through both OOD pipeline implementation and robust training. Finally, with the proposed framework we evaluated the actual impact of OOD pipeline utilization, considering the potential influence on the ID segmentation performance.

Acknowledgments. The authors acknowledge the National Cancer Institute and the Foundation for the National Institutes of Health, and their critical role in the creation of the free publicly available LIDC/IDRI Database used in this study. This research was funded by Russian Science Foundation grant number 20-71-10134.

References

1. Armato, S.G., III., et al.: The lung image database consortium (LIDC) and image database resource initiative (IDRI): a completed reference database of lung nodules on CT scans. Med. Phys. **38**(2), 915–931 (2011)
2. Bilic, P., et al.: The liver tumor segmentation benchmark (LITS). arXiv preprint arXiv:1901.04056 (2019)
3. Bitterwolf, J., Meinke, A., Augustin, M., Hein, M.: Breaking down out-of-distribution detection: Many methods based on OOD training data estimate a combination of the same core quantities. In: International Conference on Machine Learning, pp. 2041–2074. PMLR (2022)
4. Boone, L., et al.: Rood-mri: Benchmarking the robustness of deep learning segmentation models to out-of-distribution and corrupted data in mri. arXiv preprint arXiv:2203.06060 (2022)
5. Cao, T., Huang, C.W., Hui, D.Y.T., Cohen, J.P.: A benchmark of medical out of distribution detection. arXiv preprint arXiv:2007.04250 (2020)
6. Çiçek, Ö., Abdulkadir, A., Lienkamp, S.S., Brox, T., Ronneberger, O.: 3D U-net: learning dense volumetric segmentation from sparse annotation. In: Ourselin, S., Joskowicz, L., Sabuncu, M.R., Unal, G., Wells, W. (eds.) MICCAI 2016. LNCS, vol. 9901, pp. 424–432. Springer, Cham (2016). https://doi.org/10.1007/978-3-319-46723-8_49
7. Dorent, R., Kujawa, A., Cornelissen, S., Langenhuizen, P., Shapey, J., Vercauteren, T.: Cross-modality domain adaptation challenge 2022 (crossMoDA), May 2022. https://doi.org/10.5281/zenodo.6504722
8. Gal, Y., Ghahramani, Z.: Dropout as a bayesian approximation: representing model uncertainty in deep learning. In: international Conference on Machine Learning, pp. 1050–1059. PMLR (2016)
9. Geifman, Y., El-Yaniv, R.: Selective classification for deep neural networks. In: Advances in Neural Information Processing Systems, vol. 30 (2017)
10. Hendrycks, D., Gimpel, K.: A baseline for detecting misclassified and out-of-distribution examples in neural networks. arXiv preprint arXiv:1610.02136 (2016)
11. Hssayeni, M., Croock, M., Salman, A., Al-khafaji, H., Yahya, Z., Ghoraani, B.: Computed tomography images for intracranial hemorrhage detection and segmentation. Intracranial Hemorrhage Segmentation Using A Deep Convolutional Model. Data **5**(1), 14 (2020)
12. Hsu, Y.C., Shen, Y., Jin, H., Kira, Z.: Generalized ODIN: detecting out-of-distribution image without learning from out-of-distribution data. In: Proceedings of the IEEE/CVF Conference on Computer Vision and Pattern Recognition, pp. 10951–10960 (2020)

13. Karimi, D., Gholipour, A.: Improving calibration and out-of-distribution detection in deep models for medical image segmentation. IEEE Trans. Artif. Intell. **4**(2), 383–397 (2022)

14. Kompa, B., Snoek, J., Beam, A.L.: Second opinion needed: communicating uncertainty in medical machine learning. NPJ Digit. Med. **4**(1), 4 (2021)

15. Lakshminarayanan, B., Pritzel, A., Blundell, C.: Simple and scalable predictive uncertainty estimation using deep ensembles. In: Advances in Neural Information Processing Systems, vol. 30 (2017)

16. Lambert, B., Forbes, F., Doyle, S., Tucholka, A., Dojat, M.: Improving uncertainty-based out-of-distribution detection for medical image segmentation. arXiv preprint arXiv:2211.05421 (2022)

17. Litjens, G., et al.: A survey on deep learning in medical image analysis. Med. Image Anal. **42**, 60–88 (2017)

18. Mahmood, A., Oliva, J., Styner, M.: Multiscale score matching for out-of-distribution detection. arXiv preprint arXiv:2010.13132 (2020)

19. Morozov, S., Gombolevskiy, V., Elizarov, A., Gusev, M., Novik, V., Prokudaylo, S., Bardin, A., Popov, E., Ledikhova, N., Chernina, V., et al.: A simplified cluster model and a tool adapted for collaborative labeling of lung cancer CT scans. Comput. Methods Program. Biomed. **206**, 106111 (2021)

20. Salehi, M., Mirzaei, H., Hendrycks, D., Li, Y., Rohban, M.H., Sabokrou, M.: A unified survey on anomaly, novelty, open-set, and out-of-distribution detection: Solutions and future challenges. arXiv preprint arXiv:2110.14051 (2021)

21. Shapey, J., et al.: Segmentation of vestibular schwannoma from MRI, an open annotated dataset and baseline algorithm. Sci. Data **8**(1), 1–6 (2021)

22. Souza, R., et al.: An open, multi-vendor, multi-field-strength brain MR dataset and analysis of publicly available skull stripping methods agreement. NeuroImage **170**, 482–494 (2018)

23. Tsai, E.B., et al.: The RSNA international covid-19 open radiology database (RICORD). Radiology **299**(1), E204–E213 (2021)

24. Vasiliuk, A., Frolova, D., Belyaev, M., Shirokikh, B.: Limitations of out-of-distribution detection in 3d medical image segmentation. arXiv preprint arXiv:2306.13528 (2023)

25. van der Voort, S.R., et al.: The Erasmus glioma database (EGD): Structural MRI scans, who 2016 subtypes, and segmentations of 774 patients with glioma. Data in brief **37**, 107191 (2021)

26. Zimmerer, D., et al.: Medical out-of-distribution analysis challenge 2022, March 2022. https://doi.org/10.5281/zenodo.6362313

On the Use of Mahalanobis Distance for Out-of-distribution Detection with Neural Networks for Medical Imaging

Harry Anthony[1]([⊠])[iD] and Konstantinos Kamnitsas[1,2,3]

[1] Department of Engineering Science, University of Oxford, Oxford, UK
harry.anthony@eng.ox.ac.uk
[2] Department of Computing, Imperial College London, London, UK
[3] School of Computer Science, University of Birmingham, Birmingham, UK

Abstract. Implementing neural networks for clinical use in medical applications necessitates the ability for the network to detect when input data differs significantly from the training data, with the aim of preventing unreliable predictions. The community has developed several methods for out-of-distribution (OOD) detection, within which distance-based approaches - such as Mahalanobis distance - have shown potential. This paper challenges the prevailing community understanding that there is an optimal layer, or combination of layers, of a neural network for applying Mahalanobis distance for detection of any OOD pattern. Using synthetic artefacts to emulate OOD patterns, this paper shows the optimum layer to apply Mahalanobis distance changes with the type of OOD pattern, showing there is no one-fits-all solution. This paper also shows that separating this OOD detector into multiple detectors at different depths of the network can enhance the robustness for detecting different OOD patterns. These insights were validated on real-world OOD tasks, training models on CheXpert chest X-rays with no support devices, then using scans with unseen pacemakers (we manually labelled 50% of CheXpert for this research) and unseen sex as OOD cases. The results inform best-practices for the use of Mahalanobis distance for OOD detection. The manually annotated pacemaker labels and the project's code are available at: https://github.com/HarryAnthony/Mahalanobis-OOD-detection

Keywords: Out-of-distribution · Uncertainty · Distribution shift

1 Introduction

Neural networks have achieved state-of-the-art performance in various medical image analysis tasks. Yet their generalisation on data not represented by the training data - out-of-distribution (OOD) - is unreliable [12,21,33]. In the medical imaging field, this can have severe consequences. Research in the field of

C. H. Sudre et al. (Eds.): UNSURE 2023, LNCS 14291, pp. 136–146, 2023.
https://doi.org/10.1007/978-3-031-44336-7_14

OOD detection [26] seeks to develop methods that identify if an input is OOD, acting as a safeguard that informs the human user before a potentially failed model prediction affects down-stream tasks, such as clinical decision-making - facilitating safer application of neural networks for high-risk applications.

One category of OOD detection methods use an **external model for OOD detection**. These include using *reconstruction models* [1,9,20,22,27], which are trained on in-distribution (ID) data and assume high reconstruction loss when reconstructing OOD data. Some approaches employ a *classifier* to learn a decision boundary between ID and OOD data [26]. The boundary can be learned in an unsupervised manner, or supervised with exposure to pre-collected OOD data [11,25,29,31]. Other methods use *probabilistic models* [15] to model the distribution of the training data, and aim to assign low probability to OOD inputs.

Another category are **confidence-based methods** that enable discriminative models trained for a specific task, such as classification, to estimate uncertainty in their prediction. Some methods use the network's softmax distribution, such as MCP [10], MCDropout [6] and ODIN [18], whereas others use the distance of the input to training data in the model's latent space [17].

A commonly studied method of the latter category is Mahalanobis distance [17], possibly due to its intuitive nature. The method has shown mixed performance in literature, performing well in certain studies [7,14,24,32] but less well in others [2,28,30]. Previous work has explored which layer of a network gives an embedding optimal for OOD detection [3,17]. But further research is needed to understand the factors influencing its performance to achieve reliable application of this method. This paper provides several contributions towards this end:

- Identifies that measuring Mahalanobis distance at the last hidden layer of a neural network, as commonly done in literature, can be sub-optimal.
- Demonstrates that different OOD patterns are best detectable at different depths of a network, implying that there is no single layer to measure Mahalanobis distance for optimal detection of *all* OOD patterns.
- The above suggests that optimal design of OOD detection systems may require multiple detectors, at different layers, to detect different OOD patterns. We provide evidence that such an approach can lead to improvements.
- Created a benchmark for OOD detection by manually annotating pacemakers and support devices in CheXpert [13].

2   Methods

Primer on Mahalanobis Score, $\mathcal{D}_{\mathcal{M}}$: Feature extractor $\mathcal{F}$ transforms input $\mathbf{x}$ into an embedding. $\mathcal{F}$ is typically a section of a neural network pre-trained for a task of interest, such as disease classification, from which feature maps $h(\mathbf{x})$ are obtained. The mean of feature maps $h(\mathbf{x})$ are used as embedding vector $\mathbf{z}$:

$$\mathbf{z} \in \Re^M = \frac{1}{D^2} \sum_D \sum_D h(\mathbf{x}), \quad \text{where } h(\mathbf{x}) \in \Re^{D \times D \times M} \tag{1}$$

for M feature maps with dimensions $D{\times}D$. Distance-based OOD methods assume the embedded in-distribution (ID) and OOD data will deviate in latent space, ergo being separable via a distance metric. In the latent space $\Re^M$, N_c *training* data points for class c have a mean and covariance matrix of

$$\boldsymbol{\mu_c} = \frac{1}{N_c} \sum_{i=1}^{N_c} \mathbf{z_{i_c}}, \quad \boldsymbol{\Sigma_c} = \frac{1}{N_c} \sum_{i=1}^{N_c} (\mathbf{z_{i_c}} - \boldsymbol{\mu_c}) \, (\mathbf{z_{i_c}} - \boldsymbol{\mu_c})^T \quad (2)$$

where $\boldsymbol{\mu_c}$ is vector of length M and $\boldsymbol{\Sigma_c}$ is a $M{\times}M$ matrix. Mahalanobis distance $\mathcal{D}_{\mathcal{M}_c}$ between embedding $\mathbf{z}$ of a *test* data point and the *training* data of class c can be calculated as a sum over M dimensions [19]. The **Mahalanobis score** $\mathcal{D}_\mathcal{M}$ for OOD detection is defined as the minimum Mahalanobis distance between the test data point and the class centroids of the training data,

$$\mathcal{D}_{\mathcal{M}_c}(\mathbf{x}) = \sum_{i=1}^{M} (\mathbf{z} - \boldsymbol{\mu_c}) \, \boldsymbol{\Sigma_c}^{-1} \, (\mathbf{z} - \boldsymbol{\mu_c})^T, \quad \mathcal{D}_\mathcal{M}(\mathbf{x}) = \min_c \{\mathcal{D}_{\mathcal{M}_c}(\mathbf{x})\}. \quad (3)$$

Threshold t, chosen empirically, is then used to separate ID ($\mathcal{D}_\mathcal{M} < t$) from OOD data ($\mathcal{D}_\mathcal{M} > t$). Score $\mathcal{D}_\mathcal{M}$ is commonly measured at a network's last hidden layer (LHL) [2,4,5,23,28,30]. To analyse the score's effectiveness with respect to where it is measured, we extracted a separate vector $\mathbf{z}$ after each network module (Fig. 1). Herein, a *module* refers to a network operation: convolution, batch normalisation (BN), ReLU, addition of residual connections, pooling, flatten. Stats $\boldsymbol{\mu_c}^\ell$ and $\boldsymbol{\Sigma_c}^\ell$ (Eq. 2) of the training data were measured after each module ℓ, and for each input an OOD score $\mathcal{D}_\mathcal{M}^\ell$ was calculated per module (Eq. 3).

Weighted Combination: Weighted combination of Mahalanobis scores $\mathcal{D}_\mathcal{M}^\ell$, measured at different layers ℓ, was developed [17] to improve OOD detection:

$$\mathcal{D}_{\mathcal{M},comb}(\mathbf{x}) = \sum_\ell \alpha_\ell \, \mathcal{D}_\mathcal{M}^\ell(\mathbf{x}), \quad (4)$$

using $\alpha_l \in \Re$ to down-weight ineffective layers. Coefficients α_l are optimised using a logistic regression estimator on pre-collected OOD data [17].

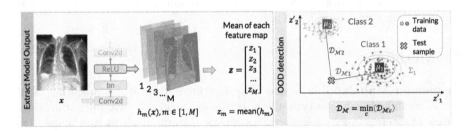

Fig. 1. (Left) Method to extract embeddings after a network module. (Right) Mahalanobis score $\mathcal{D}_\mathcal{M}$ of an input to the closest training class centroid.

Fast Gradient Sign method (FGSM) [8,17]: Empirical evidence showed that the rate of change of Mahalanobis distance with respect to a small input perturbation is typically greater for ID than OOD inputs [17,18]. Therefore, perturbations $\mathbf{x}' = \mathbf{x} - \varepsilon \cdot \text{sign}(\nabla_x \mathcal{D}_\mathcal{M}(\mathbf{x}))$ of magnitude ε are added to image $\mathbf{x}$, to minimise distance $\mathcal{D}_{\mathcal{M}_c}$ to the nearest class centroid. Mahalanobis score $\mathcal{D}_\mathcal{M}(\mathbf{x}')$ of the perturbed image $\mathbf{x}'$ is then used for OOD detection.

Multi-branch Mahalanobis (MBM): During this work it was found that different OOD patterns are better detected at different depths of a network (Sect. 3). This motivated the design of a system with multiple OOD detectors, operating at different network depths. We divide a network into parts, separated by downsampling operations. We refer to each part as a *branch* hereafter. For each branch b, we combine (with summation) the scores $\mathcal{D}_\mathcal{M}^\ell$, measured at modules $\ell \in L_b$, where L_b is the set of modules in the branch (visual example in Fig. 5). For each branch, we normalise each score $\mathcal{D}_\mathcal{M}^\ell$ before summing them, to prevent any single layer dominating. For this, the mean ($\mu_b^\ell = \mathbb{E}_{\mathbf{x} \in X_{train}}[D_M^\ell(\mathbf{x})]$) and standard deviation ($\sigma_b^\ell = \mathbb{E}_{x \in X_{train}}[(D_M^\ell(\mathbf{x}) - \mu_b^\ell)^2]^{\frac{1}{2}}$) of Mahalanobis scores of the *training data* after each module were calculated, and used to normalise $\mathcal{D}_\mathcal{M}^\ell$ for any *test* image $\mathbf{x}$, as per Eq. 5. This leads to a different Mahalanobis score and OOD detector per branch (4 in experiments with ResNet18 and VGG16).

$$\mathcal{D}_{\mathcal{M},branch-b}(\mathbf{x}) = \sum_{\ell \in L_b} \frac{\mathcal{D}_\mathcal{M}^\ell(\mathbf{x}) - \mu_b^\ell}{\sigma_b^\ell}. \tag{5}$$

3   Investigation of the Use of $\mathcal{D}_\mathcal{M}$ with Synthetic Artefacts

The abilities of Mahalanobis score $\mathcal{D}_\mathcal{M}$ were studied using CheXpert [13], a multi-label collection of chest X-rays. Subsequent experiments were performed under three settings, summarised in Fig. 2. In the first setting, studied here, we used scans containing either Cardiomegaly or Pneumothorax. We trained a ResNet18 on 90% of these images to classify between the two classes (ID task), and held-out 10% of the data as ID test cases. We generated an OOD test set by adding a synthetic artefact at a random position to these held-out images.

Set.	ID Classification Task	# ID images	Train:test split	OOD Task	# OOD images
1	Cardiomegaly	23,365	90:10	Synthetic artefacts	4319
	Pneumothorax	15,505			
2	Pleural Effusion	3606	5-fold split	Unseen Pacemaker	4862
	Not PE	5193			
3	PE (male only)	1877	5-fold split	Unseen Sex	4149
	Not PE (male only)	2773			

Synthetic artefacts: Square   Ring   a)   b)

Fig. 2. a) Visual and b) quantitative summary of the synthetic (setting 1) and real (setting 2 & 3) ID and OOD data used to evaluate OOD detection performance.

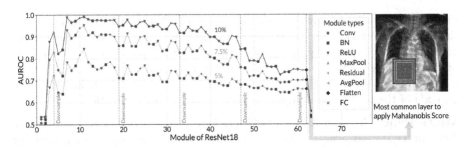

Fig. 3. AUROC (mean of 3 seeds) for Mahalanobis score over the modules of ResNet18 for synthetic square artefacts of size 10% (purple), 7.5% (green) and 5% (blue) of the image. The module types of ResNet18 are visualised, showing AUROC is typically improved after a ReLU module. The downsample operations are shown by dashed grey lines. The AUROC at the last hidden layer (LHL) is highlighted in orange, exhibiting a comparatively poor performance. (Color figure online)

Square Artefact: Firstly, grey squares, of sizes 10, 7.5 and 5 % of the image area, were introduced to create the OOD cases. We processed ID and OOD data, measured their $\mathcal{D}_{\mathcal{M}}$ after every module in the network and plotted the AUROC score in Fig. 3. We emphasize the following observations. The figure shows that larger square artefacts are easier to detect, with this OOD pattern being easier to detect in earlier layers. Moreover, we observed that AUROC is poor at the last hidden layer (LHL), which is a common layer to apply $\mathcal{D}_{\mathcal{M}}$ in the literature [2,4, 5,23,28,30]. The performance of this sub-optimal configuration may be diverting the community's attention, missing the method's true potential. The results also show AUROC performance in general improves after a ReLU module, compared to the previous convolution and BN of the corresponding layer. Similar results were found with VGG16 but not shown due to space constraints.

Ring Artefact: The experiments were repeated with a white ring as the synthetic artefact, and results were compared with the square artefact (Fig. 4). The figure shows the AUROC for different OOD patterns peak at different depths of the network. The figure shows the layers and optimised linear coefficients α_l for each artefact for $\mathcal{D}_{\mathcal{M},comb}$ (Eq. 4), highlighting that the ideal weighting of distances for one OOD pattern can cause a degradation in the performance for another, there is no single weighting that optimally detects both patterns. As the types of OOD patterns that can be encountered are unpredictable, the idea of searching for an optimal weighting of layers may be ill-advised - implying a different application of this method is required.

4   Investigation of the Use of $\mathcal{D}_{\mathcal{M}}$ with Real Artefacts

To create an OOD benchmark, we manually labelled 50% of the frontal scans in CheXpert based on whether they had a) no support device, b) any support devices (e.g. central lines, catheters, pacemakers), c) definitely containing a pacemaker, d) unclear. This was performed because CheXpert's "support devices"

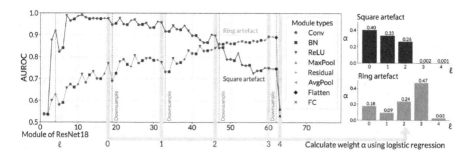

Fig. 4. AUROC (mean of 3 seeds) for Mahalanobis score over the modules of ResNet18 for synthetic grey square (purple) and white ring (orange) artefacts. The layers used for $\mathcal{D}_{\mathcal{M},comb}$ [17] (Sect. 2) are highlighted in blue, and the weightings α_l for each layer (Eq. 4) are shown on the right for each artefact. The results show the ideal weighting for one artefact causes a degradation in performance for another - implying there's no one-fits-all weighting. (Color figure online)

class is suboptimal, and to separate pacemakers (distinct OOD pattern). Findings from the synthetic data were validated on two real OOD tasks (described in Fig. 2). For the first benchmark, models were trained with scans with no support devices to classify if a scan had Pleural Effusion or not (ID task). Images containing pacemakers were then used as OOD test cases. For the second benchmark, models were trained on males' scans with no support devices to classify for Pleural Effusion, then females' scans with no support devices were used as OOD test cases. For both cases, the datasets were split using 5-fold cross validation, using 80% of ID images for training and the remaining 20% as ID test cases.

Where to Measure $\mathcal{D}_{\mathcal{M}}$: Figure 5 shows the AUROC for unseen pacemaker and sex OOD tasks when $\mathcal{D}_{\mathcal{M}}$ is measured at different modules of a ResNet18. The figure validates the findings on synthetic artefacts: applying $\mathcal{D}_{\mathcal{M}}$ on the LHL can result in poor performance, and the AUROC performance after a ReLU module is generally improved compared to the preceding BN and convolution. Moreover, it shows that the unseen pacemaker and sex OOD tasks are more detectable at different depths of ResNet18 (modules 51 and 44 respectively). As real-world OOD patterns are very heterogeneous, this motivates an optimal OOD detection system having multiple detectors, each processing features of a network at different layers responsible for identifying different OOD patterns.

Compared Methods: The OOD detection performance of multi-branch Mahalanobis (MBM) was studied. MBM was also investigated using only distances after ReLUs, as experiments on synthetic OOD patterns suggested this may be beneficial. The impact of FGSM (Sect. 2) on MBM was also studied. This was compared to OOD detection baselines. The softmax-based methods used were MCP [10], MCDropout [6], Deep Ensembles [16] (using 3 networks per k-fold), ODIN [18] (optimising temperature $T \in [1, 100]$ and perturbation $\varepsilon \in [0, 0.1]$). The performance was also compared to distance-based OOD detection methods such as $\mathcal{D}_{\mathcal{M}}$, $\mathcal{D}_{\mathcal{M},comb}$ ($\alpha_l = 1 \ \forall l$), $\mathcal{D}_{\mathcal{M}}$ with FGSM (using an optimised perturbation $\varepsilon \in [0, 0.1]$) and $\mathcal{D}_{\mathcal{M}}$ at the best performing network module.

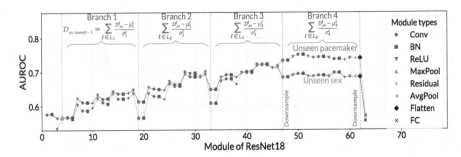

Fig. 5. AUROC (mean of 5 folds) for Mahalanobis score at different modules of ResNet18 for unseen pacemaker (green) and unseen sex (pink) OOD tasks. The figure shows the modules in each branch for MBM with grey brackets. (Color figure online)

Performance of OOD methods for both ResNet18 and VGG16 are shown in Table 1. Results show that $\mathcal{D}_{\mathcal{M},comb}$ without LHL outperforms the original weighted combination, showing that the LHL can have a degrading impact on OOD detection. MBM results for ResNet18 in Table 1 show that the OOD patterns are optimally detected at different branches of the network (branch 4 and 3 respectively), further motivating an ideal OOD detector using multiple depths for detecting different patterns. For VGG16 these specific patterns both peak in the deepest branch, but other patterns, such as synthetic squares, peak at different branches (these results are not shown due to space limits). MBM results show that if one could identify the optimal branch for detection of a specific OOD pattern, the MBM approach not only outperforms a sum of all layers, but also outperforms the best performing single layer for a given pattern in some cases. Deducing the best branch for detecting a specific OOD pattern has less degrees-of-freedom than the best layer, meaning an ideal system based on MBM would be easier to configure. The results also show MBM performance can be improved by only using ReLU modules, and optimised with FGSM.

Finding Thresholds: Using multiple OOD detectors poses the challenge of determining OOD detection thresholds for each detector. To demonstrate the potential in the MBM framework, a grid search optimised the thresholds for four OOD detectors of MBM using ReLU modules for ResNet18 trained on setting 3 (described in Fig. 2). Thresholds were set to classify an image as OOD if any detector labeled it as such. Unseen pacemakers and unseen sex were used as OOD tasks to highlight that thresholds could be found to accommodate multiple OOD tasks. The performance of these combined OOD detectors was compared to $\mathcal{D}_{\mathcal{M},comb}$ w/o LHL ($\alpha_l = 1 \ \forall l$) and $\mathcal{D}_{\mathcal{M},comb}$ with optimised α_l (Eq. 4) where both require a single threshold, using balanced accuracy as the metric (Table 2). Although optimising thresholds for all OOD patterns in complex settings would be challenging, these results show the theoretically attainable upper bound outperforms both single-layer or weighted combination techniques. Methods for configuring such multi-detector systems can be an avenue for future research.

Table 1. AUROC (mean for 5 folds) for OOD detection methods for a) unseen pace-maker and b) unseen sex OOD tasks. **Bold** highlights the best result of methods, not including oracle methods which represent a theoretical upper bound. * methods with hyperparameters optimised on OOD data.

a) Unseen pacemaker OOD task

	ResNet18 (AUROC ↑)				VGG16 (AUROC ↑)			
MCP [10]	58.4				58.3			
Monte Carlo Dropout [6]	58.4				58.4			
Deep Ensemble [16]	59.7				60.0			
ODIN* [18]	66.1				70.3			
Mahal. Score (LHL)[17]	57.1				55.8			
Mah. Score (LHL) + FGSM[17]	57.4				57.5			
Mahal. Score (weight. comb)[17]	64.5				66.0			
M. Score (w. comb w/o LHL)	71.4				67.4			
*M. Score (Opt. Layer - Oracle)**	*75.1 (after module 51)*				*76.4 (after module 40)*			
Multi-branch Mahal. (MBM)	61.9	66.2	69.6	76.1	60.4	60.3	67.1	75.0
MBM (only ReLUs)	63.6	68.8	71.7	76.2	61.2	63.8	71.7	76.2
MBM (only ReLUs) + FGSM*	63.6	68.8	73.1	**76.8**	61.2	63.8	74.1	**77.0**

b) Unseen sex OOD task

	ResNet18 (AUROC ↑)				VGG16 (AUROC ↑)			
MCP [10]	57.0				56.6			
Monte Carlo Dropout [6]	57.0				56.7			
Deep Ensemble [16]	58.3				57.7			
ODIN* [18]	60.4				64.4			
Mahal. Score (LHL) [17]	55.6				55.2			
Mah. Score (LHL) + FGSM[17]	55.8				57.0			
Mahal. Score (weight. comb)[17]	64.3				63.0			
M. Score (w. comb w/o LHL)	70.3				66.7			
*M. Score (Opt. Layer - Oracle)**	*72.2 (after module 44)*				*76.3 (after module 43)*			
Multi-branch Mahal. (MBM)	63.4	67.5	70.8	70.6	62.7	64.2	67.8	74.7
MBM (only ReLUs)	64.9	69.3	71.8	70.2	63.8	66.2	69.7	76.4
MBM (only ReLUs) + FGSM*	64.9	69.3	**72.1**	71.4	63.8	66.2	70.4	**78.0**

Table 2. Balanced Accuracy for simultaneous detection of 2 OOD patterns, showing a multi-detector system can improve OOD detection over single-detector systems based on the optimal layer or optimal weighted combination of layers.

OOD detection method	OOD task (balanced accuracy ↑)		
	Both tasks	Unseen sex	Pacemakers
Mahal. score (equally weighted comb w/o LHL)	67.64	64.63	70.37
Mahal. score (weighted comb with optimised α_l)	68.14	64.89	70.90
Multi-branch Mahal. (ReLU only)	**71.40**	**67.26**	**75.16**

5   Conclusion

This paper has demonstrated with both synthetic and real OOD patterns that different OOD patterns are optimally detectable using Mahalanobis score at different depths of a network. The paper shows that the common implementations using the last hidden layer or a weighted combination of layers are sub-optimal, and instead a more robust and high-performing OOD detector can be achieved by using multiple OOD detectors at different depths of the network - informing best-practices for the application of Mahalanobis score. Moreover, it was demonstrated that configuring thresholds for multi-detector systems such as MBM is feasible, motivating future work into developing an ideal OOD detector that encompasses these insights.

Acknowledgments. HA is supported by a scholarship via the EPSRC Doctoral Training Partnerships programme [EP/W524311/1]. The authors also acknowledge the use of the University of Oxford Advanced Research Computing (ARC) facility in carrying out this work (http://dx.doi.org/10.5281/zenodo.22558).

References

1. Baur, C., Denner, S., Wiestler, B., Navab, N., et al.: Autoencoders for unsupervised anomaly segmentation in brain MR images: a comparative study. Med. Image Anal. **69**, 101952 (2021)
2. Berger, C., Paschali, M., Glocker, B., Kamnitsas, K.: Confidence-based out-of-distribution detection: a comparative study and analysis. In: Sudre, C.H., et al. (eds.) UNSURE/PIPPI -2021. LNCS, vol. 12959, pp. 122–132. Springer, Cham (2021). https://doi.org/10.1007/978-3-030-87735-4_12
3. Çallı, E., Murphy, K., Sogancioglu, E., Van Ginneken, B.: Frodo: free rejection of out-of-distribution samples: application to chest x-ray analysis. arXiv preprint arXiv:1907.01253 (2019)
4. Du, X., Wang, X., Gozum, G., Li, Y.: Unknown-aware object detection: learning what you don't know from videos in the wild. In: 2022 IEEE/CVF CVPR, pp. 13668–13678. IEEE, New Orleans, LA, USA (2022)
5. Fort, S., Ren, J., Lakshminarayanan, B.: Exploring the limits of out-of-distribution detection. Adv. Neural Inf. Process. Syst. **34**, 7068–7081 (2021)
6. Gal, Y., Ghahramani, Z.: Dropout as a bayesian approximation: representing model uncertainty in deep learning. In: Proceedings of The 33rd International Conference on Machine Learning, pp. 1050–1059. PMLR (2016)
7. González, C., Gotkowski, K., Fuchs, M., Bucher, A., et al.: Distance-based detection of out-of-distribution silent failures for covid-19 lung lesion segmentation. Med. Image Anal. **82**, 102596 (2022)
8. Goodfellow, I. J., Shlens, J., Szegedy, C.: Explaining and harnessing adversarial examples. arXiv preprint arXiv:1412.6572 (2015)
9. Graham, M.S., Pinaya, W.H., Tudosiu, P.-D., Nachev, P., et al.: Denoising diffusion models for out-of-distribution detection. In: Proceedings of the IEEE/CVF CVPR, pp. 2947–2956 (2023)
10. Hendrycks, D., Gimpel, K.: A baseline for detecting misclassified and out-of-distribution examples in neural networks. arXiv preprint arXiv:1610.02136 (2018)

11. Hendrycks, D., Mazeika, M., Dietterich, T.: Deep anomaly detection with outlier exposure. In: International Conference on Learning Representations (2018)
12. Hu, Y., Jacob, J., Parker, G.J.M., Hawkes, D.J., et al.: The challenges of deploying artificial intelligence models in a rapidly evolving pandemic. Nat. Mach. Intell. **2**(6), 298–300 (2020)
13. Irvin, J., Rajpurkar, P., Ko, M., Yu, Y., et al.: Chexpert: a large chest radiograph dataset with uncertainty labels and expert comparison. In: Proceedings of the AAAI Conference on Artificial Intelligence, vol. 33, pp. 590–597 (2019)
14. Kamoi, R., Kobayashi, K.: Why is the mahalanobis distance effective for anomaly detection? arXiv preprint arXiv:2003.00402 (2020)
15. Kobyzev, I., Prince, S.J., Brubaker, M.A.: Normalizing flows: an introduction and review of current methods. IEEE TPAMI **43**(11), 3964–3979 (2021)
16. Lakshminarayanan, B., Pritzel, A., Blundell, C.: Simple and scalable predictive uncertainty estimation using deep ensembles. In: Advances in Neural Information Processing Systems, vol. 30 (2017)
17. Lee, K., Lee, K., Lee, H., Shin, J.: A simple unified framework for detecting out-of-distribution samples and adversarial attacks. In: Advances in Neural Information Processing Systems, vol. 31 (2018)
18. Liang, S., Li, Y., Srikant, R.: Enhancing the reliability of out-of-distribution image detection in neural networks. arXiv preprint arXiv:1706.02690 (2020)
19. Mahalanobis, P.C.: On the generalised distance in statistics. Proc. Natl. Inst. Sci. India **12**, 49–55 (1936)
20. Pawlowski, N., Lee, M.C.H., Rajchl, M., McDonagh, S., et al.: Unsupervised lesion detection in brain CT using bayesian convolutional autoencoders. In: MIDL (2018)
21. Perone, C.S., Ballester, P., Barros, R.C., Cohen-Adad, J.: Unsupervised domain adaptation for medical imaging segmentation with self-ensembling. NeuroImage **194**, 1–11 (2019)
22. Pinaya, W.H., Tudosiu, P.-D., Gray, R., Rees, G., et al.: Unsupervised brain imaging 3d anomaly detection and segmentation with transformers. Med. Image Anal. **79**, 102475 (2022)
23. Ren, J., Fort, S., Liu, J., Roy, A.G., et al.: A simple fix to mahalanobis distance for improving near-ood detection. arXiv preprint arXiv:2106.09022 (2021)
24. Rippel, O., Mertens, P., König, E., Merhof, D.: Gaussian anomaly detection by modeling the distribution of normal data in pretrained deep features. IEEE TIM **70**, 1–13 (2021)
25. Roy, A.G., Ren, J., Azizi, S., Loh, A., et al.: Does your dermatology classifier know what it doesn't know? detecting the long-tail of unseen conditions. Med. Image Anal. **75**, 102274 (2022)
26. Ruff, L., Kauffmann, J.R., Vandermeulen, R.A., Montavon, G., et al.: A unifying review of deep and shallow anomaly detection. Proc. IEEE **109**(5), 756–795 (2021)
27. Schlegl, T., Seeböck, P., Waldstein, S.M., Langs, G., et al.: f-anogan: fast unsupervised anomaly detection with generative adversarial networks. Med. Image Anal. **54**, 30–44 (2019)
28. Song, Y., Sebe, N., Wang, W.: Rankfeat: rank-1 feature removal for out-of-distribution detection. NeurIPS **35**, 17885–17898 (2022)
29. Steinbuss, G., Böhm, K.: Generating artificial outliers in the absence of genuine ones - a survey. ACM Trans. Knowl. Disc. Data **15**(2), 1–37 (2021)
30. Sun, Y., Li, Y.: DICE: Leveraging sparsification for out-of-distribution detection. In: Avidan, S., Brostow, G., Cissé, M., Farinella, G.M., Hassner, T. (eds.) Computer Vision - ECCV 2022. ECCV 2022. LNCS, vol. 13684, pp. 691–708. Springer, Cham (2022). https://doi.org/10.1007/978-3-031-20053-3_40

31. Tan, J., Hou, B., Batten, J., Qiu, H., et al.: Detecting outliers with foreign patch interpolation. Mach. Learn. Biomed. Imaging **1**, 1–27 (2022)
32. Uwimana, A., Senanayake, R.: Out of distribution detection and adversarial attacks on deep neural networks for robust medical image analysis. In: ICML 2021 Workshop on Adversarial Machine Learning (2021)
33. Zech, J.R., Badgeley, M.A., Liu, M., Costa, A.B., et al.: Variable generalization performance of a deep learning model to detect pneumonia in chest radiographs: a cross-sectional study. PLoS Med. **15**(11), e1002683 (2018)

Dimensionality Reduction for Improving Out-of-Distribution Detection in Medical Image Segmentation

McKell Woodland[1,2(✉)] [ID], Nihil Patel[1] [ID], Mais Al Taie[1] [ID], Joshua P. Yung[1] [ID], Tucker J. Netherton[1] [ID], Ankit B. Patel[2,3] [ID], and Kristy K. Brock[1] [ID]

[1] The University of Texas MD Anderson Cancer Center, Houston, TX 77030, USA
mewoodland@mdanderson.org
[2] Rice University, Houston, TX 77005, USA
[3] Baylor College of Medicine, Houston, TX 77030, USA

Abstract. Clinically deployed deep learning-based segmentation models are known to fail on data outside of their training distributions While clinicians review the segmentations, these models do tend to perform well in most instances, which could exacerbate automation bias. Therefore, it is critical to detect out-of-distribution images at inference to warn the clinicians that the model likely failed. This work applies the Mahalanobis distance post hoc to the bottleneck features of a Swin UNETR model that segments the liver on T1-weighted magnetic resonance imaging. By reducing the dimensions of the bottleneck features with principal component analysis, images the model failed on were detected with high performance and minimal computational load. Specifically, the proposed technique achieved 92% area under the receiver operating characteristic curve and 94% area under the precision-recall curve and can run in seconds on a central processing unit.

Keywords: Out-of-distribution detection · Swin UNETR · Mahalanobis distance · Principal component analysis

1 Introduction

Deep learning (DL) models struggle to generalize to information that was not present while the model was being trained [29]. This problem is exacerbated in the medical field where collecting large-scale, annotated, and diverse training datasets is challenging due to the cost of labeling, presence of rare cases, and patient privacy. Even models that have demonstrated high-performance during external validation may fail when presented with novel information after clinical deployment. This can be demonstrated by the work of Anderson et al. [2]. On

---

Supplementary Information The online version contains supplementary material available at https://doi.org/10.1007/978-3-031-44336-7_15.

test data, 96% of their DL-based liver segmentations were deemed clinically acceptable, with the majority of their autosegmentations being preferred over manual segmentations. The two images that the model failed on contained cases that were not present during training - namely, ascites and a stent.

While autosegmentations are typically manually evaluated and corrected, if need be, by a clinician before they are used in patient treatment, the main concern is automation bias, where physicians may become too reliant on model output. Protecting against automation bias is especially important for clinically deployed segmentation models, since these segmentations influence the amount of radiation that a patient will receive during treatment. In a review study, Goddard et al. found that automation bias in healthcare can be reduced by displaying low confidence values for recommendations that are likely incorrect [7].

Displaying confidence values that correspond to the likelihood that a DL-based prediction is correct is a non-trivial problem because DL models are inherently poorly calibrated [9]. Accordingly, some techniques in related literature endeavor to calibrate the model. Common calibration approaches include temperature scaling and input perturbations [19], truncating activations [27], Monte Carlo dropout [6], and ensembling [16]. On the other hand, other methods ignore confidence values and instead define an out-of-distribution (OOD) detection score. For example, Lee et al. calculate a score using the Mahalanobis distance [18], while Liu et al. define an energy score [20]. OOD detection operates under the assumption that the model is unlikely to perform well on data outside of the model's training distribution. While these methods perform well in theoretical settings, they often do not perform well in real-world scenarios [26]. This is especially true when these techniques are applied to medical images [3]. In fact, Cao et al. found that no method performed better than random guessing when applied to unseen medical conditions or artifacts [4].

The Mahalanobis distance is one of the most utilized OOD detection methods, due to its simplicity [18]. One of the major reasons it struggles in practice is due to the curse of dimensionality. As it is a distance, it loses meaning in high-dimensional spaces and thus cannot be applied to images directly. In the classification domain, great success was achieved when the Mahalanobis distance was applied to embeddings extracted from pretrained transformers [5]. Similarly, Gonzalez et al., applied the Mahalanobis distance to embeddings extracted from an nnU-Net for medical image segmentation [8]. The major problem is that embeddings from 3D segmentation models are an order of magnitude larger than the embeddings from 2D classification models.

We build upon previous work by applying the Mahalanobis distance to principal component analysis (PCA) projected embeddings extracted from a Swin Transformer-based segmentation model. The main contributions of our paper are as follows:

1. Applying the Mahalanobis distance to a transformer-based segmentation model for OOD detection.

2. Reducing the dimensionality of bottleneck features using PCA before the Mahalanobis distance is applied.
3. Proposing a successful OOD detection pipeline that has minimal computation load and can be applied post hoc to any U-Net-based segmentation model.

2   Methods

2.1   Data

The training dataset was comprised of 337 T1-weighted liver magnetic resonance imaging exams (MRIs). The T1-weighted images came from the Duke Liver MRI [22], AMOS [11,12], and CHAOS [14,15] datasets. 27 T1-weighted liver MRIs from The University of Texas MD Anderson Cancer Center were employed for testing the segmentation model.

To protect against automation bias, OOD images should be defined as images that differ enough from the training distribution that the segmentation model is likely to fail on them. As such, the model's test data is split into in-distribution (ID) and OOD categories based on model performance. Specifically, an image is labelled ID if it has a Dice similarity coefficient (DSC) of at least 95%. Accordingly, an image is labelled OOD if it has a DSC under 95%. This follows Hendrycks et al., in the classification domain, who defined OOD data to be data that was incorrectly classified [10].

An additional 23 T1-weighted liver MRIs were acquired from The University of Texas MD Anderson Cancer Center for the OOD evaluation. All these images were flagged by physicians for poor image quality in a clinical setting. 14 images contained motion artifacts, 7 contained truncation artifacts, and the other two images contained a single artifact: magnetic susceptibility and spike noise. None had associated ground truth liver segmentations.

All test images were retrospectively acquired under an approved internal review board protocol. All images were preprocessed by reorientation to Right-Anterior-Superior (RAS), resampling to a uniform spacing (1.5, 1.5, 2.0) mm, and normalization using each image's mean and standard deviation. Example test images are shown in Fig. 1.

2.2   Segmentation Model

A Swin UNETR model [28] was trained to segment the T1-weighted MRIs. The encoder portion of the model was pretrained using self-distilled masked imaging (SMIT) [13] utilizing 3,610 unlabeled head and neck computed tomography scans (CTs) from the Beyond the Cranial Vault (BTCV) Segmentation Challenge dataset [17]. The official Swin UNETR codebase , built on top of the Medical Open Net-work for AI (MONAI) [25], was utilized for the pretrained weights and training. All default parameters were used, with no hyperparameter searches performed. Models were trained on a single node of a Kubernetes cluster with eight A100 graphic processing units. The final model was selected according to the weights with the highest validation DSC. It was evaluated on test images with the DSC and the Hausdorff distance.

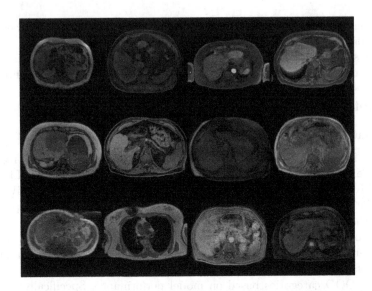

Fig. 1. Sample images from the test dataset. (Top) Images that were determined to be ID by good performance of the segmentation algorithm. (Middle) Images that were determined to be OOD by poor performance of the segmentation algorithm. (Bottom) Images that were flagged by clinicians for poor image quality. From left to right, the images had motion, magnetic susceptibility, truncation, and motion artifacts.

2.3   Out-of-Distribution Detection

The Mahalanobis distance D measures the distance between a point x and a distribution with mean μ and covariance matrix Σ, $D^2 = (x - \mu)^T \Sigma^{-1} (x - \mu)$ [23]. Lee et al. first proposed using the Mahalanobis distance for OOD detection by using it to calculate the distance between test images embedded by a classifier and a Gaussian distribution fit to class-conditional embeddings of the training images [18]. Similarly, Gonzalez et al. used the Mahalanobis distance for OOD detection in segmentation networks by extracting embeddings from the encoder of a nnU-Net [8]. As distances in high dimensions are subject to the curse of dimensionality, both sets of authors decreased the dimensionality of the embeddings through average pooling. Lee et al. suggested pooling the embeddings such that the height and width dimensions are singular [18].

In our work, encoded representations of all images were extracted from the bottleneck features of the Swin UNETR models. Images were resized to (256, 128, 128) to ensure a uniform size of the encoded representations (768, 8, 4, 4). A Gaussian distribution was fit on the encodings of the training data. The Mahalanobis distance between the embedding of each test image and the Gaussian distribution was calculated. All calculations were performed on an Intel Xeon E5-2698 v4 @ 2.20 GHz central processing unit (CPU).

As distances in extremely high-dimensional spaces often lose meaning [1], experiments were performed on the effect of decreasing the size of the bottleneck features with average pooling, principal component analysis (PCA), uniform manifold approximation and projection (UMAP) [24], and t-distributed stochastic neighbor embeddings (t-SNE) [21]. For average pooling, features were pooled in both 2- and 3-dimensions with kernel size j and stride k for $(j, k) \in \{(2, 1), (2, 2), (3, 1), (3, 2), (4, 1)\}$. For PCA, each embedding was flattened and standardized. For both PCA and UMAP, a hyperparameter search was performed over the number of components n such that $n \in \{2, 4, 8, 16, 32, 64, 128, 256\}$. Average pooling was performed using the PyTorch Python package and PCA and t-SNE were performed using the scikit-learn Python package. UMAP was performed using the UMAP Python package [24]. Outside of the hyperparameter searches mentioned above, default parameters were used.

OOD detection was evaluated with the area under the receiver operating characteristic curve (AUROC), area under the precision-recall curve (AUPR), and false positive rate at 75% true positive rate (FPR75). For all calculations, OOD was considered as the positive class. As both UMAP and t-SNE are stochastic, the average was taken over 10 iterations of the algorithms. Our code can be found at https://github.com/mckellwoodland/dimen_reduce_mahal.

3 Results

The Swin UNETR achieved a mean DSC of 96% and a mean Hausdorff distance of 14 mm. 13 images had a DSC over 95% and were thus classified as ID. The remaining 14 images were classified as OOD. Figure 3 displays visual examples of the segmentation quality of the model.

The calculation of the Mahalanobis distance, as originally defined, was computationally intractable. The inverse of the covariance matrix took ∼72 min to compute (Table 1). Once saved, it takes 75.5 GB to store the inverse. Once the matrix is in memory, it takes ∼2 s for each Mahalanobis distance calculation. The average ($\pm$ SD) Mahalanobis distance on training data was 1203.02 ($\pm$ 24.66); whereas, the average ($\pm$ SD) Mahalanobis distance on test data was 1.47×10^9 ($\pm 8.66 \times 10^8$) and $1.52 \times 10^9 (\pm 9.10 \times 10^8)$ for ID and OOD images respectively. The high dimensionality of the calculation resulted in poor OOD detection performance (Table 1).

Reducing the dimensionality of the embeddings not only made the Mahalanobis distance calculation more computationally feasible, but also improved the OOD detection (Table 1). While the search over average pooling hyperparameters proved to be volatile (Table S1 in the Supplementary Material), the best results were achieved with 3D convolutions that resulted in the height and width dimensions being singular, supporting the suggestion of Lee et al. [18].

The best results were achieved with PCA (Table 1). Reducing the dimensionality to only two principal components was sufficient to achieve 90% AUROC, 93% AUPR, and 8% FPR75. Figure 2 demonstrates that most in-distribution test images were mapped within one standard deviation of the mean of the training distribution (the image that was not contained a motion artifact); whereas,

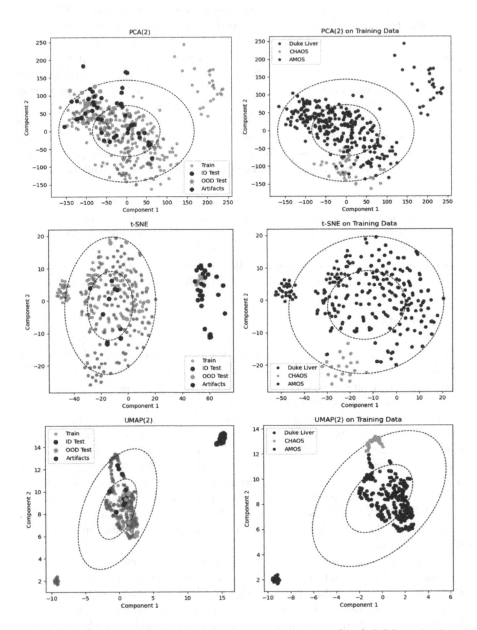

Fig. 2. Visualization of embeddings with two components. (Top) PCA projections. (Middle) t-SNE projections. (Bottom) UMAP projections. Projections for all data are in the left column. Projections for the training data by class are in the right column. The black ellipses are the covariance ellipses (one and two standard deviations) for the training distribution. (Color figure online)

Table 1. The AUROCs, AUPRs, and FPR75s for the OOD detection. ↑ means that higher is better, whereas ↓ means lower is better. Computation time is the time it takes to compute the inverse of the covariance matrix in seconds. Bold text denotes the best performance. The "no reduction" experiment is the Mahalanobis distance calculated on the original bottleneck features. AveragePool2D(j, k) represents embeddings that were 2D average pooled with kernel size j and stride k. Similar notation applies for 3D embeddings. UMAP(n) and PCA(n) represent the respective dimensionality reduction technique being performed with n components. Only the best performing average pooling, UMAP, PCA results were included in this table. Refer to Tables S1-S3 in the Material for the results of the full hyperparameter searches.

Experiment	AUROC ↑	AUPR ↑	FPR75 ↓	Computation Time (seconds)
No reduction	0.51	0.60	0.85	4327.4080
AveragePool3D(3,2)	0.76	0.84	0.38	0.1450
AveragePool3D(4,1)	0.70	0.75	0.31	0.5721
UMAP(2), $n = 10$	0.79 (±0.05)	0.85 (±0.04)	0.36 (±0.13)	0.0002 (±0.0000)
t-SNE, $n = 10$	0.82 (±0.05)	0.87 (±0.04)	0.27 (±0.14)	0.0003 (±0.0003)
PCA(2)	0.90	0.93	**0.08**	0.0001
PCA(256)	**0.92**	**0.94**	0.15	0.0118

Images with Low and High Mahalanobis Distances

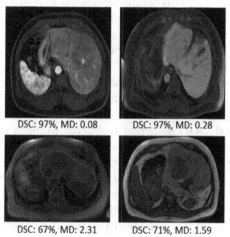

DSC: 97%, MD: 0.08   DSC: 97%, MD: 0.28

DSC: 67%, MD: 2.31   DSC: 71%, MD: 1.59

Fig. 3. Segmentations of images that contain low and high Mahalanobis distances (calculated on the PCA-projected embeddings with two components). Sample images with low Mahalanobis distances are on the top row; those with high distances are on the bottom row. Green is the ground truth segmentation; red is the automated segmentation. MD refers to the Mahalanobis distance. DSC refers to the Dice similarity coefficient. A higher DSC corresponds with better segmentation performance, whereas a higher distance corresponds to the image being OOD. (Color figure online)

most OOD test images were mapped between outside of the first standard deviation. The four OOD images mapped within one standard deviation had an average DSC of 88%; whereas, the OOD images mapped outside of one standard deviation had an average DSC of 79%. Additionally, 18 out of the 23 images that contained MRI artifacts were mapped outside of the first standard deviation. Furthermore, the two principal components visually cluster the different distributions within the training distribution. The 26 images from the AMOS dataset that were mapped outside of the second standard deviation were blurry. While UMAP and t-SNE did not perform as well as PCA, they still clustered the datasets in the training distribution and mapped OOD data outside of the first standard deviation. Notably, both UMAP and t-SNE mapped the data with imaging artifacts far from the training distribution. Visually, high Mahalanobis distances were associated with poor segmentation performance (Fig. 3). A one-sided permutation test revealed a statistically significant difference in mean Mahalanobis distances between the ID and OOD populations ($p < 0.001$).

4   Conclusion

In this work, the Mahalanobis distance was applied to dimensionality-reduced bottleneck features of a Swin UNETR. The resulting pipeline was able to embed an entire 3D medical image into only two principal components. These two components were sufficient to visually cluster datasets drawn from different institutions. Additionally, only two components were required for detecting images that the segmentation model performed poorly on with high performance and low cost (<1 s on a CPU).

While promising in regards to computation and performance, this work has several limitations. First, the analysis is limited in scope. In future work, we will apply the Mahalanobis distance to embeddings reduced by PCA for multiple imaging modalities, segmentation architectures, and OOD artifacts. Additionally, we will compare our work to state-of-the-art methods in related literature. Second, the proposed OOD detection technique cannot explain why an image was classified as OOD. In future work, we aspire to integrate more interpretable methods with the Mahalanobis distance.

In a clinical setting, a warning that the model likely failed could be added to images with large Mahalanobis distances. This would protect against automation bias, which would in turn protect patients whose scans have irregular attributes. The entire pipeline could be added post hoc to any trained segmentation model and would incur minimal computational costs.

Acknowledgements. Research reported in this publication was supported in part by the Tumor Measurement Initiative through the MD Anderson Strategic Initiative Development Program (STRIDE), the Helen Black Image Guided Fund, the Image Guided Cancer Therapy Research Program at The University of Texas MD Anderson Cancer Center, a generous gift from the Apache Corporation, and the National Cancer Institute of the National Institutes of Health under award numbers R01CA221971, P30CA016672, and R01CA235564.

References

1. Aggarwal, C.C., Hinneburg, A., Keim, D.A.: On the surprising behavior of distance metrics in high dimensional space. In: Van den Bussche, J., Vianu, V. (eds.) ICDT 2001. LNCS, vol. 1973, pp. 420–434. Springer, Heidelberg (2001). https://doi.org/10.1007/3-540-44503-X_27

2. Anderson, B.M., et al.: Automated contouring of contrast and non-contrast computed tomography liver images with fully convolutional networks. Adv. Radiat. Oncol. 6(1), 100464 (2021). https://doi.org/10.1016/j.adro.2020.04.023

3. Berger, C., Paschali, M., Glocker, B., Kamnitsas, K.: Confidence-based out-of-distribution detection: a comparative study and analysis. In: Sudre, C.H., et al. (eds.) UNSURE/PIPPI -2021. LNCS, vol. 12959, pp. 122–132. Springer, Cham (2021). https://doi.org/10.1007/978-3-030-87735-4_12

4. Cao, T., Huang, C.W., Hui, D.Y.T., Cohen, J.P.: A benchmark of medical out of distribution detection. . arXiv preprint arXiv:2007.04250 (2020)

5. Fort, S., Ren, J., Lakshminarayanan, B.: Exploring the limits of out-of-distribution detection. In: Ranzato, M., Beygelzimer, A., Dauphin, Y., Liang, P., Vaughan, J.W. (eds.) Advances in Neural Information Processing Systems, vol. 34, pp. 7068–7081. Curran Associates, Inc. (2021)

6. Gal, Y., Ghahramani, Z.: Dropout as a Bayesian approximation: representing model uncertainty in deep learning. In: Balcan, M.F., Weinberger, K.Q. (eds.) Proceedings of The 33rd International Conference on Machine Learning. PMLR, vol. 48, pp. 1050–1059. PMLR, New York, New York, USA (2016)

7. Goddard, K., Roudsari, A., Wyatt, J.C.: Automation bias: a systematic review of frequency, effect mediators, and mitigators. JAMIA 19(1), 121–127 (2011). https://doi.org/10.1136/amiajnl-2011-000089

8. Gonzalez, C., Gotkowski, K., Bucher, A., Fischbach, R., Kaltenborn, I., Mukhopadhyay, A.: Detecting when pre-trained nnU-Net models fail silently for COVID-19 lung lesion segmentation. In: de Bruijne, M., et al. (eds.) MICCAI 2021. LNCS, vol. 12907, pp. 304–314. Springer, Cham (2021). https://doi.org/10.1007/978-3-030-87234-2_29

9. Guo, C., Pleiss, G., Sun, Y., Weinberger, K.Q.: On calibration of modern neural networks. In: Precup, D., Teh, Y.W. (eds.) ICML 2017. PMLR, vol. 70, pp. 1321–1330. PMLR (2017)

10. Hendrycks, D., Gimpel, K.: A baseline for detecting misclassified and out-of-distribution examples in neural networks. arXiv preprint arXiv:1610.02136 (2018)

11. Ji, Y.: AMOS: a large-scale abdominal multi-organ benchmark for versatile medical image segmentation (2022). https://doi.org/10.5281/zenodo.7155725

12. Ji, Y., et al.: AMOS: A large-scale abdominal multi-organ benchmark for versatile medical image segmentation. In: Koyejo, S., Mohamed, S., Agarwal, A., Belgrave, D., Cho, K., Oh, A. (eds.) Advances in Neural Information Processing Systems, vol. 35, pp. 36722–36732. Curran Associates, Inc. (2022)

13. Jiang, J., Tyagi, N., Tringale, K., Crane, C., Veeraraghavan, H.: Self-supervised 3D anatomy segmentation using self-distilled masked image transformer (SMIT). In: Wang, L., Dou, Q., Fletcher, P.T., Speidel, S., Li, S. (eds.) MICCAI 2022, pp. 556–566. Springer Nature Switzerland, Cham (2022). https://doi.org/10.1007/978-3-031-16440-8_53

14. Kavur, A.E., et al.: Chaos challenge - combined (CT-MR) healthy abdominal organ segmentation. Med. Image Anal. 69, 101950 (2021). https://doi.org/10.1016/j.media.2020.101950

15. Kavur, A.E., Selver, M.A., Dicle, O., Barış, M., Gezer, N.S.: CHAOS - Combined (CT-MR) Healthy Abdominal Organ Segmentation Challenge Data (2019). https://doi.org/10.5281/zenodo.3431873
16. Lakshminarayanan, B., Pritzel, A., Blundell, C.: Simple and scalable predictive uncertainty estimation using deep ensembles. In: Guyon, I., Luxburg, U.V., et al (eds.) Advances in Neural Information Processing Systems, vol. 30. Curran Associates, Inc. (2017)
17. Landman, B., Xu, Z., Igelsias, J., Styner, M., Langerak, T., Klein, A.: MICCAI multi-atlas labeling beyond the cranial vault-workshop and challenge. In: Proceedings MICCAI Multi-Atlas Labeling Beyond Cranial Vault-Workshop Challenge, vol. 5, p. 12 (2015)
18. Lee, K., Lee, K., Lee, H., Shin, J.: A simple unified framework for detecting out-of-distribution samples and adversarial attacks. In: Bengio, S., Wallach, H., Larochelle, H., Grauman, K., Cesa-Bianchi, N., Garnett, R. (eds.) Advances in Neural Information Processing Systems, vol. 31. Curran Associates, Inc. (2018)
19. Liang, S., Li, Y., Srikant, R.: Enhancing the reliability of out-of-distribution image detection in neural networks. arXiv preprint arXiv:1706.02690 (2020)
20. Liu, W., Wang, X., Owens, J., Li, Y.: Energy-based out-of-distribution detection. In: Larochelle, H., Ranzato, M., Hadsell, R., Balcan, M., Lin, H. (eds.) Advances in Neural Information Processing Systems, vol. 33, pp. 21464–21475. Curran Associates, Inc. (2020)
21. Van der Maaten, L., Hinton, G.: Visualizing data using t-SNE. J. Mach. Learn. Res. 9(11), 2579–2605 (2008)
22. Macdonald, J.A., Zhu, Z., Konkel, B., Mazurowski, M., Wiggins, W., Bashir, M.: Duke liver dataset (MRI) (2020). https://doi.org/10.5281/zenodo.6328447
23. Mahalanobis, P.C.: On the generalized distance in statistics. Sankhyā: the Indian Journal of Statistics, Series A (2008-) **80**, pp. S1–S7 (2018)
24. McInnes, L., Healy, J., Melville, J.: UMAP: Uniform manifold approximation and projection for dimension reduction. arXiv preprint arXiv:1802.03426 (2020)
25. MONAI Consortium: MONAI: Medical open network for AI (2021). https://doi.org/10.5281/zenodo.5728262
26. Shafaei, A., Schmidt, M., Little, J.J.: A less biased evaluation of out-of-distribution sample detectors. arXiv preprint arXiv:1809.04729 (2019)
27. Sun, Y., Guo, C., Li, Y.: ReAct: Out-of-distribution detection with rectified activations. In: Ranzato, M., Beygelzimer, A., Dauphin, Y., Liang, P., Vaughan, J.W. (eds.) Advances in Neural Information Processing Systems, vol. 34, pp. 144–157. Curran Associates, Inc. (2021)
28. Tang, Y., et al..: Self-supervised pre-training of SWIN transformers for 3D medical image analysis. In: CVPR 2022, pp. 20730–20740 (2022)
29. Zech, J.R., Badgeley, M.A., Liu, M., Costa, A.B., Titano, J.J., Oermann, E.K.: Variable generalization performance of a deep learning model to detect pneumonia in chest radiographs: a cross-sectional study. PLoS Med. **15**(11), 1–17 (2018). https://doi.org/10.1371/journal.pmed.1002683

Breaking Down Covariate Shift on Pneumothorax Chest X-Ray Classification

Bogdan Bercean[1,2]([✉]), Alexandru Buburuzan[2,3], Andreea Birhala[2], Cristian Avramescu[1,2], Andrei Tenescu[1,2], and Marius Marcu[1]

[1] Politehnica University of Timisoara, Timisoara, Romania
[2] Rayscape, Bucharest, Romania
bogdan@rayscape.ai
[3] The University of Manchester, Manchester, UK

Abstract. Domain shift poses significant problems to computer-aided diagnostic (CAD) systems when deployed in clinical scenarios. There's still no definite fix nor an in-depth understanding of the exact factors driving domain shifts in medical X-rays. Here, we conduct an exploratory study on three covariate shift factors in X-ray classification by controlling for different variables. This is possible by leveraging a homogenously-relabelled mix of public and private X-ray data spanning 23 medical institutions over four continents and 17 classes of pathologies. We show that the acquisition parameter, device manufacturer and geographical shifts degrade out-of-distribution (OOD) F1 by 6%, 3.2% and 3.3%, respectively. Pneumothorax was found to be the most impaired pathology, suffering a mean F1 generalisation gap of 13.3%, despite being one of the most clinically-consequential radiological findings. To this end, we introduced LISA-topK, a multi-label adaptation of Learning Invariant Predictors with Selective Augmentation (LISA), that we showed to narrow down the OOD gap, surpassing other methods consistently. These pragmatic results shed light on some of the elements of OOD generalisation in X-ray classification, which are essential to researching, understanding and deploying CAD systems. Code is available at https://github.com/RayscapeAI/LISA-topK

Keywords: Domain generalization · Chest X-rays · Pneumothorax

1 Introduction

Clinical adoption of CAD systems in radiology went from none to a third of radiologists in just a few years [2,5]. This is mainly due to the remarkable progress of computer vision and its rapid translation to clinical practice. Yet, the high performance of these learning systems at the validation stage shows no sign of the ways

---

B. Bercean and A. Buburuzan—Equal contribution.

Supplementary Information The online version contains supplementary material available at https://doi.org/10.1007/978-3-031-44336-7_16.

they often crash when tested outside the source environment. For instance, supervised models trained on data from source hospitals fail to grasp essential information needed to generalise to other target hospitals. They struggle to perform when shifting seemingly-unimportant factors such as exposure parameters, geographical area or acquisition devices. It's often easier to fit spurious correlations prone to change with the domain instead of the genuine causal features deriving the labels. Despite efforts [21, 27] to aid domain generalisation (DG), prior validation works repeatedly showed that the current methods do not achieve any significant gains over properly-tuned empirical risk minimisation (ERM) on medical data [25].

Meanwhile, pneumothorax is a recognised treatable cause of morbidity and mortality. Its silent radiological appearance on chest X-rays makes it sometimes easier to miss by physicians. So much so that Occult Pneumothorax is an accepted medical definition for a clinically non-evident X-ray case, only later discovered through other means. This should make the perfect use case for CAD on chest X-rays, although, as this work will uncover, domain shift turns it into its weakness. Even more so, studying pneumothorax classification DG on chest X-rays proves difficult. The lack of homogenous public data, aggressive deidentification, and its strikingly low prevalence are just some of the reasons.

Having outlined why the acute need for research on this topic, our **contributions** can be summarised as follows:

- We investigate three suspect covariate shift factors on chest X-rays. This was possible only by collecting a diverse, uniformly-labelled, private dataset spanning 23 medical facilities over five countries;
- We show for the first time that, despite its clinical gravity, pneumothorax is consistently the most impaired chest X-ray pathology by covariate shift;
- We introduce LISA-topK, to our knowledge, the first successful pneumothorax DG method. It works on medical multi-label setups and exceeds ERM and other X-ray DG methods;
- We conduct a quantitative concept-shift analysis on existing public datasets. We present evidence that DG research is hindered by unreliable label-extraction mechanisms and large inconsistencies in radiological conventions.

2   Related Work

Effective research of distribution shifts in deep learning requires complex data setups. DomainBed [10] and WILDS [15] are the two reference benchmarks in general computer vision, allowing the research of domain shift in realistic settings. They comprise several computer vision applications with only one medical imaging representative, Camelyon17 [4], a benchmark for binary tumour classification in histopathological images from five hospitals. Some smaller-scale medical imaging challenges proposed studying DG under minimal setups. The MIDOG 2022 challenge [3] published a dataset of 413 cases of different tumour types. The Shifts 2022 challenge [1] put together four existing datasets to aggregate 172 MRI studies for white matter multiple sclerosis segmentation.

Similarly, due to a complete lack of distribution shift datasets of chest x-rays, researchers usually merge multiple single-source datasets by forcing label alignment [18]. This is done on top of already noisy labels extracted from radiological reports using NLP [12]. [18] warns about the actual label accuracies being 10–30% lower than initially reported and insufficiently capturing the required heterogeneity for studying DG. Likewise, [7] presents evidence that the resulting concept shift overshadows the covariate shift in which DG research may interest. For instance, [18] forces the alignment by creating new labels by joining masses and nodules together on CheXpert [12] or seven types of atelectasis-related findings on Padchest [6]. They show evidence that even when labels seemingly align (e.g., pneumothorax), the different radiological conventions and schools of thought generate significant conceptual shifts. As an alternate approach, [25] introduces an empirical framework for inducing synthetic shifts on X-rays.

Yet, the exact causal variables that can drive realistic domain shift on X-rays are not precisely known. The DG literature [18] and industry vendors usually mention factors such as geographical area and device manufacturers, or they simply conjecture a shift with each medical institution. This may be a helpful oversimplification in research but an impractical assumption when deploying models in clinical practice. At the time of writing, [14] are the only ones that studied imaging parameters as a significant driver of domain shift in a private mammography dataset. Apart from that, there is no quantitative validation of which other factors derive domain shift in medical imaging or X-ray analysis. This is partly due to the aggressive deidentification of imaging metadata on all important public X-ray datasets. MIMIC-CXR [13], CheXpert [12], Padchest [6], Brax [19], ChestX-ray14 [22] are stripping the necessary metadata.

Despite localised successes, the large-scale benchmarks [10,15] found that existing DG methods do not outperform ERM consistently. [25] found that the eight most promising methods do not yield any significant gains over ERM on X-rays. Other promising recent works in DG on thoracic X-rays, involve env-aware neural style transfer [28] or cross-domain mixup [20], although it is not clear how well they handle clinical covariate shift given the aforementioned reasons.

3   Methods

3.1   Data

To effectively study DG, a pool of chest X-ray data was collected retrospectively from 19 hospitals to which four public datasets were joined: Brax, Padchest, CheXpert and VinDR-CXR. A naturally-distributed sample of 50,000 frontal X-rays was labelled by a team of three diagnostic radiologists with a minimum of eight years of experience. The studies were relabeled by a second radiologist independently, and the final annotations were reached through forced consensus. The process was designed to ensure **label homogeneity** and maximise accuracy.

After manually refiltering heavily-artifacted images and left-out pediatric patients (i.e., ≤16 years), a total of 47,735 chest X-rays spanning 23 medical institutions from four continents were successfully annotated for 17 most common classes of chest pathologies. The studies sampled from public datasets largely lacked device, acquisition or patient metadata, while the images acquired privately span 26 X-ray devices from 12 manufacturers.

All data collection procedures were conducted in conformity with the Declaration of Helsinki and International Conference on Harmonisation Good Clinical Practice guidelines and EU General Data Protection Regulation. The action received approval from the Ethical Review Boards of each institution.

3.2 Experimental Setup

Throughout experiments, we used an ID-OOD setup with domain partitions distributed between training and testing. The training subset was, in turn, split into training and validation with a 3:1 ratio, to be used in fine-tuning and model selection. Likewise, the OOD testing subset was split with a 3:1 ratio for OOD and ID usage, respectively. To assess ID performance, we utilized a mixed-to-test setting [15] wherein the model was trained on a combination of train and test data, and evaluated on a separate testing subset. The stratified splits were carefully selected with no patient overlap.

In line with prior X-ray classification baselines, we used a DenseNet-121 [11] with ImageNet [8] pretraining to prevent domain leaks, at a resolution of 256×256 pixels. Baseline augmentations were employed in all experiments, including ERM. All runs were trained with Adam optimiser, reduce learning rate on plateau initialised at 1e-4, a weight decay of 1e-4 and batch size of 32, over 45 epochs, on four NVidia Tesla V100s.

3.3 Isolating Domain Shift Factors

In clinical scenarios, for an AI vendor to leverage the understanding of X-ray domain shifts, they first need to recognise its main causes. In the following experiments, we isolate and explore three notorious yet unvalidated DG factors affecting CAD systems, chosen such that they allowed for complete, strong ID-OOD setups, and were based on the authors' experience with deploying AI.

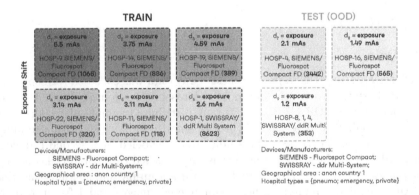

Fig. 1. The experimental configuration for studying exposure shift. All other factors indicated at the bottom, are matched in train and test domains.

Exposure Shift. refers to varying acquisition parameters. Although they usually differ from scan to scan, they are set by human radiographers, which determines hospital-specific patterns. We use the Exposure DICOM tag (0018,1152), which indicates the total amount of radiation produced by the X-ray tube, defined as:

$$Exposure\ (mAs) = Exposure\ time\ (s) * Xray\ tube\ current\ (mA) \qquad (1)$$

To isolate the exposure shift, we design an experiment in which we control the other main variables: hospital types, geography and manufacturers. Both training and testing environments match all variables except for the mean exposure, at the cost of discarding some data (Fig. 1).

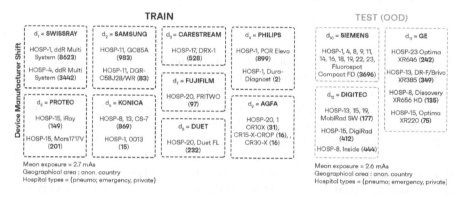

Fig. 2. The experimental configuration for studying manufacturer shift. All other factors indicated at the bottom, are matched in train and test domains.

Manufacturer Shift. is supposedly provoked by the change in X-ray device particularities specific to each large manufacturer. In short, different manufacturers use different hardware, processing algorithms or calibration, which affects the overall appearance of the image. X-rays from different manufacturers might appear different, despite matching all environment factors.

To investigate how this affects DG, 12 disjoint domains, one for each manufacturer, were split into training and testing (Fig. 2). The other factors (i.e., exposure, geography, hospital type) were evenly distributed. Additionally, we held one device from each testing manufacturer to measure how training on a single device improves the generalisation on all other devices from the same manufacturer. We call this regime Pseudo-ID, where the model has some knowledge of OOD manufacturers but not of the exact devices, as traditional ID does. This is meant to answer whether seeing a single device from each manufacturer completely closes the DG gap of manufacturer shift or if all devices are needed.

Geographical Shift. assumes that differences between patient populations might be visible on X-ray studies [9]. Different geographical areas deal with different diseases with various prevalences. To this end, we capitalise on the data by modelling the five countries into different domains, as shown in Fig. 3.

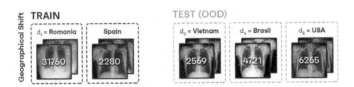

Fig. 3. The experimental configuration for studying geographical shift. Each country represents a distinct environment.

LISA-TopK. By deriving from a previous method for Learning Invariant Predictors with Selective Augmentation (LISA) [24], we propose LISA-topK. The original method uses mixup [26] to interpolate multi-class samples with the same label (intra-label), but different domains, and samples with the same domain (intra-domain), but different labels, alternatively. It is worth pointing out that LISA, which was validated only on multi-class classification, does not translate to the multi-label setting since exact matches of the target vectors are highly unlikely to occur. To account for the large number of possible target vectors in multi-label classification, our method performs intra-label mixup by only considering the labels of the topK classes with the worst generalisation gaps (e.g., pneumothorax and support devices).

Furthermore, LISA-topK removes one additional hard constraint that LISA enforces, allowing the interpolation of same-domain, same-label pairs. This second adaptation ensures that LISA-topK, for large K, can always identify a match given a training sample. Moreover, it avoids aggressive oversampling on imbalanced classes, where the cross-label component of the intra-domain mixup would force samples from the majority classes to be matched with those from the minority ones. Statistically, given the large number of domains and target vectors, there will still exist enough matches with conflicting labels or domains, that could diminish spurious correlations.

4   Results

4.1   Isolating Domain Shift Factors

All three shift types caused significant DG gaps in mean F1 (Table 1). Pneumothorax generalisation consistently underperformed with gaps between 200%-350% larger than the average of the 17 classes. The exposure yielded the most significant generalisation drops, which were expected given the importance of contrast and brightness in medical imaging interpretation.

Table 1. Average test F1 scores for the three types of distribution shifts. All experiments are run with five seeds and discard the fifth most distant to minimise variance. Pneumothorax consistently shows up in the top three worst-performing classes throughout all experiments. (PTX - Pneumothorax; SD - Support devices; TBC - Tuberculosis; DD - Diaphragmatic Dysfunction)

	Exposure Shift		Manufacturer Shift			Geographical Shift	
	ID	OOD (ERM)	ID	PseudoID	OOD (ERM)	ID	OOD (ERM)
Mean	54.8	48.8 (−6.0)	51	48.3 (−2.7)	47.2 (−3.2)	53.4	50.1 (−3.3)
Pneumothorax	44.9	22.2 (−22.7)	40.1	35.9 (−4.2)	29.7 (−10.4)	46	39.8 (−6.2)
Worst top 3 classes	1. **PTX**, 2. SD, 3. EMP		1. DD, 2. SD, **3. PTX**			1. **PTX**, 2. SD, 3. TBC	

The Pseudo-ID strategy in the manufacturer shift did not fix the DG issue, although it notably closed the gap from −3.1 (OOD F1) to −2.7 (Pseudo-ID F1). This result debunks an industry myth that training on at least one device from each manufacturer ensures generalisation over all devices.

So far, all factors have been analysed through the lens of covariate shift. However, the literature experiments and reports on joint public datasets with unknown degrees of concept shift embedded. In a subsequent analysis, we isolated a subset of 15,835 radiographs, representing all X-rays originating from the four public datasets. Figure 4 quantitatively compares the public and private labels (ours) on these data. The wildly different values of Cohen's Kappa [17] coefficients mark the larger-than-taught magnitude of the concept shift between public hospitals.

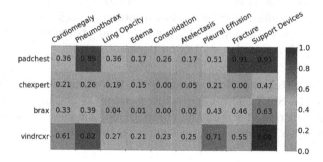

Fig. 4. Cohen's kappa coefficients between public labels and our relabelling on the public data subsets.

4.2   LISA-topK

LISA-top2, where the value for K was determined using hyperparameter tuning (see Appendix), achieves consistent improvements over ERM both on mean F1 and worst-class F1 (i.e., pneumothorax). Table 2 confirms standard LISA struggles with multi-label classification in a multi-label X-ray setup, and, consistent with prior works, other methods fail to outperform ERM in most scenarios. In the first experiment, the method proposed by Zunaed et al. [28] achieves the best mean F1 since their style transfer could be regarded as a targeted augmentation in the context of exposure shift.

Table 2. Comparative test F1 scores of LISA-top2 and other generalisation methods. All experiments are run with five seeds and the fifth most distant is discarded to minimise variance.

	Exposure Shift		Manufacturer Shift		Geographical Shift	
	PTX	Mean	PTX	Mean	PTX	Mean
ERM w/ Augm	22.2	48.8	29.7	47.2	39.1	**50.1**
Cross-domain [20]	28.5 (+6.3)	49.4 (+1.1)	17 (−12.7)	44.7 (−2.5)	27 (−12.1)	44.1 (−6.0)
Style transfer [28]	28.2 (+6.0)	**51.7** (+2.9)	23.7 (−6.0)	46.2 (−1.0)	30.8 (−0.3)	46.6 (−3.5)
LISA [24]	16.2 (−6.0)	48.9 (+0.1)	31.3 (+1.6)	46.9 (−0.3)	36.8 (−2.2)	48.7 (−1.4)
LISA-top2 (ours)	**37.9** (+15.7)	51.1 (+2.3)	**38.2** (+8.5)	**47.9** (+0.7)	**40.2** (+1.1)	48.8 (−1.3)

5   Outlook and Broader Impact

Following are the main key takeaways that we converged upon:

Pneumothorax is Consistently One of the Worst Performers w. r. t. DG. Moreover, due to its low prevalence, the impact of domain shift on pneumothorax CAD systems is dangerously well-hidden. Even randomised clinical trials, the gold standard in evidence-based medicine, might fail to underrepresent the generalisation gap if the shifting environments are not understood and accounted for. LISA-top2 boosts DG on pneumothorax.

The Labelling-Related Conceptual Shift Overshadows the more Relevant Covariate Shift. This raises some questions regarding the legitimacy of public dataset merging for studying covariate shift on chest X-rays and might be a root cause for the sparse advancements on the topic.

There are no Benchmarks and Little Research on Multi-label X-ray DG. Most of the existing methods and benchmarks are centred around tasks such as CMNIST [23] or PACS [16], which are not representative of textural medical imaging. The single-source public X-ray data suffer from overly-aggressive deidentification, stripping required metadata for distribution shift research.

Finally, DG on chest X-rays reveals multiple layers of complexity. In this work, we take a bottom-up approach and understand how three individual factors influence covariate shift, on top of which conceptual shift further adds up to disturb OOD generalisation. Pneumothorax classification specifically proves to be a weak link, which LISA-topK, consistently improves upon. The results may have practical implications for how CAD systems are deployed and researched.

References

1. Shifts challenge 2022 - grand challenge. www.shifts.grand-challenge.org/. Accessed 10 Mar 2023
2. Allen, B., Agarwal, S., Coombs, L., Wald, C., Dreyer, K.: 2020 ACR data science institute artificial intelligence survey. J. Am. Coll. Radiol. **18**(8), 1153–1159 (2021)
3. Aubreville, M., Bertram, C., Breininger, K., Jabari, S., Stathonikos, N., Veta, M.: Mitosis domain generalization challenge 2022 (2022). https://doi.org/10.5281/zenodo.6362337
4. Bandi, P., et al.: From detection of individual metastases to classification of lymph node status at the patient level: the CAMELYON17 challenge. IEEE Trans. Med. Imaging **38**(2), 550–560 (2018)
5. European Society of Radiology (ESR). Current practical experience with artificial intelligence in clinical radiology: a survey of the European Society of Radiology. Insights Imaging **13**, 107 (2022). https://doi.org/10.1186/s13244-022-01247-y
6. Bustos, A., Pertusa, A., Salinas, J.M., de la Iglesia-Vayá, M.: PadChest: a large chest X-ray image dataset with multi-label annotated reports. Med. Image Anal. **66**, 101797 (2020)
7. Cohen, J.P., Hashir, M., Brooks, R., Bertrand, H.: On the limits of cross-domain generalization in automated X-ray prediction. In: Medical Imaging with Deep Learning, pp. 136–155. PMLR (2020)
8. Deng, J., Dong, W., Socher, R., Li, L.J., Li, K., Fei-Fei, L.: ImageNet: a large-scale hierarchical image database. In: 2009 IEEE Conference on Computer Vision and Pattern Recognition, pp. 248–255. IEEE (2009)
9. Gichoya, J.W., et al.: AI recognition of patient race in medical imaging: a modelling study. Lancet Digital Health **4**(6), e406–e414 (2022)
10. Gulrajani, I., Lopez-Paz, D.: In search of lost domain generalization. In: International Conference on Learning Representations
11. Huang, G., Liu, Z., Van Der Maaten, L., Weinberger, K.Q.: Densely connected convolutional networks. In: Proceedings of the IEEE Conference on Computer Vision and Pattern Recognition, pp. 4700–4708 (2017)
12. Irvin, J., et al.: CheXpert: a large chest radiograph dataset with uncertainty labels and expert comparison. In: Thirty-Third AAAI Conference on Artificial Intelligence (2019)
13. Johnson, A.E., et al.: Mimic-CXR, a de-identified publicly available database of chest radiographs with free-text reports. Sci. Data **6**(1), 317 (2019)
14. Kilim, O., Olar, A., Joó, T., Palicz, T., Pollner, P., Csabai, I.: Physical imaging parameter variation drives domain shift. Sci. Rep. **12**(1), 21302 (2022)
15. Koh, P.W., et al.: WILDS: a benchmark of in-the-wild distribution shifts. In: International Conference on Machine Learning, pp. 5637–5664. PMLR (2021)
16. Li, D., Yang, Y., Song, Y.Z., Hospedales, T.M.: Deeper, broader and artier domain generalization. In: Proceedings of the IEEE International Conference on Computer Vision, pp. 5542–5550 (2017)
17. McHugh, M.L.: Interrater reliability: the kappa statistic. Biochemia Med. **22**(3), 276–282 (2012)
18. Pooch, E.H.P., Ballester, P., Barros, R.C.: Can we trust deep learning based diagnosis? The impact of domain shift in chest radiograph classification. In: Petersen, J., et al. (eds.) TIA 2020. LNCS, vol. 12502, pp. 74–83. Springer, Cham (2020). https://doi.org/10.1007/978-3-030-62469-9_7

19. Reis, E.P., et al.: Brax, Brazilian labeled chest X-ray dataset. Sci. Data **9**(1), 487 (2022)
20. Wang, H., Xia, Y.: Domain-ensemble learning with cross-domain mixup for thoracic disease classification in unseen domains. Biomed. Sig. Process. Control **81**, 104488 (2023)
21. Wang, J., et al.: Generalizing to unseen domains: a survey on domain generalization. IEEE Trans. Knowl. Data Eng. **35**(8), 8052–8072 (2022)
22. Wang, X., Peng, Y., Lu, L., Lu, Z., Bagheri, M., Summers, R.M.: ChestX-ray8: hospital-scale chest X-ray database and benchmarks on weakly-supervised classification and localization of common thorax diseases. In: Proceedings of the IEEE Conference on Computer Vision and Pattern Recognition, pp. 2097–2106 (2017)
23. Wenkel, S.: Concatenated MNIST (CMNIST). making 784 pixels challenging again. (2019). www.simonwenkel.com/publications/articles/pdf/20190924_CMNIST.pdf
24. Yao, H., et al.: Improving out-of-distribution robustness via selective augmentation. In: International Conference on Machine Learning, pp. 25407–25437. PMLR (2022)
25. Zhang, H., Dullerud, N., Seyyed-Kalantari, L., Morris, Q., Joshi, S., Ghassemi, M.: An empirical framework for domain generalization in clinical settings. In: Proceedings of the Conference on Health, Inference, and Learning, pp. 279–290 (2021)
26. Zhang, H., Cisse, M., Dauphin, Y.N., Lopez-Paz, D.: mixup: Beyond empirical risk minimization. arXiv preprint arXiv:1710.09412 (2017)
27. Zhou, K., Liu, Z., Qiao, Y., Xiang, T., Loy, C.C.: Domain generalization: a survey. IEEE Trans. Pattern Anal. Mach. Intell. **45**(4), 4396–4415 (2022)
28. Zunaed, M., Haque, M., Hasan, T., et al.: Learning to generalize towards unseen domains via a content-aware style invariant framework for disease detection from chest x-rays. arXiv preprint arXiv:2302.13991 (2023)

Robustness Stress Testing in Medical Image Classification

Mobarakol Islam[1,2(✉)], Zeju Li[1,3], and Ben Glocker[1]

[1] BioMedIA Group, Department of Computing, Imperial College London, London, UK
[2] Wellcome/EPSRC Centre for Interventional and Surgical Sciences(WEISS) and Department of Medical Physics and Biomedical Engineering, University College London, London, UK
`mobarakol.islam@ucl.ac.uk`
[3] FMRIB Centre, Nuffield Department of Clinical Neurosciences, University of Oxford, Oxford, UK

Abstract. Deep neural networks have shown impressive performance for image-based disease detection. Performance is commonly evaluated through clinical validation on independent test sets to demonstrate clinically acceptable accuracy. Reporting good performance metrics on test sets, however, is not always a sufficient indication of the generalizability and robustness of an algorithm. In particular, when the test data is drawn from the same distribution as the training data, the iid test set performance can be an unreliable estimate of the accuracy on new data. In this paper, we employ stress testing to assess model robustness and subgroup performance disparities in disease detection models. We design progressive stress testing using five different bidirectional and unidirectional image perturbations with six different severity levels. As a use case, we apply stress tests to measure the robustness of disease detection models for chest X-ray and skin lesion images, and demonstrate the importance of studying class and domain-specific model behaviour. Our experiments indicate that some models may yield more robust and equitable performance than others. We also find that pretraining characteristics play an important role in downstream robustness. We conclude that progressive stress testing is a viable and important tool and should become standard practice in the clinical validation of image-based disease detection models.

1 Introduction

Despite expert-level performance of artificial intelligence (AI) systems on some image-based disease detection tasks [6,9,12], there remain concerns regarding the generalizability and robustness of such systems when deployed in clinical

Source code: https://github.com/mobarakol/Robustness_Stress_Testing.

Supplementary Information The online version contains supplementary material available at https://doi.org/10.1007/978-3-031-44336-7_17.

© The Author(s), under exclusive license to Springer Nature Switzerland AG 2023
C. H. Sudre et al. (Eds.): UNSURE 2023, LNCS 14291, pp. 167–176, 2023.
https://doi.org/10.1007/978-3-031-44336-7_17

practice [10]. The systems may need to process new data with different characteristics compared to the development data. The performance on such new data
may be different from the one observed previously during clinical validation, in
particular, when the previous test data was drawn from the same distribution
as the training data. This commonly occurs in controlled experimental settings
where the final model performance is established on an independent and identically distributed (iid) test set. But even when external datasets are being used
as part of the validation, the observed performance in terms of true and false
positive rates (TPR/FPR), or threshold-agnostic metrics such as area under the
receiver operating characteristic curve (AUC), may be different after deployment
when the data characteristics change. Such performance drift of AI models can
occur due to changes in the image acquisition, upgrades to scanner hardware,
or other distribution shifts, for example, in the patient population [4]. The performance drift between the development and deployment stage with robustness
concern has been associated with (i) spurious correlations between the training data and the output target labels [20], and (ii) underspecification [5] where
deep neural networks are notoriously underspecified regarding the 'to be learned
mechanism' mapping inputs to outputs. While two models may perform similarly well on the majority of patients, there can be significant differences in the
performance across subgroups [19] or underrepresented populations [21,22]. In
order to identify and differentiate between models that otherwise have similar iid
test set performance, stress testing was proposed as a valuable tool for analysing
model robustness [5,8]. We argue that stress testing needs to extend to subgroup
performance analysis if the goal is to deliver equitable solutions that work across
the entire patient population.

Computational stress testing is a well known tool in AI to assess model performance by deliberately modifying the input data to simulate various real-world
conditions. Most recently, there are attempts to design stress testing for the
assessment of deep neural networks in medical applications [1,8,25,26]. Inspired
by [5], the study [8] discusses a framework for identifying model underspecification using stress testing by stratifying test sets according to input perturbations.
Stress testing can be done with a variety of clinically meaningful transformations
to assess model performance beyond the commonly reported metrics [26]. The
study presented in [26] finds that a model with acceptable performance on conventional metrics may not necessarily pass the stress test. Adversarial attacks are
also found to be utilized in stress testing to reveal the vulnerability of medical
images compared to natural images [25]. However, most of these works investigate overall, aggregated performance changes by stratifying test data according
to the input perturbation only, ignoring potential performance disparities across
subgroups and input domains.

In this work, we highlight the importance of extending stress testing to
include subgroup performance analysis. We use two real-world applications of
chest X-ray disease detection and skin lesion classification for which we design
meaningful stress tests using uni- and bi-directional image perturbation with
multiple levels of perturbation severity. We use systematic changes to the image

appearance in order to modify the iid test set as illustrated in Fig. 1(a). This allows us to investigate model robustness and analyse subgroup disparities of disease detection models. We employ four different neural network architectures, comparing state-of-the-art convolutional neural networks (DenseNet-121 [15] and ResNet-34 [13]) with the emerging vision transformers (ViT [7] and Swin-Transformer [18]). We measure the classification accuracy in terms of TPR and FPR for a specific operating point, and the general ability of the models to identify disease via the threshold-agnostic AUC metric. Our key findings are (i) Stress testing is capable of identifying performance differences beyond iid test set accuracy; (ii) Transformer-based models may potentially be more robust compared to traditional CNNs; (iii) Subgroup performance should be analysed using class-specific stress testing to check for disparities; (iv) Stress testing reveals that changes in performance across subgroups can relate to jointly shifting TPR and FPR while the AUC remains similar across groups. The last observation is of particular importance as it raises questions about the clinical utility of these models. A model that shows a shift in TPR/FPR but performs equally well in terms of AUC on different subgroups requires careful analysis of the underlying causes of the performance shift, which could be related to various types of dataset and model bias [2].

2 Stress Testing via Image Perturbations

In stress testing, model performance is assessed by applying meaningful perturbations to the input images. In this way, a model can be tested systematically to measure the robustness under simulated yet realistic conditions. Perturbation techniques such as blurring, changes to the brightness and contrast, or pixelation have been previously employed. In addition to appearance changes, spatial transformations such as horizontal flipping and rotations have been used [26]. Several studies have employed extensive perturbations to determine model robustness [14,23,24]. In this work, we design stress tests using four bidirectional and one unidirectional image perturbations with six different severity levels. The perturbations are applied during test time. We use systematic changes via gamma correction (GC), contrast (Con), brightness (Bri), sharpness (Sha), and Gaussian blur (Blur) in order to modify the iid test set. Figure 1(a)) visualizes the effect of the perturbations on an example input image with different levels of severity. Positive and negative adjustments can be applied for contrast, brightness, gamma correction, and sharpness. We adopt the implementation of these transformations from the torchvision functional library which facilitates straightforward reproducibility of our experiments[1]. The choice of suitable stress tests is data and task-specific. We consider perturbations that are meaningful for X-ray and skin lesion imaging and directly relate to key aspects of any image acquisition. Other perturbations may be considered for providing a more complete picture of the model performance. For a specific application and clinical use, the stress tests should be designed according to the characteristics of the application.

---

[1] https://pytorch.org/vision/stable/transforms.html.

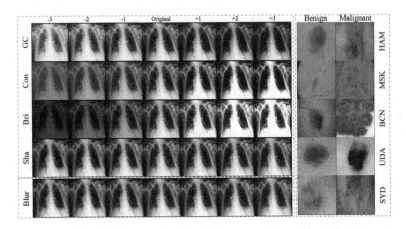

Fig. 1. Stress testing via image perturbations: (left) Effects of different perturbations shown for an example chest X-ray image; (right) Benign and malignant images from five different sites with domain shift in ISIC skin lesion dataset.

Use case 1 (Chest X-ray disease detection): We utilise the publicly available CheXpert dataset [16] as the method development domain and the MIMIC-CXR dataset [17] as the external validation domain. In CheXpert, there are 127,118 chest X-ray scans with 14 different disease multi-label annotations and split into training (76,205), validation (12,673), and testing (38,240) following the setup in [11]. The dataset also contains demographic information including racial identity (78% White, 15 % Asian, 7% Black) and biological sex (41% female and 59% of male). In MIMIC-CXR [17], there are 183,207 chest X-ray scans with 14 disease annotation as CheXpert and 30% of the scans are used for external testing in this work. The dataset contains racial identity and biological sex information of 77% White, 4% Asian, 19% Black, 52% Female and 48% Male.

Use case 2 (Skin lesion classification): We use the publicly available ISIC [3] skin lesion detection dataset with 52,710 images consisting complete meta-information from 5 different sites (HAM, MSK, BCN, UDA, and SYD) as shown in Fig. 1(b) and split into 60% / 40% for training and testing. We defined five subgroups of male (48%), female (52%), young (24%, age < 39), mid-aged (47%, 39 < age > 59) and old (29%, age > 59).

3   Experimental Setup

To evaluate the performance of medical image classification under stress testing, we train chest X-ray disease detection and skin lesion classification models employing different types of state-of-the-art deep neural network architectures. We use two popular CNN-based architectures, DenseNet-121 [15] and ResNet-34 [13], and two recent transformer-based models, the Vision Transformer (ViT) [7] and Swin-Transformer [18]. ViT is a transformer-like architecture over patches of the image where Swin-transformer introduce hierarchical

Table 1. Performance of the disease detection in chest X-ray on iid test set (CheXpert), external test set (MIMIC-CXR) and skin lesion on multi-site test set(ISIC) for DenseNet and ViT.

| | | | CheXpert | | | | | | MIMIC-CXR | | | | | | ISIC Skin Lesion | | | |
| | | | No Finding | | | Pleural Effusion | | | No Finding | | | Pleural Effusion | | | | | | |
		Subgrp	w pretr.	w/o pretr.	waug.	w pretr.	w/o pretr.	waug.	w pretr.	w/o pretr.	wpretr.	w pretr.	w/o pretr.	waug.	Subgrp	w pretr.	w/o pretr.	waug.
AUC	DenseNet	White	0.87	0.87	0.87	0.86	0.86	0.86	0.82	0.82	0.83	0.88	0.88	0.89	Young	0.79	0.81	0.82
		Asian	0.88	0.87	0.86	0.88	0.88	0.88	0.83	0.83	0.83	0.88	0.89	0.89	Mid-aged	0.80	0.78	0.82
		Black	0.88	0.89	0.89	0.86	0.86	0.86	0.83	0.82	0.83	0.90	0.89	0.89	Old	0.70	0.72	0.72
		Female	0.87	0.87	0.87	0.87	0.87	0.87	0.84	0.83	0.84	0.89	0.90	0.90	Female	0.79	0.78	0.81
		Male	0.87	0.87	0.87	0.86	0.86	0.87	0.81	0.82	0.82	0.88	0.88	0.88	Male	0.79	0.79	0.81
	ViT	White	0.87	0.86	0.88	0.87	0.86	0.87	0.82	0.81	0.82	0.89	0.88	0.89	Young	0.86	0.82	0.87
		Asian	0.87	0.87	0.88	0.88	0.87	0.88	0.83	0.83	0.84	0.89	0.88	0.89	Mid-aged	0.84	0.82	0.85
		Black	0.89	0.88	0.89	0.87	0.86	0.87	0.83	0.82	0.83	0.90	0.88	0.90	Old	0.82	0.77	0.88
		Female	0.87	0.86	0.88	0.87	0.87	0.87	0.83	0.83	0.84	0.90	0.89	0.90	Female	0.86	0.82	0.87
		Male	0.88	0.87	0.88	0.87	0.86	0.87	0.81	0.81	0.81	0.88	0.88	0.88	Male	0.83	0.81	0.83
F1	DenseNet	White	0.40	0.40	0.40	0.74	0.74	0.74	0.64	0.64	0.65	0.68	0.69	0.69	Young	0.43	0.44	0.43
		Asian	0.42	0.42	0.41	0.77	0.76	0.76	0.68	0.69	0.69	0.69	0.70	0.70	Mid-aged	0.49	0.46	0.49
		Black	0.46	0.47	0.46	0.70	0.68	0.70	0.69	0.68	0.70	0.62	0.62	0.61	Old	0.22	0.22	0.20
		Female	0.41	0.41	0.41	0.75	0.74	0.75	0.68	0.67	0.68	0.68	0.69	0.68	Female	0.38	0.37	0.38
		Male	0.41	0.40	0.40	0.74	0.74	0.74	0.63	0.64	0.64	0.67	0.67	0.68	Male	0.56	0.52	0.60
	ViT	White	0.40	0.40	0.41	0.75	0.74	0.75	0.63	0.63	0.64	0.69	0.69	0.69	Young	0.47	0.44	0.47
		Asian	0.43	0.42	0.43	0.77	0.77	0.77	0.67	0.68	0.69	0.71	0.69	0.70	Mid-aged	0.52	0.48	0.55
		Black	0.46	0.48	0.47	0.71	0.71	0.71	0.69	0.68	0.69	0.63	0.60	0.63	Old	0.24	0.18	0.26
		Female	0.40	0.41	0.42	0.75	0.75	0.75	0.67	0.66	0.68	0.69	0.68	0.69	Female	0.43	0.41	0.43
		Male	0.42	0.41	0.42	0.75	0.74	0.75	0.63	0.62	0.64	0.68	0.67	0.68	Male	0.63	0.60	0.62

feature maps and shifted window attention. For training, we employ the Adam optimizer with a learning rate of 0.001 and binary cross-entropy loss for multi-label (14 classes) chest X-ray disease detection and a binary cross-entropy loss for skin lesion classification.

4 Results and Findings

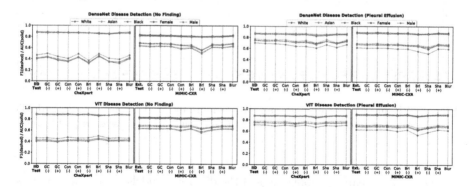

Fig. 2. F1 and AUC across patient subgroups for a DenseNet (top) and ViT (bottom) disease detection model for a variety of stress tests on the development data (CheXpert) and the external validation data (MIMIC-CXR). Performance for 'no-finding' is shown on the left, and 'pleural effusion' on the right.

The performance for the chest X-ray disease detection model on iid (CheXpert), external (MIMIC-CXR) test sets (without any perturbations applied) and the skin lesion classification on multi-site (ISIC) test sets are given in Table 1. To

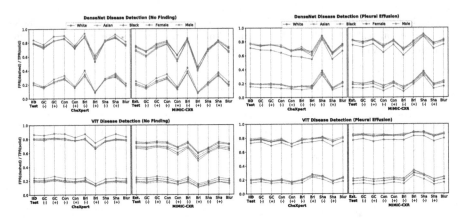

Fig. 3. TPR and FPR change across patient subgroups for a DenseNet (top) and ViT (bottom) disease detection model for a variety of stress tests on the development data (CheXpert) and the external validation data (MIMIC-CXR). Performance for 'no-finding' on the left, and 'pleural effusion' on the right.

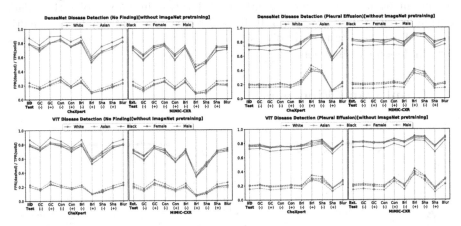

Fig. 4. TPR and FPR change across patient subgroups for a DenseNet (top) and ViT (bottom) disease detection model trained from scratch (without ImageNet pretraining).

analyse and compare the robustness of the different models, we employ progressive stress testing via image perturbations. We apply 30 different image perturbations to assess model robustness. In the following we only choose one positive (+2) and negative (−2) adjustment for each bidirectional perturbation and only one positive (+2) adjustment for the unidirectional one (as in Fig. 1), as we found that the change in performance is monotonic. The results of the stress testing of the chest X-ray disease detection models are shown in Fig. 2 and Fig. 3. To investigate the somewhat surprising robustness of the ViT, we also trained both models from randomly initialized weights instead of using ImageNet pretraining, keeping all other settings unchanged as shown in Fig. 4. To further analyse the

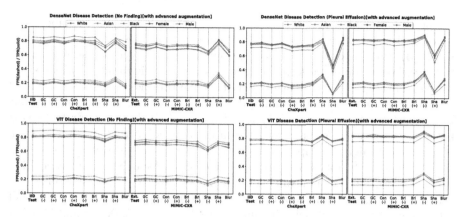

Fig. 5. TPR and FPR change across subgroups for DenseNet and ViT trained with advanced augmentations including gamma correction, contrast, and brightness.

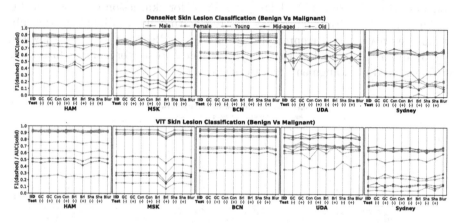

Fig. 6. F1 and AUC change across patient subgroups over five different test domains for a DenseNet (top) and ViT (bottom) disease detection model.

mixing effects of pretraining and data augmentation on model robustness, we utilized additional appearance augmentation techniques during training including gamma correction, contrast, and brightness (cf. Fig. 5). We also observe a much higher degree of robustness of ViT compared to DenseNet across the different stress tests on skin lesion classification task as shown in Fig. 6 and Fig. 7. Additional figures and observations on advanced augmentation, ResNet vs Swin-Transformer, and robustness in model calibration can be found in the materials.

From the experimental results, figures, and tables, our observation can be summarized as: (i) Transformer-based networks (ViT or Swin-Transformer) yield much more stable TPR/FPR performance across perturbations compared to the CNN-based networks (DenseNet, ResNet) (as shown in Fig. 3). (ii) The effect of the perturbations is larger for certain classes, which highlights the importance of using class-specific stress testing for complete robustness analysis (as shown in Fig. 3). (iii) In terms of the AUC metric alone, all types of network architectures show a robust performance across stress tests in most of the cases but varying TPR/FPR performance under the same threshold (as shown in Fig. 2 and Table 1). (iv) ViT substantially degrades in robustness if training without ImageNet pretraining weights, which indicates that the ImageNet pretraining is not only important to obtain downstream robustness but that the exact nature of pretraining might be important (as shown in Fig. 4). (v) Advanced augmentations improve the robustness, in particular for the DenseNet in corresponding perturbations, but ViT appears overall more robust even to perturbations outside the data augmentation strategy (as shown in Fig. 5). (vi) In terms of model robustness under domain shift, iid and external test sets CheXpert and MIMIC-CXR seem largely consistent with similar fluctuations (as shown in Fig. 3); however, we observe significant changes in overall performance across the test domains (HAM, MSK, BCN, UDA, and SYD) for skin lesion classification (as shown in Fig. 7). (vii) The progressive stress testing also can highlight the subgroup disparity for underrepresented groups (e.g., Black patients) (as shown in Fig. 3) and negatively affect the group of female patients for some architectures with advanced data augmentation (as shown in Fig. 5).

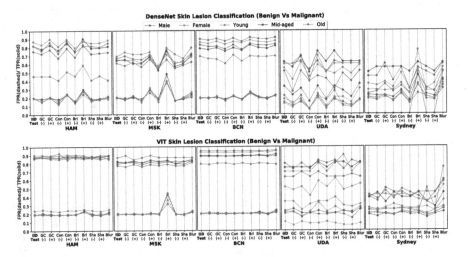

Fig. 7. TPR and FPR change across patient subgroups over five different test domains for a DenseNet (top) and ViT (bottom) skin lesion classification model.

5   Discussion and Conclusion

In this work, we have explored progressive stress testing as a comprehensive tool to assess robustness in image classification models. Our work extends previous frameworks, arguing that it is important to include subgroup analysis and class-specific performance monitoring. The example applications of chest X-ray disease detection and skin lesion classification highlight the value of progressive stress testing to reveal robustness characteristics that otherwise remain hidden when using traditional test set evaluation. We found differences in robustness between state-of-the-art neural network architectures. We found a connection between ImageNet pretraining and downstream robustness which potentially has a larger contribution than the choice of the neural network architecture. The transformer-based models, ViT and Swin-Transformer, appear generally more robust than the CNN-based models, DenseNet and ResNet. The future direction of this work is to consider adversarial attacks to design adversarial stress testing.

Acknowledgements. This project has received funding from the European Research Council (ERC) under the European Union's Horizon 2020 research and innovation programme (grant agreement No 757173, project MIRA, ERC-2017-STG).

References

1. Araujo, V., Carvallo, A., Aspillaga, C., Thorne, C., Parra, D.: Stress test evaluation of biomedical word embeddings. arXiv preprint arXiv:2107.11652 (2021)
2. Bernhardt, M., Jones, C., Glocker, B.: Potential sources of dataset bias complicate investigation of underdiagnosis by machine learning algorithms. Nat. Med., 1–2 (2022)
3. Cassidy, B., Kendrick, C., Brodzicki, A., Jaworek-Korjakowska, J., Yap, M.H.: Analysis of the ISIC image datasets: usage, benchmarks and recommendations. Med. Image Anal. **75**, 102305 (2022)
4. Castro, D.C., Walker, I., Glocker, B.: Causality matters in medical imaging. Nat. Commun. **11**(1), 1–10 (2020)
5. D'Amour, A., et al.: Underspecification presents challenges for credibility in modern machine learning. arXiv preprint arXiv:2011.03395 (2020)
6. De Fauw, J., et al.: Clinically applicable deep learning for diagnosis and referral in retinal disease. Nat. Med. **24**(9), 1342–1350 (2018)
7. Dosovitskiy, A., et al.: An image is worth 16×16 words: transformers for image recognition at scale. arXiv preprint arXiv:2010.11929 (2020)
8. Eche, T., Schwartz, L.H., Mokrane, F.Z., Dercle, L.: Toward generalizability in the deployment of artificial intelligence in radiology: role of computation stress testing to overcome underspecification. Radiology: Artif. Intell. **3**(6), e210097 (2021)
9. Esteva, A., et al.: Dermatologist-level classification of skin cancer with deep neural networks. Nature **542**(7639), 115–118 (2017)
10. Finlayson, S.G., et al.: The clinician and dataset shift in artificial intelligence. N. Engl. J. Med., 283–286 (2020)
11. Gichoya, J.W., et al.: AI recognition of patient race in medical imaging: a modelling study. The Lancet Digital Health (2022)
12. Gulshan, V., et al.: Development and validation of a deep learning algorithm for detection of diabetic retinopathy in retinal fundus photographs. Jama **316**(22) (2016)
13. He, K., Zhang, X., Ren, S., Sun, J.: Deep residual learning for image recognition. In: Proceedings of the IEEE Conference on Computer Vision and Pattern Recognition, pp. 770–778 (2016)

14. Hendrycks, D., Dietterich, T.: Benchmarking neural network robustness to common corruptions and perturbations. arXiv preprint arXiv:1903.12261 (2019)

15. Huang, G., Liu, Z., Van Der Maaten, L., Weinberger, K.Q.: Densely connected convolutional networks. In: Proceedings of the IEEE Conference on Computer Vision and Pattern Recognition, pp. 4700–4708 (2017)

16. Irvin, J., et al.: CheXpert: a large chest radiograph dataset with uncertainty labels and expert comparison. In: Proceedings of the AAAI Conference on Artificial Intelligence, vol. 33, pp. 590–597 (2019)

17. Johnson, A.E., et al.: MIMIC-CXR, a de-identified publicly available database of chest radiographs with free-text reports. Sci. Data **6**(1), 1–8 (2019)

18. Liu, Z., et al.: Swin transformer: hierarchical vision transformer using shifted windows. In: Proceedings of the IEEE/CVF International Conference on Computer Vision, pp. 10012–10022 (2021)

19. Oakden-Rayner, L., Dunnmon, J., Carneiro, G., Ré, C.: Hidden stratification causes clinically meaningful failures in machine learning for medical imaging. In: Proceedings of the ACM Conference on Health, Inference, and Learning, pp. 151–159 (2020)

20. Saab, K., Hooper, S., Chen, M., Zhang, M., Rubin, D., Ré, C.: Reducing reliance on spurious features in medical image classification with spatial specificity. In: Machine Learning for Healthcare Conference, pp. 760–784. PMLR (2022)

21. Seyyed-Kalantari, L., Liu, G., McDermott, M., Chen, I.Y., Ghassemi, M.: CheXclusion: fairness gaps in deep chest X-ray classifiers. In: BIOCOMPUTING 2021: Proceedings of the Pacific Symposium, pp. 232–243. World Scientific (2020)

22. Seyyed-Kalantari, L., Zhang, H., McDermott, M., Chen, I.Y., Ghassemi, M.: Underdiagnosis bias of artificial intelligence algorithms applied to chest radiographs in under-served patient populations. Nat. Med., 1–7 (2021)

23. Taori, R., Dave, A., Shankar, V., Carlini, N., Recht, B., Schmidt, L.: Measuring robustness to natural distribution shifts in image classification. Adv. Neural. Inf. Process. Syst. **33**, 18583–18599 (2020)

24. Wiles, O., et al.: A fine-grained analysis on distribution shift. arXiv preprint arXiv:2110.11328 (2021)

25. Yao, Q., He, Z., Lin, Y., Ma, K., Zheng, Y., Zhou, S.K.: A hierarchical feature constraint to camouflage medical adversarial attacks. In: de Bruijne, M., Cattin, P.C., Cotin, S., Padoy, N., Speidel, S., Zheng, Y., Essert, C. (eds.) MICCAI 2021. LNCS, vol. 12903, pp. 36–47. Springer, Cham (2021). https://doi.org/10.1007/978-3-030-87199-4_4

26. Young, A.T., et al.: Stress testing reveals gaps in clinic readiness of image-based diagnostic artificial intelligence models. NPJ Digit. Med. **4**(1), 1–8 (2021)

Confidence-Aware and Self-supervised Image Anomaly Localisation

Johanna P. Müller[1]([✉]) [ID], Matthew Baugh[2] [ID], Jeremy Tan[3] [ID],
Mischa Dombrowski[1] [ID], and Bernhard Kainz[1,2] [ID]

[1] Friedrich-Alexander University Erlangen-Nürnberg, Erlangen, Germany
johanna.paula.mueller@fau.de
[2] Imperial College London, London, England
[3] ETH Zurich, Zurich, Switzerland

Abstract. Universal anomaly detection still remains a challenging problem in machine learning and medical image analysis. It is possible to learn an expected distribution from a single class of *normative samples*, *e.g.*, through epistemic uncertainty estimates, auto-encoding models, or from synthetic anomalies in a self-supervised way. The performance of self-supervised anomaly detection approaches is still inferior compared to methods that use examples from *known unknown* classes to shape the decision boundary. However, outlier exposure methods often do not identify *unknown unknowns*. Here we discuss an improved self-supervised single-class training strategy that supports the approximation of probabilistic inference with loosen feature locality constraints. We show that up-scaling of gradients with histogram-equalised images is beneficial for recently proposed self-supervision tasks. Our method is integrated into several out-of-distribution (OOD) detection models and we show evidence that our method outperforms the state-of-the-art on various benchmark datasets.

Keywords: Anomaly detection · Out-of-distribution detection · Poisson image interpolation · Self-supervision

1 Introduction

Out-of-distribution (OOD) detection builds upon the assumption that the division into normal and abnormal data is distinct, however, OOD data can overlap in-distribution (ID) data and may exhibit an infinite number of descriptive features. We assume for medical imaging data a finite ID ("healthy") distribution space and an infinite OOD ("anomalous") distribution space. Furthermore, we assume ID consistency for healthy medical images such that the compatibility condition holds, based on the impossibility theorems for OOD detection by [8]. As a result, OOD detection algorithms can be capable of learning the finite ID space and also a finite but sufficient number of ODD features for inference. We can approximate density-based spaces based on drawn samples from real

© The Author(s), under exclusive license to Springer Nature Switzerland AG 2023
C. H. Sudre et al. (Eds.): UNSURE 2023, LNCS 14291, pp. 177–187, 2023.
https://doi.org/10.1007/978-3-031-44336-7_18

unknown (conditioned) probability distributions for covering uncertainty in the annotation of data, and, therefore, assume the Realisability assumption [8] for learnable OOD detection referring to the proposed problem formulation.

The OOD problem for medical imaging can also be seen from a practical, intuitive point of view. To reflect that multiple human medical experts can come by different diagnoses given the same image of a patient, we integrate uncertainty estimates for both ID and OOD data in the form of probability distributions. Intuitively, we tend to imagine a finite ID space, since we observe a consistency between ID features which are exhibited by healthy human individuals from an anatomical point of view. By assuming that, we postulate that we can present learnable OOD detection through training different types of algorithms on normal data with synthetically generated anomalies.

Learning from synthetically generated anomalies became a research focus in medical image analysis research recently [11]. In a medical context, labelling requires medical expertise and, hence, human resources for generating reliable ground truth masks for anomaly detection algorithms. Self-supervised tasks that base on synthetically generated anomalies are considered convenient mitigation for limited robustness and generalisation abilities that result from small datasets. An extension of this idea is to leverage the natural variations in normal anatomy to create a range of synthetic abnormalities. For example, image patch regions can be extracted from two independent samples and replaced with an interpolation between both patches [15,25]. The interpolation factor, patch size, and patch location can be randomly sampled from uniform distributions. Any encoder-decoder architecture can be trained to give a pixel-wise prediction of the patch and its interpolation factor. This encourages a deep network to learn what features to expect normally and to identify where foreign patterns have been introduced. The estimate of the interpolation factor lends itself nicely to the derivation of an outlier score. Meanwhile, the pixel-wise output allows for pixel- and subject-level predictions using the same model. However, such synthesis strategies feature obvious discontinuities. [22,26] solve the discontinuity problem by using Poisson image editing, but the resulting anomalies can be so subtle that they may represent variations of the normal class rather than true anomalies and these approaches do not provide prediction confidence estimates. Therefore we propose a new approach to model the ID space and make the following contributions:

1. We propose a revised Poisson Image-interpolation framework for the generation of salient but still smoothly interpolated anomalies for self-supervision in unsupervised image anomaly localisation.
2. We propose self-supervision with a probabilistic feature extractor – Probabilistic PII (P-PII) – which allows the generation of stochastic anomalies with which we are able to simulate multiple annotators.
3. We evaluate P-PII on 2D chest radiograph images and 3D CT scans and show that our method outperforms recently proposed self-supervised anomaly localisation approaches.

4. We show that it is possible to learn feature distributions for 'normal' tissue in a self-supervised way from databases that exclusively contain patients with the disease.

Related Work. The most prominent direction for unsupervised medical anomaly localisation [27] is dominated by reconstruction-based methods like VAEs [10,16,28,33] as well as other generative models like GANs [1,21,31] , especially, for image synthesis and data augmentation [7,9,11]. New advances are expected by Diffusion models, which shine with detailed reconstructions and anomaly maps for detection [29] but they are computationally very challenging and have not been evaluated in detail yet. Other commonly used methods include one-class Support Vector Machines, k-Nearest Neighbors and extensions of these approaches for dimensionality-reduced feature spaces [6,17]. Probabilistic methods have not been researched in detail for OOD detection yet. However, they are known for probabilistic segmentation approaches. For example, the Probabilistic Hierarchical Segmentation (PHISeg) combines a conditional variational autoencoder (cVAE) with a U-NET setup proposed by [4], Bayesian U-Nets [23] can model epistemic uncertainty with weak labels and Monte Carlo estimates [5,19,20].

In a medical context, labelling requires medical expertise and, hence, human resources for generating reliable ground truth masks for anomaly detection algorithms. Self-supervised tasks are considered as convenient extensions for improving robustness, uncertainty and generalisation abilities of models and replace expensive labelling [12,13,18,32]. We modify our backbone models to allow for OOD detection. To do this, we form a self-supervised task which is easily interchangeable. The self-supervised principle relies on patch interpolation from the same or a different source image into a target image. Since more research work focuses on alleviating the labelling effort by experts for image data, different generation methods for anomalies emerged. For Foreign patch interpolation (FPI) [25], two patches of the same location are extracted from two independent samples and replaced with an interpolation between both patches. CutPaste [15] updates the original method by translating patches within an image and allows the effective detection of anomalies in industrial datasets. Poisson Image Interpolation (PII) [26] overcomes sharp discontinuities with Poisson editing as an interpolation strategy and generates more organic and subtle outliers. Natural Synthetic Anomalies (NSA) [22] are introduced by rescaling, shifting and a new Gamma-distribution-based patch shape sampling without the use of interpolation factors for an end-to-end model for anomaly detection.

2   Method

Self-supervised tasks were considered convenient extensions for improving the robustness, uncertainty and generalisation abilities of models [12,13,18]. Our proposed Probabilistic PII self-supervision task is based on [25] and builds upon the Poisson image editing implementation by [3]. PII relies on the relative changes of the source image, the image gradient field $\mathbf{v_{pq}}$, in the patch

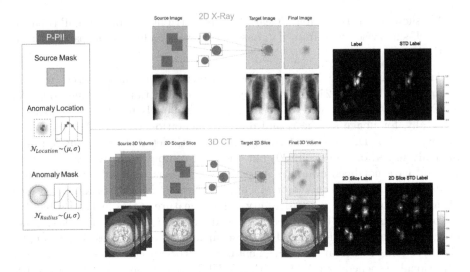

Fig. 1. Probabilistic PII takes patches from a source image of a given size. A second mask of circular size, drawn from two normal distributions for radius and location inside the source patches, allows aggregated anomalies with smoothly interpolated boundaries. We obtain probabilistic and salient anomalies.

region and the patch boundary of the target image δh, see Eq. 1. The solution of the underlying mathematical problem represents the discretised Poisson equation with Dirichlet boundary conditions, see Eq. 2 and Eq. 4. The intensity values within the patch h are given by the scalar function f_{in} and $\langle p, q \rangle$ are denoted as a pixel pair such that $q \in N_p$ denote the four directly adjacent neighbour pixel of p. For PII, α determines the influence of the individual image gradients on the interpolation task.

$$v_{pq} = \begin{cases} (1-\alpha)(x_{i_p} - x_{i_q}), & \text{if } \left|(1-\alpha)(x_{i_p} - x_{i_q})\right| > \left|\alpha(x_{i_p} - x_{i_q})\right| \\ \alpha(x_{i_p} - x_{i_q}), & \text{otherwise.} \end{cases} \quad (1)$$

$$\nabla f_{in} = \text{div}\mathbf{v} \text{ over } h \quad (2)$$

The PII task can be reformulated to the following minimisation problem (Eq. 3), given the projection of $\mathbf{v}(\frac{p+q}{2})$ onto the oriented edge (Eq. 1) [26] and the field of intensity image gradients (Eq. 2). The problem formulation can be solved via a discrete linear system solver.

$$\min_{f_{in}} \iint_h |\nabla f_{in} - \mathbf{v}|^2, \text{ with } f_{in}\Big|_{\delta h} = f_{out}\Big|_{\delta h} \quad (3)$$

$$\min_{f_{in}|_h} \sum_{\langle p,q \rangle \cap h \neq 0} (f_{in,p} - f_{in,q} - v_{pq})^2, \text{ with } f_{in}\Big|_{\delta h} = f_{out}\Big|_{\delta h}, \forall p \in \delta h, q \in N_p \quad (4)$$

Our proposed Probabilistic PII (P-PII) builds upon these mathematical foundations but incorporates new features and approaches for addressing current limitations and rethinking its application.

First, we apply P-PII pairwise on allegedly non-anomalous training data samples but those pairs can be also, *e.g.*, easily reduced to one and single non-anomalous image sample for reduced memory and time consumption. If pairwise applied, the allocation of image pairs is randomly drawn from the image batch. Second, we take patches from different locations of the source image and interpolate them into different locations inside the target image, hence, we latch on the patch drawing by NSA [22]. Third, we overcome the current limitation of PII and PII-based anomaly generation methods regarding the grade of abnormality of the interpolated patches. If both, source and target images, are normalised, these anomalous regions are very subtle and difficult to recognise - compared to real lesions as well. For intensifying these abnormal features, we introduce an amplification of gradients, through a scaling factor, during the interpolation into the source patch. This approach generates less subtle, salient anomalies which are still smoothly interpolated into the target image. Fourth, we mitigate class imbalance of normal and anomalous pixels through the generation of $k > 1$ anomalies per image with which we speed up learning to differentiate both classes. Fifth, we introduce the Probabilistic feature into PII. For simulating the variance of annotations by multiple raters, as *e.g.*, annotation of lesions by multiple medical experts, we generate circular anomalies, inside each extracted patch from the source image. Therefore, we draw anomaly masks whose parameters, radius $\mathbf{r}$ and location $(\mathbf{x,y})$ (Eq. 5), we sample from normal distributions. We ensure with fixed boundaries of location and radius that the generated anomaly only touches the boundaries.

$$\mathbf{r} \sim \mathcal{N}_{Radius}(\mu, \sigma) \qquad (\mathbf{x}, \mathbf{y}) \sim \mathcal{N}_{Location}(M = \langle \mu_\mathbf{x}, \mu_\mathbf{y} \rangle, \Sigma = \langle \sigma_\mathbf{x}, \sigma_\mathbf{y} \rangle) \qquad (5)$$

For using P-PII as the self-supervised task for OOD detection, we decided on intensity-based label generation. Based on the mean of all anomalies of each patch, we use the absolute difference between the original target image and the mean final image as the label. Additionally, we have a variance map of all anomalies which can be used for further statistical evaluation or integration into the optimisation problem.

3   Evaluation and Results

Data. We use the JSRT database [24] as an exemplary smaller medical imaging dataset which includes 154 conventional chest radiographs with lung nodules and 93 radiographs without a nodule. For each patient, only one image is attributed. We re-scaled all images from 2048 × 2048 matrix size to 512 × 512 in order to hold the conditions for all datasets equal. The subset without pathological findings serves as our training dataset. LIDC-IDRI [2] covers 1018 cases in the form of CT scans with 7371 lesions, which were marked by at least one radiologist. We also divide the dataset into lesion slices and anomaly-free slices by extracting the context slices from each volume with a margin of about 5 slices on either side of the lesion, which approximates the maximum possible margin of lesions given slice thickness and lesion diameter. We use the first 800 cases as a training dataset, and the rest for validation and testing. The large-scale dataset DeepLesion [30] contains 32,735 lesions in 32,120 computed tomography (CT) slices from 10,594 studies of 4,427 unique patients. Since the image size varies throughout the dataset, we resize each image to the smallest occurring size, 512×512. Each lesion slice is provided as part of an imaging volume which provides the 3D context of the lesion. We divide the dataset into lesion slices and anomaly-free slices by extracting the context slices from each volume with a margin of about 10 mm on either side of the lesion. As a result, we have 386,587 anomaly-free slices and 4831 annotated anomalous slices. We test the quality of performance for all models on ID and OOD data samples, which were not seen during training. For JSRT, the test set consists of 19 ID samples and 154 OOD samples. For the large datasets, we drew a test cohort of 500 ID and 500 (478 for LIDC-IDRI) OOD samples. For LIDC-IDRI and DeepLesion, both ID and OOD samples are from patients not occurring in the training dataset. Note that the models are trained on healthy tissue of ill patients for the datasets LIDC-IDRI and DeepLesion, which is different to the dataset JSRT for which we only differentiate between ill and healthy patients/samples.

Pre-processing and Training. We use histogram equalisation to the normalised images for contrast enhancement, adopted from MIMIC-CXR-JPG [14]. We apply this type of equalisation to all datasets. We train all models for a fixed number of $100,000$ steps with a fixed batch size of 16. We used PNY NVIDIA A100s with at least 18 GB of memory per job. The training runtime was approx. 4 d. The backbone models and P-PII were implemented in Python and TensorFlow.

Metrics. Choosing suitable metrics for evaluating OOD detection methods is important to effectively evaluate the performance of a method and make valid comparisons with other approaches. We chose the Area under the receiver operating characteristic (AUROC) for sample- and pixel-wise binary classification between OOD and ID samples/pixels as a threshold-less metric. We refer with *OOD* to anomalous samples/pixels and with *ID* to normal ('healthy') input samples/pixels. Average Precision (AP) takes both precision and recall into account and is considered a sample-based evaluation metric here. In medical imaging analysis, false negatives are more critical than false positives, especially, in lesion detection. Therefore, we include the Free-response receiver operating characteristic (FROC) score as an evaluation measure.

Sensitivity Analysis. We perform an ablation study to investigate the impact of revised PII as a self-supervision task for various backbone models (U-Net, Monte-Carlo Dropout (rate=0.1) U-Net, PHiSeg). All backbone models have the same depth of five levels, PHiSeg includes two additional resolution levels. We examine the influence of selected augmentation functions for small-scale datasets or datasets suffering from class imbalance for improving the performance of self-supervised training.

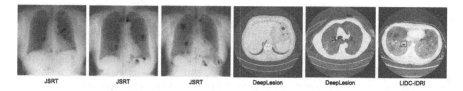

Fig. 2. Exemplary anomaly prediction on test data with U-net, input image in grey, heatmap of prediction in red, ground truth bounding box in blue. (Color figure online)

Results. We evaluated all models with the training checkpoint for best dice. We show quantitative results in Table 1 for all backbone models. We observed an increase of pixel-wise AUROC of up to 13% for U-net and PHiSeg and 18% for Dropout U-net, for the JSRT dataset. For LIDC-IDRI, we achieve values improved by up to 53% for PHiSeg. For DeepLesion, we determined an increase of 34% with PHiSeg and 9% with U-net for pixel-wise AUROC. Emphasising the sensitivity level of 0.27 for 10 avg. FPS, we increased the performance of the U-net, trained with PII, threefold with our proposed self-supervision task. Sample-wise AUROC was improved the most for the JSRT dataset with 45%, whereas we observed AUROC values < 0.5 for LIDC-IDRI and, partially, for DeepLesion and JSRT. An increased amount of false positives in predicting anomalous samples results for sample-wise AP for the large datasets. We show qualitative results for the prediction of U-net as a backbone model in Fig. 2. The prediction on JSRT is quantitatively better, but there are still false positive pixels in all examples, especially, for the larger datasets. We compare augmentation functions for further enhancing the performance of P-PII, see Table 2. We compare both best-performing models and obtain an increase of 1% with scaling of the input image and combining scaling, random rotation in between ±10° and elastic deformation. Further improvement was achieved by scaling the input for the Dropout U-net which resulted in enhancing image-wise AUROC about 3%. The highest improvement can be achieved through the use of augmentation functions yielding a sensitivity of 11% for U-net with combined augmentation, and 19% for Dropout U-net with scaling.

Discussion. Self-supervision with P-PII enables all models to detect also very small lesions, see Fig. 2, which is still a major challenge for other anomaly localisation models, in both, a supervised and self-supervised context. We improve upon the issue of decreasing sensitivity for increasing average FPs in FROC, which we observe for the baseline method. With augmentation functions the performance of models trained with PII increases the sensitivity significantly by up to 19%. The limited quantitative performance on DeepLesion and LIDC-IDRI is likely due to the fixed training steps which could be insufficient for large datasets and also the foreground-background class imbalance could influence the

Table 1. Results; for PHiSeg, mean of 50 drawn samples from likelihood network; AUC - Area under the Receiver operating characteristic (AUROC), FC - Free-response Receiver operating characteristic (FROC) for 10 average FPs

| | | JSRT [24] | | | | DeepLesion [30] | | | | LIDC-IDRI [2] | | | |
| | | Pixel | | Sample | | Pixel | | Sample | | Pixel | | Sample | |
	Model	AUC	FC	AUC	AP	AUC	FC	AUC	AP	AUC	FC	AUC	AP
PII [25]	U-Net	0.80	0.08	0.44	0.87	0.68	0.00	0.50	0.49	0.50	0.00	0.36	0.39
	MC U-Net	0.76	0.01	0.55	0.90	**0.74**	0.00	0.53	**0.55**	0.59	**0.01**	0.40	0.43
	PHiSeg	0.67	0.00	0.51	0.90	0.41	**0.01**	0.47	0.48	0.43	0.00	**0.52**	**0.50**
Ours P-PII	U-Net	**0.90**	**0.27**	**0.64**	**0.94**	0.74	0.01	**0.56**	0.52	**0.69**	0.01	0.33	0.38
	MC U-Net	**0.90**	0.26	**0.64**	0.93	0.72	**0.01**	0.47	0.49	0.67	**0.01**	0.38	0.41
	PHiSeg	0.76	0.06	0.63	0.93	0.55	**0.01**	0.55	0.51	0.66	**0.01**	0.41	0.44

Table 2. Sensitivity analysis of augmentation functions for small-scale datasets on P-PII for JSRT [24]; scaling, combined (rotation $\pm 10°$, elastic deformation, scaling).

| | Model | Augmentation | AUROC | | AP | FROC |
			Pixel	Image	Image	10FPs
Ours P-PII	U-Net	scaling	**0.91**	0.60	0.93	0.27
	MC U-Net	scaling	**0.91**	**0.66**	**0.94**	**0.31**
	U-Net	combined	**0.91**	0.60	0.92	0.30
	MC U-Net	combined	**0.91**	0.59	0.93	0.25

results for large datasets. These issues need to be approached in further studies. Considering the number of false positive predicted regions, we would require expert analysis if those regions are correlated with real aberrations in the input images. For now, we can only interpret them as visually perceived abnormal regions in the input images, *e.g.*, dense regions in the lung hilum. Compared to the original PII implementation we achieved a shortening of at least half of the training time through the usage of Poisson image editing through discrete sine transformation [3]. This allows us to sample from different source images multiple times for probabilistic representations of anomalies while still being faster than the baseline.

4   Conclusion

We analyse the proposed self-supervised learning method, P-PPI, on multiple three backbone models and three small- and large-scale datasets from the medical imaging domain. We exploit the influence of augmentation functions for the self-supervision task and present probabilistic anomalies, which are described for the first time for applications in OOD detection. Our investigations highlight previous limitations when using Poisson image interpolation for the generation of synthetic anomalies. We improve pixel-wise AUROC by up to 18% and sample-wise AUROC by up to 45% in comparison to baseline methods.

Additionally, we enhanced the pixel-wise sensitivity to 10 avg. FPs up to 38%. We also show that it is possible to learn feature distributions for normal tissue in a self-supervised way from databases that exclusively contain patients with the disease (DeepLesion and LIDC-IDRI). In future work, the integration of the generated variance maps into the loss function has a high potential for pushing unsupervised probabilistic learning further towards integration into clinical workflows.

Acknowledgements. The authors gratefully acknowledge the scientific support and HPC resources provided by the Erlangen National High Performance Computing Center (NHR@FAU) of the Friedrich-Alexander-Universität Erlangen-Nürnberg (FAU) under the NHR projects b143dc and b180dc. NHR funding is provided by federal and Bavarian state authorities. NHR@FAU hardware is partially funded by the German Research Foundation (DFG) - 440719683. Additional support was also received by the ERC - project MIA-NORMAL 101083647, DFG KA 5801/2-1, INST 90/1351-1 and by the state of Bavaria.

References

1. Akcay, S., Atapour-Abarghouei, A., Breckon, T.P.: GANomaly: semi-supervised anomaly detection via adversarial training. In: Jawahar, C.V., Li, H., Mori, G., Schindler, K. (eds.) ACCV 2018. LNCS, vol. 11363, pp. 622–637. Springer, Cham (2019). https://doi.org/10.1007/978-3-030-20893-6_39

2. Armato, S.G., III., et al.: The lung image database consortium (LIDC) and image database resource initiative (IDRI): a completed reference database of lung nodules on CT scans. Med. Phys. **38**(2), 915–931 (2011)

3. Baugh, M.: PIE-torch. www.github.com/matt-baugh/pytorch-poisson-image-editing

4. Baumgartner, C.F., et al.: PHiSeg: capturing uncertainty in medical image segmentation. In: Shen, D., et al. (eds.) MICCAI 2019. LNCS, vol. 11765, pp. 119–127. Springer, Cham (2019). https://doi.org/10.1007/978-3-030-32245-8_14

5. Baur, C., Wiestler, B., Albarqouni, S., Navab, N.: Bayesian skip-autoencoders for unsupervised hyperintense anomaly detection in high resolution brain MRI. In: 2020 IEEE 17th International Symposium on Biomedical Imaging (ISBI), pp. 1905–1909. IEEE (2020)

6. Cao, T., Huang, C.W., Hui, D.Y.T., Cohen, J.P.: A benchmark of medical out of distribution detection. arXiv preprint arXiv:2007.04250 (2020)

7. Chen, X., Pawlowski, N., Rajchl, M., Glocker, B., Konukoglu, E.: Deep generative models in the real-world: an open challenge from medical imaging. arXiv preprint arXiv:1806.05452 (2018)

8. Fang, Z., Li, Y., Lu, J., Dong, J., Han, B., Liu, F.: Is out-of-distribution detection learnable? arXiv preprint arXiv:2210.14707 (2022)

9. Guan, S., Loew, M.: Breast cancer detection using synthetic mammograms from generative adversarial networks in convolutional neural networks. J. Med. Imaging **6**(3), 031411 (2019)

10. Guo, X., Gichoya, J.W., Purkayastha, S., Banerjee, I.: CVAD: a generic medical anomaly detector based on cascade VAE. arXiv preprint arXiv:2110.15811 (2021)

11. Han, C., et al.: Synthesizing diverse lung nodules wherever massively: 3D multiconditional GAN-based CT image augmentation for object detection. In: 2019 International Conference on 3D Vision (3DV), pp. 729–737. IEEE (2019)
12. Henaff, O.: Data-efficient image recognition with contrastive predictive coding. In: International Conference on Machine Learning, pp. 4182–4192. PMLR (2020)
13. Hendrycks, D., Mazeika, M., Kadavath, S., Song, D.: Using self-supervised learning can improve model robustness and uncertainty. arXiv preprint arXiv:1906.12340 (2019)
14. Johnson, A., et al.: MIMIC-CXR-JPG-chest radiographs with structured labels (2019)
15. Li, C.L., Sohn, K., Yoon, J., Pfister, T.: CutPaste: self-supervised learning for anomaly detection and localization. In: Proceedings of the IEEE/CVF Conference on Computer Vision and Pattern Recognition, pp. 9664–9674 (2021)
16. Li, X., Lu, Y., Desrosiers, C., Liu, X.: Out-of-distribution detection for skin lesion images with deep isolation forest. In: Liu, M., Yan, P., Lian, C., Cao, X. (eds.) MLMI 2020. LNCS, vol. 12436, pp. 91–100. Springer, Cham (2020). https://doi.org/10.1007/978-3-030-59861-7_10
17. Liang, S., Li, Y., Srikant, R.: Enhancing the reliability of out-of-distribution image detection in neural networks. arXiv preprint arXiv:1706.02690 (2017)
18. Mohseni, S., Pitale, M., Yadawa, J., Wang, Z.: Self-supervised learning for generalizable out-of-distribution detection. In: Proceedings of the AAAI Conference on Artificial Intelligence, vol. 34, pp. 5216–5223 (2020)
19. Nakao, T., Hanaoka, S., Nomura, Y., Hayashi, N., Abe, O.: Anomaly detection in chest 18F-FDG PET/CT by Bayesian deep learning. Japan. J. Radiol., 1–10 (2022)
20. Pawlowski, N., et al.: Unsupervised lesion detection in brain CT using Bayesian convolutional autoencoders (2018)
21. Schlegl, T., Seeböck, P., Waldstein, S.M., Langs, G., Schmidt-Erfurth, U.: f-AnoGAN: fast unsupervised anomaly detection with generative adversarial networks. Med. Image Anal. **54**, 30–44 (2019)
22. Schlüter, H.M., Tan, J., Hou, B., Kainz, B.: Self-supervised out-of-distribution detection and localization with natural synthetic anomalies (NSA). arXiv preprint arXiv:2109.15222 (2021)
23. Seeböck, P., et al.: Exploiting epistemic uncertainty of anatomy segmentation for anomaly detection in retinal oct. IEEE Trans. Med. Imaging **39**(1), 87–98 (2019)
24. Shiraishi, J., et al.: Development of a digital image database for chest radiographs with and without a lung nodule: receiver operating characteristic analysis of radiologists' detection of pulmonary nodules. Am. J. Roentgenol. **174**(1), 71–74 (2000)
25. Tan, J., Hou, B., Batten, J., Qiu, H., Kainz, B.: Detecting outliers with foreign patch interpolation. arXiv preprint arXiv:2011.04197 (2020)
26. Tan, J., Hou, B., Day, T., Simpson, J., Rueckert, D., Kainz, B.: Detecting outliers with poisson image interpolation. In: de Bruijne, M., et al. (eds.) MICCAI 2021. LNCS, vol. 12905, pp. 581–591. Springer, Cham (2021). https://doi.org/10.1007/978-3-030-87240-3_56
27. Tschuchnig, M.E., Gadermayr, M.: Anomaly detection in medical imaging-a mini review. Data Sci.-Anal. Appl., 33–38 (2022)
28. Venkatakrishnan, A.R., Kim, S.T., Eisawy, R., Pfister, F., Navab, N.: Self-supervised out-of-distribution detection in brain CT scans. arXiv preprint arXiv:2011.05428 (2020)
29. Wolleb, J., Bieder, F., Sandkühler, R., Cattin, P.C.: Diffusion models for medical anomaly detection. arXiv preprint arXiv:2203.04306 (2022)

30. Yan, K., Wang, X., Lu, L., Summers, R.M.: DeepLesion: automated mining of large-scale lesion annotations and universal lesion detection with deep learning. J. Med. Imaging **5**(3), 036501 (2018)
31. Zenati, H., Foo, C.S., Lecouat, B., Manek, G., Chandrasekhar, V.R.: Efficient GAN-based anomaly detection. arXiv preprint arXiv:1802.06222 (2018)
32. Zhao, H., et al.: Anomaly detection for medical images using self-supervised and translation-consistent features. IEEE Trans. Med. Imaging **40**(12), 3641–3651 (2021)
33. Zhou, L., Deng, W., Wu, X.: Unsupervised anomaly localization using VAE and beta-VAE. arXiv preprint arXiv:2005.10686 (2020)

Uncertainty Estimation in Liver Tumor Segmentation Using the Posterior Bootstrap

Shishuai Wang[1]([⊠])[iD], Johan Nuyts[2][iD], and Marina Filipovic[2][iD]

[1] Faculty of Medicine, KU Leuven, Leuven, Belgium
shishuai.wang@student.kuleuven.be
[2] MIRC, Department of Imaging and Pathology, Nuclear Medicine and Molecular Imaging, KU Leuven, Leuven, Belgium

Abstract. Deep learning-based medical image segmentation is widely used and has achieved the state-of-the-art segmentation performance, in which nnU-Net is a particularly successful pipeline due to its pre-processing and auto-configuration features. However, the output predicted probabilities from neural networks are generally not properly calibrated and don't necessarily indicate segmentation errors, which are problematic for clinical use. Bayesian deep learning is a promising way to address these problems by improving the probability calibration and error localisation ability. In this paper, we proposed a novel Bayesian approach based on posterior bootstrap theory to sample the neural network parameters from a posterior distribution. Based on nnU-Net, we implemented our method and other Bayesian approaches, and evaluated their uncertainty estimation quality. The results show that the proposed posterior bootstrap method provides improvement on uncertainty estimation with equivalent segmentation performance. The proposed method is easy to implement, compatible with any deep learning-based image segmentation pipeline, and doesn't require additional hyper-parameter tuning, enabling it to totally preserve nnU-Net's auto-configuration feature.

Keywords: Bayesian deep learning · Uncertainty estimation · nnU-Net · Image segmentation

1 Introduction

Semantic image segmentation is an essential part of medical image analysis. While manual delineation is the gold standard, it is expensive, tedious, and suffers from inter-operator variability and inconsistency between slices of 3D images. With the development of deep neural networks and the increasing amount of annotated data, deep learning-based segmentation has been popularised and become the state-of-the-art technique in some applications. Particularly, based on the idea that the bottleneck to further improve neural network's performance depends much more on its configuration and data pre-processing rather than on the modification of its architecture, nnU-Net was proposed [9]. It implements an

© The Author(s), under exclusive license to Springer Nature Switzerland AG 2023
C. H. Sudre et al. (Eds.): UNSURE 2023, LNCS 14291, pp. 188–197, 2023.
https://doi.org/10.1007/978-3-031-44336-7_19

automated pre-processing, configuration and training pipeline, without modifying the U-Net architecture [16] and without manual tuning. It was reported to have superior or similar segmentation performance compared to its counterparts designed for specific applications in various tasks. However, there are still concerns about the robustness of deep learning tools and their use in large-scale and diverse medical data [2]. The heterogeneity of data due to different modalities, artifacts and tissue properties lead to silent failure of the segmentation results, especially in difficult tasks. Estimating and taking into account different sources of uncertainty is a promising approach for addressing this problem.

In deep learning-based segmentation tools, the *Softmax* or similar output is commonly used as a proxy for the pixel-wise categorical probability distribution of a pixel belonging to a certain class. However, in practice, the output probabilities are not well calibrated in general [8] and their interpretation remains difficult (e.g. sources of uncertainty). In addition, the usual training procedure produces only a single set of values for neural network parameters. Hence, the epistemic uncertainty (due to network parameter values) is not taken into account. Bayesian approaches aim at estimating and taking into account the epistemic uncertainty using a posterior distribution of network parameters, given the training data and the architecture. They may also improve the calibration of the segmentation network outputs [18]. The estimated high-uncertain regions could also be used to guide the manual correction or to improve the network segmentation performance.

Multiple Bayesian approaches have been proposed. Variational inference (VI) aims to approximate the analytical form of a posterior distribution of neural network parameters [3]. By keeping dropout layers active during prediction, Monte-Carlo dropout [7] allows the use of a unique model at each prediction, which can be viewed as a sample from a posterior distribution. Deep ensemble [11,15] uses the average over the predictions from several neural networks that are different in architecture and separately trained. Time-checkpoint ensemble [19] samples neural network's parameters from a posterior distribution at specific epochs and makes the final prediction by averaging the sampled models predictions.

In this paper, we propose a novel Bayesian approach by applying the posterior bootstrap method [5,6,12,14] to the liver tumor segmentation from contrast-enhanced CT images. The method draws realisations from a posterior distribution of network parameters by repeating the training with a differently weighted loss per subject, where the random weights are drawn from a chosen Dirichlet process. Predictions from all the sampled models are averaged to produce the final softmax output (segmentation and uncertainty estimation). The implementation is easy and can be integrated with any deep learning segmentation pipeline, without modifying the architecture or the type of loss function.

We apply the proposed posterior bootstrap method, as well as Monte-Carlo dropout and time-checkpoint ensemble, within the nnU-Net framework to make use of its successful pre-processing pipeline. Then we evaluate their performance in terms of both segmentation accuracy and quality of uncertainty estimation.

2 Theory

Assume the images $x_{1:N}$ in the training dataset are observed realisations from an unknown distribution F_0, i.e., $x_{1:N} \overset{iid}{\sim} F_0$. A set of neural network parameters can be trained by using the following optimisation process

$$\hat{w}\,(F_0) = \arg\min_{w} \int l(y, x, w) dF_0(x) \tag{1}$$

where w denotes the neural network parameters, d is the differential symbol, F_0 is the probability distribution of the images, x is the input image, y is the ground truth label, and $l(y, x, w)$ is the loss function that can be freely chosen [6]. A single set of parameters $\hat{w}_i$ can be estimated using a sample from F_0. We would like instead to estimate a posterior distribution of $\hat{w}$. For this, we can put a prior on F_0. As we are not ready to specify an actual prior on the distribution of (here liver CT) images yet, we chose a non-informative prior. It conveys no prior information and the sampling from the posterior distribution of $\hat{w}$ becomes simplified, as described in [6].

First, we draw a set of weighting factors b_i and then we optimise the randomised loss function as Eq. 2 shows.

$$\hat{w}_i = \arg\min_{w} \sum_{j=1}^{N} b_{ij} l\,(y_j, x_j, w) \tag{2}$$

where i indexes the realisations (i.e. neural network parameter values) from the posterior distribution, j indexes the subjects in the training dataset, and N is the total number of subjects in the training dataset. Within one training, say, the ith training, b_i is one set of weighting factors (with length N) used only for this training, and $l\,(y_j, x_j, w)$ is the loss computed on each subject.

We can draw b_i for suitably enough times, and optimise the corresponding randomised loss functions to acquire a larger sample of realisations $\hat{w}_i$. The latter corresponds to a distribution of neural network parameters which is posterior with respect to a prior on the data distribution (here the distribution of relevant CT images). The weighting factors b_i can encapsulate our prior knowledge about the data distribution. For the initial tests, we choose a special case, providing a non-informative prior (no prior information) over the data distribution, $b_i \sim$ Dirichlet$(1, ..., 1)$. This is equivalent to applying the Bayesian bootstrap [17] to the data, and then training the network parameters. The sampled distribution can also be seen as an approximation of a posterior distribution with respect to a prior on the network parameters, which prior can be defined by the chosen random weighting factors distribution.

The loss function can be defined using any target criterion. In nnU-Net the default loss function is the sum of Dice loss and cross-entropy loss [4]. Note that we don't change the way to calculate the loss for each individual subject or each batch, but only change the contribution of each subject by weighting it using b_{ij}. The procedure is scalable with respect to the number of posterior realisations and it is trivially parallelisable.

3   Methods

3.1   Experiment Setup

The liver and tumour segmentation task from the challange dataset Medical Segmentation Decathlon (MSD) [1] was used for training and evaluation. It contains 131 3D contrast-enhanced CT images with ground truth labels acquired from patients with primary or metastatic liver cancer. We randomly selected 15 images as test dataset while the remaining 116 images were used for training and validation.

Two existing Bayesian methods (Monte-Carlo dropout and time-checkpoint ensemble) and the proposed posterior bootstrap method were implemented on top of nnU-Net. We strived to minimise the changes to the original nnU-Net, in order to preserve its excellent features. Deep ensemble approach was not implemented in this work because it would imply modifying the optimised nnU-Net pipeline and potentially compromising the segmentation performance. We monitored the segmentation performance through Dice coefficient to make sure that after implementing Bayesian approaches the segmentation performance is not affected.

Uncertainty was quantified using the binary (tumor vs not tumor) Shannon entropy computed from the *Softmax* output. For the baseline nnU-Net, the single *Softmax* output was used for uncertainty estimation and for the segmentation prediction. For Bayesian methods, the average of the sampled posterior predictive *Softmax* outputs was used for uncertainty estimation and for the final segmentation prediction. The implementation details are:

1) **Baseline:** nnU-Net with default settings (1000 epochs, polynominal learning rate, loss function of the sum of cross-entropy loss and Dice loss, deep supervision).

2) **Monte-Carlo Dropout (MCD):** Several dropout rates in the range $[0.05, 0.4]$ were tested and 0.1 was empirically selected as a trade-off between slower convergence and better exploration of the posterior distribution. As the training took a longer time to converge, we used 2000 epochs in total aiming to achieve the same global Dice as baseline. We saved the model at $epoch = 1000$ and $epoch = 2000$, denoted as *MCD-1000* and *MCD-2000* respectively. For each subject in the test dataset, 15 predictions were made.

3) **Time-checkpoint Ensemble (TimeChk):** We used the same parameters within the learning rate scheme as those in [19], except that we increased the number of epochs per period to 1000 (3 periods in total). The interval of sampling was set to 10 epochs. In total 15 models were sampled from epoch 955 to 995, 1955 to 1995 and 2955 to 2995, which are in the constant-learning-rate region. Each model was used to produce a prediction.

4) **Posterior Bootstrap (PB-15):** The configuration of the nnU-Net was the same as for the baseline except that we added the random weighting factors in the loss function. We thus trained 15 models with different weights to generate 15 realisations from a posterior distribution of network parameters. Each model was used to produce a prediction.

The network parameters were randomly initialized using the same seed for all the training tasks.

3.2 Evaluation Metrics

The performance of uncertainty estimation was evaluated for all the approaches using a modified version of Expected Calibration Error (ECE) [13] and the Uncertainty-Error overlap (U-E overlap) [10]. These metrics were firstly computed on the dataset level, in which all voxels from all subjects in the test dataset were considered together. The same metrics were also computed on each test subject separately, which emphasises the per subject uncertainty and may be more related to the application in real practice.

In the case of large imbalance between tumor and background volumes, ECE may be dominated by the background area. Hence, we constructed a global mask including tumor areas (both ground truth and predicted) and used it to exclude a large irrelevant part of the background. ECE ranges from 0 to 1 and we reported it in percentage. Lower ECE means better probability calibration.

U-E overlap ranges from 0 to 1. A higher U-E overlap means better ability to localise errors. Although other thresholds for calculating high-uncertain region may also be relevant and may achieve a higher U-E overlap, we chose 0.5 as the threshold for all subjects and methods for consistency.

4 Results

4.1 Dataset Level

Dataset level evaluation is shown in Table 1. All methods achieved a similar global Dice coefficient, in which *Baseline* has the lowest global Dice coefficient 0.811 and *PB-15* has the highest global Dice coefficient 0.824. *MCD-1000* achieved the best global ECE 2.08%, and the proposed method *PB-15* has the second best global ECE 2.35%. All Bayesian approaches provide a lower global ECE than *Baseline* (3.58%). *PB-15* has the highest global U-E overlap 0.463, while the other 3 Bayesian approaches are not able to exceed *Baseline* (0.458).

Table 1. Dataset Level Metrics

	Global Dice	Global ECE (%)	Global U-E Overlap
Baseline	0.811	3.58	0.458
MCD-1000	0.818	**2.08**	0.452
MCD-2000	0.822	2.85	0.448
TimeChk	0.817	2.44	0.419
PB-15	0.824	2.35	**0.463**

4.2   Subject Level

The average values of subject level evaluation are shown in Table 2. The segmentation performance is comparable in average, with the Bayesian methods having a slightly lower average subject level Dice coefficient compared to the *Baseline*. An exception is the *MCD-1000* method which achieves a much lower average Dice coefficient. The proposed method *PB-15* achieves the best average ECE 8.78%. Other Bayesian approaches also achieved a better average ECE compared with *Baseline* (average ECE 9.72%) except *MCD-1000* (average ECE 10.23%). Our method also achieves the best average U-E overlap 0.408, while the other 3 Bayesian approaches can't outperform *Baseline* (average U-E overlap 0.390).

Table 2. Subject Level Metrics

	Average Dice	Average ECE (%)	Average U-E Overlap
Baseline	0.727	9.72	0.390
MCD-1000	0.641	10.23	0.333
MCD-2000	0.709	9.53	0.380
TimeChk	0.703	9.03	0.373
PB-15	0.718	**8.78**	**0.408**

Distribution of evaluation metrics over test subjects is shown in Fig. 1. Our method achieves a relatively narrower spread of ECE and U-E overlap, showing its ability to deal with various situations (e.g. different tumor size).

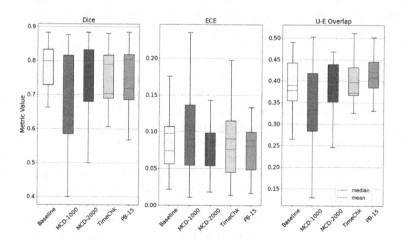

Fig. 1. Distribution of subject level metrics

4.3 Visual Evaluation

Figure 2 (a) shows a case with slight segmentation errors, where all methods have comparable error-localisation performance. The segmentation errors around the largest tumor as well as other smaller tumors are highlighted by the uncertain region. Figure 2 (b) shows a case in which all the methods make severe errors as they predict a tumor that doesn't exist. High uncertain regions produced by *Baseline* and *MCD-2000* overlap poorly with the error inside the falsely predicted tumor. *TimeChk* makes least mistakes but produces the broadest high-uncertain regions. For *MCD-1000* and *PB-15* the high-uncertain regions indicate well the segmentation errors. The proposed method shows the best visual overlap between the segmentation errors and the high-uncertainty regions, both for the edge of main part and for the missed part in the peripheral region.

5   Discussion

On the contrary to other implemented Bayesian methods, posterior bootstrap doesn't involve any hyper-parameter tuning, but it implies a choice for the data prior, for which a non-informative prior is initially selected. Monte-Carlo dropout requires the choice of the dropout rate, which in our case showed to be a trade-off between slower convergence (higher dropout rate) and slower exploration of the posterior distribution (lower dropout rates). Time-checkpoint ensemble relies on its cyclical learning rate scheme, hence a careful learning rate design based on the given dataset properties is required, which may compromise the auto-configuration feature of nnU-Net. In our implementation, the fact that the optimal hyper-parameter values may not have been achieved could be one reason why the other Bayesian approaches failed to outperform the baseline nnU-Net in terms of U-E overlap, though it outperformed it in terms of ECE. Admittedly, the currently implemented non-informative prior is merely the simplest case. We suppose that informative prior is promising to further improve the performance and is still compatible with nnU-Net as well as any other image segmentation pipelines.

The proposed method is scalable: the computations (i.e. training multiple models) can be done in parallel without any adjustments, and more computations should lead to improvement in results. In the training stage, it is more computationally expensive compared to other Bayesian approaches, which generally need only one training. The time required for inference is comparable with that of the other Bayesian approaches.

At the current stage, improvements in uncertainty estimation quality made by using Bayesian approaches can only be reflected by a relatively small change of the selected metrics. However, it is also the case in other studies focusing on tumor [10] or other tissue type [19]. Several confounding factors should be noticed. Firstly, we used 0.5 as the threshold to calculate high-uncertain region, which doesn't necessarily produce the highest U-E overlap for all subjects. Secondly, as we can see from some cases (e.g. on the edge of the largest tumor in Fig. 2 (a)), a very small error region could be entirely encompassed by a large

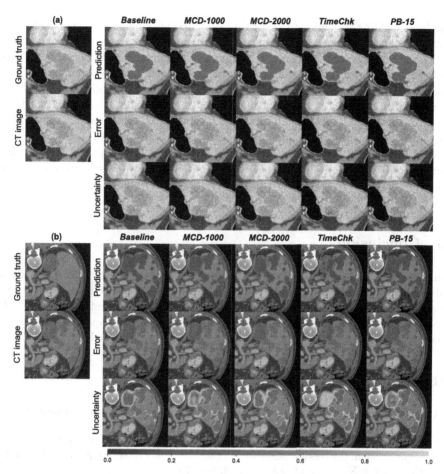

Fig. 2. Visual evaluation for (a) a case with slight segmentation errors, (b) a case with severe segmentation errors

high-uncertain region. In this situation, the U-E overlap is lower by its definition, but the high-uncertain region can still provide useful error localisation. Furthermore, ideally, we would like to have the exact same predicted label from all methods, so that we can attribute the improvement of uncertainty estimation entirely to the corresponding Bayesian method itself. However, in practice it is not achievable. Although Dice coefficients show a comparable segmentation performance, we cannot totally exclude that the slightly better segmentation performance may contribute to the improvement of uncertainty estimation.

Future work will produce more network parameters realisations using a larger test dataset and cross-validation to mitigate the influence of these confounding factors. Besides, here we mainly consider epistemic uncertainty due to the choice of network parameter values for a given deep learning segmentation framework, without tackling the sources of miscalibration and without exploring other frameworks, which could also be the subject of future work.

The error localisation ability is especially useful when high segmentation accuracy is needed, e.g. in tumor segmentation. Although the proposed method doesn't necessarily provide better uncertainty estimation quality for each individual subject, it does provide some improvement on the dataset level metrics and on the statistics of the subject level metrics. The estimated high-uncertain region could be used to guide the manual correction. We can also encode the spatial information of high-uncertain region, where the segmentation is usually error-prone, in the loss function, forcing the neural network to learn more from this region. In this way, the neural network's performance could be boosted especially for the challenging regions.

6   Conclusion

In this work, we proposed a novel posterior bootstrap method as a Bayesian approach for better uncertainty estimation. The results show that our method mostly outperforms the baseline as well as other Bayesian counterparts. Though computationally expensive, the proposed method is easy to implement and compatible with any deep learning-based image segmentation pipeline.

References

1. Antonelli, M., et al.: The medical segmentation decathlon. Nat. Commun. **13**(1), 4128 (2022)
2. Bakas, S., et al.: Identifying the best machine learning algorithms for brain tumor segmentation, progression assessment, and overall survival prediction in the brats challenge. arXiv preprint arXiv:1811.02629 (2018)
3. Blei, D.M., Kucukelbir, A., McAuliffe, J.D.: Variational inference: a review for statisticians. J. Am. Stat. Assoc. **112**(518), 859–877 (2017)
4. Drozdzal, M., Vorontsov, E., Chartrand, G., Kadoury, S., Pal, C.: The importance of skip connections in biomedical image segmentation. In: Carneiro, G., et al. (eds.) LABELS/DLMIA -2016. LNCS, vol. 10008, pp. 179–187. Springer, Cham (2016). https://doi.org/10.1007/978-3-319-46976-8_19
5. Filipović, M., Dautremer, T., Comtat, C., Stute, S., Barat, É.: Reconstruction, analysis and interpretation of posterior probability distributions of PET images, using the posterior bootstrap. Phys. Med. Biol. **66**(12), 125018 (2021)
6. Fong, E., Lyddon, S., Holmes, C.: Scalable nonparametric sampling from multimodal posteriors with the posterior bootstrap. In: Chaudhuri, K., Salakhutdinov, R. (eds.) Proceedings of the 36th International Conference on Machine Learning. Proceedings of Machine Learning Research, vol. 97, pp. 1952–1962. PMLR (2019)
7. Gal, Y., Ghahramani, Z.: Dropout as a Bayesian approximation: representing model uncertainty in deep learning. In: Proceedings of the 33rd International Conference on International Conference on Machine Learning, vol. 48, pp. 1050–1059. ICML'16, JMLR.org (2016)

8. Guo, C., Pleiss, G., Sun, Y., Weinberger, K.Q.: On calibration of modern neural networks. In: Proceedings of the 34th International Conference on Machine Learning, vol. 70, pp. 1321–1330. ICML'17, JMLR.org (2017)

9. Isensee, F., Jaeger, P.F., Kohl, S.A.A., Petersen, J., Maier-Hein, K.H.: nnU-Net: a self-configuring method for deep learning-based biomedical image segmentation. Nat. Methods **18**(2), 203–211 (2021)

10. Jungo, A., Balsiger, F., Reyes, M.: Analyzing the quality and challenges of uncertainty estimations for brain tumor segmentation. Front. Neurosci. **14**, 282 (2020)

11. Lakshminarayanan, B., Pritzel, A., Blundell, C.: Simple and scalable predictive uncertainty estimation using deep ensembles. In: Proceedings of the 31st International Conference on Neural Information Processing Systems, pp. 6405–6416. NIPS'17, Curran Associates Inc., Red Hook, NY, USA (2017)

12. Lyddon, S., Walker, S., Holmes, C.: Nonparametric learning from Bayesian models with randomized objective functions. In: Proceedings of the 32nd International Conference on Neural Information Processing Systems, pp. 2075–2085. NIPS'18, Curran Associates Inc., Red Hook, NY, USA (2018)

13. Naeini, M.P., Cooper, G.F., Hauskrecht, M.: Obtaining well calibrated probabilities using Bayesian binning. Proc. AAAI Conf. Artif. Intell. **2015**, 2901–2907 (2015)

14. Newton, M.A., Polson, N.G., Xu, J.: Weighted Bayesian bootstrap for scalable posterior distributions. Can. J. Stat. **49**(2), 421–437 (2021)

15. Ovadia, Y., et al.: Can you trust your model's uncertainty? Evaluating predictive uncertainty under dataset shift. In: Proceedings of the 33rd International Conference on Neural Information Processing Systems, pp. 14003–14014. Curran Associates Inc. (2019)

16. Ronneberger, O., Fischer, P., Brox, T.: U-Net: convolutional networks for biomedical image segmentation. In: Navab, N., Hornegger, J., Wells, W.M., Frangi, A.F. (eds.) MICCAI 2015. LNCS, vol. 9351, pp. 234–241. Springer, Cham (2015). https://doi.org/10.1007/978-3-319-24574-4_28

17. Rubin, D.B.: The Bayesian bootstrap. Ann. Stat. **9**(1), 130–134 (1981)

18. Wilson, A.G., Izmailov, P.: Bayesian deep learning and a probabilistic perspective of generalization. In: Larochelle, H., Ranzato, M., Hadsell, R., Balcan, M., Lin, H. (eds.) Advances in Neural Information Processing Systems, vol. 33, pp. 4697–4708. Curran Associates, Inc. (2020)

19. Zhao, Y., Yang, C., Schweidtmann, A., Tao, Q.: Efficient Bayesian uncertainty estimation for nnU-Net. In: Wang, L., Dou, Q., Fletcher, P.T., Speidel, S., Li, S. (eds.) Medical Image Computing and Computer Assisted Intervention - MICCAI 2022, pp. 535–544. Springer Nature Switzerland, Cham (2022). https://doi.org/10.1007/978-3-031-16452-1_51

Pitfalls of Conformal Predictions
for Medical Image Classification

Hendrik Mehrtens, Tabea Bucher, and Titus J. Brinker

Deutsches Krebsforschungszentrum (DKFZ), 69120 Heidelberg, Germany
{hendrikalexander.mehrtens,tabea.bucher}@dkfz-heidelberg.de,
titus.brinker@nct-heidelberg.de

Abstract. Reliable uncertainty estimation is one of the major challenges for medical classification tasks. While many approaches have been proposed, recently the statistical framework of conformal predictions has gained a lot of attention, due to its ability to provide provable calibration guarantees. Nonetheless, the application of conformal predictions in safety-critical areas such as medicine comes with pitfalls, limitations and assumptions that practitioners need to be aware of. We demonstrate through examples from dermatology and histopathology that conformal predictions are unreliable under distributional shifts in input and label variables. Additionally, conformal predictions should not be used for selecting predictions to improve accuracy and are not reliable for subsets of the data, such as individual classes or patient attributes. Moreover, in classification settings with a small number of classes, which are common in medical image classification tasks, conformal predictions have limited practical value.

Keywords: Conformal Predictions · Uncertainty Estimation

1 Introduction

In recent years, deep learning has gained popularity in the medical domain. Nonetheless, the adaptation into clinical practice remains low, as current machine learning approaches based on deep neural networks are not able to provide reliable uncertainty estimates [1–3], which however are a necessary condition for the safe and reliable operation in and admission to clinical practice.

Over the last years many publications in the machine learning literature have been focused on estimating the predictive uncertainty of machine learning models using a plethora of approaches, however, recent publications [4,5] have shown that these methods do not consistently outperform the baseline of the confidence value of a single neural network when evaluated over a range of tasks. Moreover, these approaches are heuristic and lack calibration *guarantees*, which are essential in high-risk environments like medical classification.

Conformal Predictions (CP) [6] have emerged as a promising framework for estimating uncertainty in neural network predictions, as they can provide a

C. H. Sudre et al. (Eds.): UNSURE 2023, LNCS 14291, pp. 198–207, 2023.
https://doi.org/10.1007/978-3-031-44336-7_20

guaranteed level of true label coverage by constructing sets of predicted classes instead of single point predictions with uncertainty values, whereby larger sets indicate higher uncertainty. In this publication, we explore the viability and limitations of CP for medical image classification, where it has been used before, e.g. [7–11], addressing common misconceptions and pitfalls, underpinning our observations with experiments conducted in histopathological tissue and dermatological skin classification tasks. While some of these limitations are well-known in the CP literature, e.g. [9,12], the intend of this publication is to serve as a comprehensive guide for future practitioners that might aspire to use or learn about conformal predictions for their own work in medical image classification, to avoid misconceptions and pitfalls, that we encountered ourselves, in discussions with colleagues and found in applications in the literature.

After briefly introducing the concept of CP, we focus on the guarantees offered by conformal predictions and the challenges they pose in medical scenarios, particularly in dealing with domain shifts. Another challenge is maintaining coverage guarantees under shifts in the label distribution, which are harder to control and observe compared to changes in the input domain. We discuss the distinction between marginal and conditional coverage and its consequences for the coverage of predictive set sizes, coverage of individual classes, and other data subgroups. In this context, we also explore the connection between conformal predictions and selective classification [13] and why CP are insufficient for this task. Finally, we discuss the applicability and limitations of conformal predictions for medical image classifications, as here often tasks are considered that only have few classes or are even binary, for example, classification of benign and malignant tissue samples or the detection of a disease.

2   Conformal Predictions

Conformal predictions (CP) [6] is a low assumption posthoc calibration approach for probabilistic classification models. Given a classifier $\hat{Y}$, that was already optimized on a training dataset D_{train}, and a calibration dataset D_{cal}, CP forms a set of classes $C(\hat{Y}(x_i))$ out of the predictions of the model $\hat{Y}(x_i)$, so that

$$\mathbb{P}_{(x_i,y_i)\in D_{test}}(y_i \in C(\hat{Y}(x_i))) \geq 1 - \alpha , \tag{1}$$

which is called the marginal coverage guarantee, where $1 - \alpha$ is the desired coverage and the set-valued function C is found on the calibration set.

Conformal predictions make no assumptions on the model or the data but only necessitate the property of exchangeability between the datasets D_{cal} and D_{test}. The set-valued function C that forms predictive sets over the output of the classifier $\hat{Y}$ is found on the held out calibration data set D_{cal} using a nonparametric quantile-based algorithm. Given the exchangeability of both data collections, the properties of this function then also hold for the test data set.

Various approaches exist for forming the prediction sets using different conformity scores. In our experiments, we employ the adaptive prediction sets (APS) formulation [14], previously used in image classification [15]. While these approaches may employ different conformity scores to construct the predictive sets $C(\hat{Y}(x_i))$, they share the common goal of taking an initially uncalibrated uncertainty estimate from the trained classifier $\hat{Y}$ and finding a set of classes for each prediction that satisfies the expected marginal coverage guarantee based on the classifier's behavior on the calibration dataset and are by that nature susceptible to the in the following discussed pitfalls and limitations.

3   Conformal Prediction for Histopathology and Dermatology

To showcase our observations we first trained five ResNet-34 [16] on two medical image classification datasets each: HAM10K [17] for multi-class skin-lesion classification and CAMELYON17 [18] for histopathological whole-slide image (WSI) classification. The HAM10K dataset consists of seven skin conditions,

Dataset	CAMELYON17	HAM10K
Num. Classes	2	7
Validation Set	126672	967
Calibration Set	1000	500
Accuracy (ID)	97.56%$_{\pm 0.1}$	77.76%$_{\pm 0.4}$

Table 1. Overview of the used dataset, number of calibration points and the reached in-distribution accuracy over 5 evaluations

while the CAMELYON17 dataset includes 50 WSIs with annotated tumor regions from five different clinics. We preprocessed the WSIs into non-overlapping patches of size 256×256 pixels. Our training setup followed the approach in [5], using the same augmentations and hyperparameters for both datasets. We trained our neural networks on Centers 1, 3, and 5 of the CAMELYON17 dataset and produced predictions for the Centers 2 and 4 for domain-shift experiments. It's important to note that conformal predictions have been previously employed in histopathology [7,8] and dermatology [9]. Our goal with these experiments is to showcase the applicability and limitations of conformal predictions for medical classification tasks, rather than achieving state-of-the-art classification results. We used singular neural networks for uncertainty estimation, as they have been shown to be sufficiently competitive [4,5] to more advanced approaches like Deep Ensembles [19] or Monte-Carlo Dropout [20,21]. Table 1 provides details of the datasets and the achieved accuracies.

We utilized the APS algorithm [14,15] to compute the conformal prediction sets. We used 1000 calibration data points for CAMELYON17 and 500 for HAM10K, randomly sampled from their respective validation datasets, performing 10 calibration set samplings for each trained neural network, averaging the results over calibration sets and the five trained neural network per dataset.

The calibration curves for the APS algorithm are shown in Fig. 1, starting from the accuracy of the respective methods up to 100% coverage. For the CAMELYON17 dataset we show the calibration on the test dataset, but also under domain-shift and label-shift. For the HAM10K dataset, we show the empirical coverage on the test set, but also the coverage of predictions of different conformal set sizes and different classes.

As depicted in the figures, conformal predictions reliably guarantee marginal coverage on the test sets for both the CAMELYON17 and HAM10K datasets. Further results will be discussed in subsequent chapters.

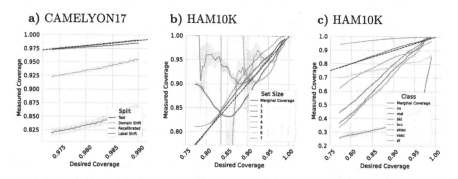

Fig. 1. Coverage of the APS algorithm on two datasets under differing conditions. All curves are averaged over 5 runs and 10 sampled calibration sets. The dotted line shows the ideal calibration. a): Coverage on the CAMELYON17 dataset on the test set and under domain-shift and label distribution shift and after recalibrating on the domain-shifted data b): Coverage of different predictive set sizes on the HAM10K test dataset c): Coverage of different individual classes on the HAM10K test dataset.

4   Guarantees of Conditional and Marginal Coverage

The conformal predictions procedure ensures marginal coverage (Eq. 1), but not conditional coverage $\mathbb{P}_{(x,y) \in D_{test}}(y \in C(\hat{Y}(x))|x) \geq 1-\alpha$. This means that while a conformal algorithm with a $1-\alpha = 90\%$ marginal coverage guarantee provides a predictive set that covers the correct class with 90% probability on average, it does not guarantee this for individual instances or structured subgroups of the data.

For example, in a dermatological classification task with a distribution of 95% white patients and 5% black patients, a 90% coverage guarantee may provide a 92% coverage to white patients, while systematically under-covering black patients with a 62% coverage. Moreover, rare and potentially dangerous classes like melanoma can be under-covered, with frequent ones like skin nevi being over-covered, which is contrary to what should be desired in clinical practice.

Figure 1c shows the coverage of the different classes of the HAM10K dataset. The *nevus* class is over-covered, all other classes, including the *melanoma* class are undercovered, even though the overall coverage guarantee is met.

The literature proposes solutions to address these issues [9,22], but they require separate calibration datasets for each combination of attributes (such as skin color, sex) and each class, which can be challenging for rare conditions or attribute combinations. Gathering such large calibration datasets may be difficult in certain settings, such as MRI or histopathological classification with rare conditions, and could limit the practical applicability of conformal predictions in such cases. Additionally, if such large datasets are available, there is a debate about whether they should be used to improve the classifier instead.

> Marginal coverage is a property over the distribution and does not give guarantees for singular prediction sets.
> Structured subgroups in heterogeneous datasets and imbalanced class-distributions might lead to false confidence in predictive sets.

5   Conformal Predictions Under Domain Shift

The core assumption of conformal predictions is the exchangeability of calibration and test data sets. However, in practical deployments, this assumption might often be violated as validation sets are typically gathered together with the training data, while the deployment data can be encountered later in different contexts, for example in different clinics, with different image-acquisition processes.

Another important pitfall for using conformal predictions, that can be easily overlooked, is to not only address shifts in the domain of the input variable, but also to consider changes in the label distribution, as the exchangeability assumption must hold for both. This pitfall can intuitively be missed by practitioners if the distribution of labels in the deployment domain differs from that of the training data, for example some diseases being more common in certain regions or populations.

We demonstrate both issues in Fig. 1a using experiments conducted on the CAMELYON17 dataset. The coverage guarantees are successfully met when evaluating on the in-distribution test dataset. However, under domain-shift the coverage guarantee is not upheld. We generate an artificial test dataset by resampling the in-distribution dataset with a shifted label distribution. It is evident that the coverage guarantee is violated under these circumstances. This observation is supported by Fig. 1c, which clearly shows that conformal predictions do not provide coverage guarantees for individual subsets of classes, making the coverage guarantee vulnerable to shifts in the class distribution.

Practitioners must ensure that the label distribution does not shift when the algorithm is deployed. If the distribution of labels in the deployment setting is known a-priori, for example through patient records of the past years, the calibration set should be resampled or weighted to match this distribution.

However, it is possible to gather a new representative calibration data set for each domain, which can then be used to recalibrate the model under domain shift.

This procedure is demonstrated in Fig. 1a, where after re-calibrating on a subset of size 1000 of the Camelyon17 domain-shifted images, we again observe the coverage guarantees. As this has to be done for each application domain, this however might be a very large burden, especially combined with the fairness concerns discussed in Sect. 4.

> Conformal predictions guarantees do not hold under distributional-shift of the input variable **or** the label distribution. In this case, re-calibration on a new calibration dataset is required.

6 Conformal Predictions and Selective Classification

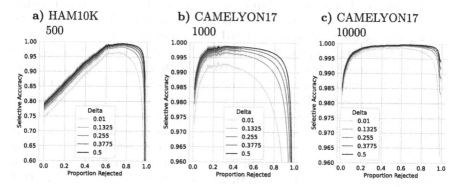

Fig. 2. Selective Accuracy curves, using the approach of [12], on HAM10K with 500 calibration points (left) and CAMELYON17 with 1000 points (middle) and 10000 (right) calibration points. We plot the curves for different values of δ, the failure rate of the algorithm, ranging from 0.01 to 0.5. All curves are averaged over 5 runs.

We have come across several publications [8, 10] that utilize conformal predictions (CP) to enhance the classification accuracy of a classifier by solely using predictive sets of size 1. However, we argue that this is an incorrect application of CP, as it offers no control over the accuracy of predictions in sets of size 1 and cannot guarantee that these predictions will have higher accuracy than the rest of the predictions. While in practice, predictive sets of size 1, which represent the most *certain* predictions of the neural network, often achieve higher accuracy than the rest of the predictions, this is a general property of the underlying uncertainty measurement of the neural network, not the conformal predictions procedure.

Figure 1b illustrates the measured coverage of different predictive set sizes. As can be seen, while the overall coverage is nearly ideally calibrated, the coverage of the individual set sizes can vary significantly, as CP does not guarantee any level of coverage over subsets of the data. As previously expected, the set size 1 predictions are in fact over-covered. However, CP does not offer control over the coverage of this subset or its size and therefore offers no additional value, compared to directly just utilizing the most confident predictions directly.

In recent years multiple publications have shown that neural networks are well capable of selective classification [4,5,13] and as such this framework should be employed when selecting predictions for higher accuracy. With this approach, one can obtain high-probability guarantees for desired accuracy levels, while conformal predictions cannot provide any coverage guarantees for prediction sets of size 1. Angelopoulos et al. [12] provide a statistical framework for selective classification in their worked examples. Their procedure guarantees the following property with a chosen probability $1 - \delta$, where λ is dependent on δ:

$$\mathbb{P}_{(x,y) \in D_{test}}(y = argmax(\hat{Y}(x)) | max(\hat{Y}(x)) \geq \lambda) \geq 1 - \alpha \qquad (2)$$

Contrary to CP, the approach produces point predictions instead of prediction sets and the number of required data points is dependent on the model, dataset, and the distribution of produced uncertainty estimates.

Figure 2 shows this approach for the HAM10K and CAMELYON17 datasets, for different failure probabilities (δ) of the algorithm. The reachable accuracy level and the required number of calibration data points are dependent on the task and the trained model. The lower the tolerated failure rate (δ), the more conservative the estimate of the reached accuracy. After a certain percentage of rejected data points, the guaranteed accuracy of each curve drops, as the distribution of estimated accuracy values becomes too wide, due to too few remaining data points. However, with more calibration data points, higher accuracies are reachable, as can be seen for the CAMELYON17 curve on the right with 10000 calibration images. The CAMELYON17 predictions require far more calibration datapoints to see any increase in estimated accuracy after a 40% rejection rate, which demonstrates the task dependency.

> Conformal predictions can neither guarantee nor control accuracies on the prediction sets of small cardinality. If selective classification is desired, practitioners can use more appropriate frameworks.

7   Classification with Few Classes

Medical classification tasks often only have a limited number of classes, contrary to some natural image classification tasks, for example, the ImageNet classification challenge [23]. Many of these tasks are binary classification tasks, e.g. detecting the presence of tumors or other illnesses, and in others, the classes can be categorized into relevant super-classes, for example, benign and malignant conditions. A binary classification setting is an extreme case for CP, due to the low number of possible uncertainty quantifications as there are only 3 possible prediction sets, both classes individually and the combination of both.

A prediction set encompassing *both* classes, or sets of classes containing benign and malignant classes, can be uninformative to the clinician. Therefore, an algorithm that produces many of these prediction sets, while faithfully ensuring the desired coverage, lacks practical value. With a rising desired level of coverage, the efficiency [12] of the CP algorithm drops, leaving the practitioner only with the most certain predictions, of set size 1, the same situation discussed in Sect. 6.

As an example consider a binary classification case with a desired marginal coverage of 90%. This could be met with (80% correct single predictions, 10% both, 10% false single predictions) or (90% both, 10% false single predictions). Conformal predictions do not provide control over the outcome, and the practical value of each case can vary significantly. Figure 3 that with rising guarantees, the proportion of set size 1 predictions declines. Even though there are seven

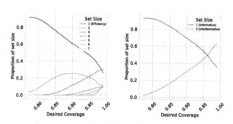

Fig. 3. Efficiency of HAM10K with the seven individual classes (left) and classes mapped to benign and malignant (right).

classes, when the classes are mapped to benign and malignant conditions, which are the most relevant for treatment decisions, most of the predictions are uninformative.

> The practical value of conformal predictions in settings with few classes or categories can be low, due to the coarse resolution of prediction sets.

8   Conclusion

Conformal predictions provide a valuable statistical framework for obtaining guarantees on uncertainty estimates, addressing the otherwise heuristic nature of neural network uncertainty estimates. However, especially in situations encountered in the medical classification context, they have limitations, assumptions, and pitfalls that practitioners should be aware of. In this publication, we have presented an overview of these limitations, pitfalls, and interpretations of conformal predictions guarantees in the context of often situation in medical image classification. Solutions to challenges like fairness, imbalance in class coverage, and domain shifts in input and label space exist but require additional calibration data, which may not always be available in sufficient quantities. Moreover, consideration should be given to whether this additional data would be better utilized for improving the classifier. Additionally, in medical classification tasks with few classes, conformal predictions may have limited practical value. Conformal predictions should not be utilized to perform selective classification, as other, better suited frameworks exist. We hope that this publication will help practitioners navigate potential pitfalls and address common misunderstandings associated with conformal predictions.

Acknowledgements. This publication is funded by the 'Ministerium für Soziales, Gesundheit und Integration', Baden Württemberg, Germany, as part of the 'KI-Translations-Initiative'. Titus Josef Brinker owns a company that develops mobile apps (Smart Health Heidelberg GmbH, Heidelberg, Germany), outside of the scope of the submitted work.

References

1. Begoli, E., Bhattacharya, T., Kusnezov, D.: The need for uncertainty quantification in machine-assisted medical decision making. Nat. Mach. Intell. **1**(1), 20–23 (2019). https://doi.org/10.1038/s42256-018-0004-1

2. Van der Laak, J., Litjens, G., Ciompi, F.: Deep learning in histopathology: the path to the clinic. Nat. Med. **27**(5), 775–784 (2021). https://doi.org/10.1038/s41591-021-01343-4

3. Kompa, B., Snoek, J., Beam, A.L.: Second opinion needed: communicating uncertainty in medical machine learning. NPJ Digit. Med. **4**(1), 4 (2021). https://doi.org/10.1038/S41746-020-00367-3

4. Jaeger, P.F., Lüth, C.T., Klein, L., Bungert, T.J.: A call to reflect on evaluation practices for failure detection in image classification. arXiv preprint arXiv:2211.15259 (2022). https://doi.org/10.48550/arXiv.2211.15259

5. Mehrtens, H.A., Kurz, A., Bucher, T.-C., Brinker, T.J.: Benchmarking common uncertainty estimation methods with histopathological images under domain shift and label noise. Med. Image Anal. (2023). https://doi.org/10.1016/j.media.2023.102914

6. Vovk, V., Gammerman, A., Shafer, G.: Algorithmic Learning in a Random World. Springer, New York (2005). https://doi.org/10.1007/b106715

7. Wieslander, H., et al.: Deep learning with conformal prediction for hierarchical analysis of large-scale whole-slide tissue images. IEEE J. Biomed. Health Inform. **25**(2), 371–380 (2020). https://doi.org/10.1109/JBHI.2020.2996300

8. Olsson, H., et al.: Estimating diagnostic uncertainty in artificial intelligence assisted pathology using conformal prediction. Nat. Commun. **13**(1), 7761 (2022). https://doi.org/10.1038/s41467-022-34945-8

9. Lu, C., Lemay, A., Chang, K., Höbel, K., Kalpathy-Cramer, J.: Fair conformal predictors for applications in medical imaging. In: Proceedings of the AAAI Conference on Artificial Intelligence, pp. 12008–12016 (2022). https://doi.org/10.1609/aaai.v36i11.21459

10. Lu, C., Chang, K., Singh, P., Kalpathy-Cramer, J.: Three applications of conformal prediction for rating breast density in mammography. arXiv preprint arXiv:2206.12008 (2022). https://doi.org/10.48550/ARXIV.2206.12008

11. Lu, C., Angelopoulos, A.N., Pomerantz, S.: Improving trustworthiness of AI disease severity rating in medical imaging with ordinal conformal prediction sets. In: International Conference on Medical Image Computing and Computer-Assisted Intervention, pp. 545–554 (2022). https://doi.org/10.48550/ARXIV.2207.02238

12. Angelopoulos, A.N., Bates, S.: A gentle introduction to conformal prediction and distribution-free uncertainty quantification. arXiv preprint arXiv:2107.07511 (2021)

13. Geifman, Y., El-Yaniv, R.: Selective classification for deep neural networks. In: Advances in Neural Information Processing Systems, vol. 30 (2017)

14. Romano, Y., Sesia, M., Candes, E.: Classification with valid and adaptive coverage. Adv. Neural. Inf. Process. Syst. **33**, 3581–3591 (2020). https://doi.org/10.48550/arXiv.2006.02544

15. Angelopoulos, A., Bates, S., Malik, J., Jordan, M.I.: Uncertainty sets for image classifiers using conformal prediction. arXiv preprint arXiv:2009.14193 (2020). https://doi.org/10.48550/arXiv.2009.14193

16. He, K., Zhang, X., Ren, S., Sun, J.: Deep residual learning for image recognition. In: Proceedings of the IEEE Conference on Computer Vision and Pattern Recognition, pp. 770–778 (2016)

17. Tschandl, P., Rosendahl, C., Kittler, H.: The HAM10000 dataset, a large collection of multi-source dermatoscopic images of common pigmented skin lesions. Sci. Data **5**(1), 1–9 (2018). https://doi.org/10.1038/sdata.2018.161

18. Bandi, P., et al.: From detection of individual metastases to classification of lymph node status at the patient level: the CAMELYON17 challenge. IEEE Trans. Med. Imaging **38**(2), 550–560 (2018). https://doi.org/10.1109/TMI.2018.2867350

19. Lakshminarayanan, B., Pritzel, A., Blundell, C.: Simple and scalable predictive uncertainty estimation using deep ensembles. In: Advances in Neural Information Processing Systems, vol. 30 (2017)

20. Gal, Y., Ghahramani, Z.: Dropout as a Bayesian approximation: representing model uncertainty in deep learning. In: International Conference on Machine Learning, pp. 1050–1059 (2016)

21. Maddox, W.J., Izmailov, P., Garipov, T., Vetrov, D.P., Wilson, A.G.: A simple baseline for Bayesian uncertainty in deep learning. In: Advances in Neural Information Processing Systems, vol. 32 (2019)

22. Vovk, V.: Conditional validity of inductive conformal predictors. In: Asian Conference on Machine Learning, pp. 475–490 (2012). https://doi.org/10.1007/s10994-013-5355-6

23. Deng, J., Dong, W., Socher, R., Li, L.-J., Li, K., Fei-Fei, L.: ImageNet: a largescale hierarchical image database. In: 2009 IEEE Conference on Computer Vision and Pattern Recognition, pp. 248–255 (2009). https://doi.org/10.1109/CVPR.2009.5206848

Proper Scoring Loss Functions Are Simple and Effective for Uncertainty Quantification of White Matter Hyperintensities

Ben Philps[1]([envelope]) [ORCID], Maria del C. Valdes Hernandez[2] [ORCID],
and Miguel Bernabeu Llinares[3,4] [ORCID]

[1] School of Informatics, University of Edinburgh, Edinburgh, UK
B.R.Philps@sms.ed.ac.uk
[2] Department of Neuroimaging Sciences, Centre for Clinical Brain Sciences,
University of Edinburgh, Edinburgh, UK
[3] Centre for Medical Informatics, Usher Institute, University of Edinburgh,
Edinburgh, UK
[4] The Bayes Centre, University of Edinburgh, Edinburgh, UK

Abstract. Uncertainty quantification is an important tool for improving the trustworthiness and clinical usefulness of medical imaging segmentation models, and many techniques exist for quantifying segmentation uncertainty. However, popular segmentation losses such as Dice loss lead to poorly calibrated models and silent failure in uncertainty maps. We compare common proper scoring rule based losses, which encourage well-calibrated models, to Dice loss and calibrated Dice loss variants, for white matter hyperintensity (WMH) segmentation in FLAIR and T1w MRI. We show that scoring rules yield strong performance (e.g., Spherical-TopK: Dice of 0.763, vs 0.717 for Dice loss) and low WMH instance detection failure rate in axial slices (Logarithmic yields 11% missing instances in the uncertainty map vs 28% for Dice). Furthermore, proper scoring rule methods do not exhibit the performance degradation in calibration error and WMH burden prediction of Dice loss in low WMH burden patients. Finally, we show temperature scaling is insufficient to overcome the drawbacks of Dice loss.

Keywords: Scoring Functions · Uncertainty Quantification · White Matter Hyperintensities

1 Introduction

Uncertainty quantification is an important consideration for improving the trust and utility of existing AI tools, particularly for downstream clinical tasks in

Supplementary Information The online version contains supplementary material available at https://doi.org/10.1007/978-3-031-44336-7_21.

medical segmentation settings. However, the most common choices of loss function used to train medical imaging segmentation methods can result in poorly calibrated models [28]. Calibration measures how well a model's predictions of an outcome match the probability of that outcome occurring in the real world. In this work, we assess the impact of loss function choice on the calibration of segmentation models for white matter hyperintensities (WMH). WMH are a clinical feature common in brain magnetic resonance imaging (MRI) of elderly individuals, and a neuroradiological feature of small vessel disease (SVD) [26]. WMH pose a difficult segmentation challenge, due to their spatial and structural heterogeneity as well as inherent aleatoric uncertainty due to unclear borders [19] and subjectivity in identifying deep isolated small WMH clusters. Therefore, various methods have been developed to segment WMH [3], with neural networks (NNs) showing strong performance [5]. Our contributions are: 1) Proper scoring functions (a measure for evaluating predictive distributions that reward calibrated probabilities) consistently yield well calibrated models and surprisingly yield stronger Dice scores for WMH segmentation than the common Dice loss. 2) We demonstrate that Dice loss is poorly calibrated and attempts to correct Dice loss are insufficient, yielding large absolute volume differences (AVD) in patients with low WMH burden. 3) Proper scoring rules yield uncertainty maps that detect a greater proportion of small WMH instances in axial slices.

2   Background

Scoring functions are a class of functions that reward a model for outputting probabilities consistent with the true event probabilities [13]. Specifically, they provide a numerical score $S(P, Q)$ for a predictive distribution P under a target distribution Q. Scoring functions are proper if $S(Q, Q) \geq S(P, Q)$ for all P, Q. Scoring functions are often used for ex-post evaluation of models to determine which model is best calibrated. However, we can use these directly as loss functions [7] to reward a well calibrated segmentation model by minimising the loss $\mathcal{L}_S = \frac{1}{N} \sum_{i=1}^{N} 1 - S(p_{ic}, y_{ic})$. Here p_{ic} is the predicted probability of voxel i belonging to class c, y_i is a one-hot encoded vector of the annotation label, and N is the number of voxels and C the number of classes. The three most common strictly proper scoring functions are the Brier score: $\frac{1}{C} \sum_{c=1}^{C} (p_{ic} - y_{ic})^2$, the Logarithmic score: $1 + \ln(p_i \cdot y_i)$ and the Spherical score: $\frac{p_i \cdot y_i}{||p_i||}$. Notably, choosing logarithmic score is equivalent to minimising cross-entropy loss. However, for segmentation, losses that aim to optimize for the intersection over union are popular, particularly in settings where there is a high class imbalance [17]. Most popular is the Dice loss function, a soft differentiable minimization of $1-$ the Dice score (Table 1). However Dice is well known to yield highly overconfident predictions [28]. One approach for improving calibration is to selectively penalize the overconfident predictions by exponentially weighting the false positive and false negative terms in the denominator of the Dice loss (Dice++ Loss [28]):

$$\mathcal{L}_{\text{Dice++}} = 1 - \frac{1}{C} \sum_{c=1}^{C} \frac{2 \sum_{i=1}^{N} p_{ic} y_{ic}}{2 \sum_{i=1}^{N} p_{ic} y_{ic} + (\sum_{i=1}^{N} (1 - p_{ic}) y_{ic})^{\gamma} + (\sum_{i=1}^{N} p_{ic}(1 - y_{ic}))^{\gamma}} \tag{1}$$

As we increase the focal parameter γ above 1, overconfident predictions incur larger penalties, with larger γ controlling the severity of the penalty. Note that $\gamma = 1$ is equivalent to the Dice loss. Alternatively, we can attempt to adapt $\mathcal{L}_S$ to a highly imbalanced task by focusing our loss only on voxels that have low confidence (and therefore likely inaccurate predictions) for the target class. TopK loss [27] computes the loss for only the top $k\%$ lowest confidence voxels for the target class, removing high confience voxels:

$$\mathcal{L}_{\text{TopK}} = \frac{1}{\sum_{i=1}^{N} \mathbb{1}(y_{ic} = 1 \wedge p_{ic} < t)} \sum_{i=1}^{N} -\mathbb{1}(y_{ic} = 1 \wedge p_{ic} < t) S(p_i, y_i) \tag{2}$$

where S is a proper scoring function, $\mathbb{1}$ is the indicator function and we adjust t each training batch such that we include only $k\%$ voxels.

Finally, we can treat calibration not as an ex-ante design consideration, but an ex-post correction to our model. A simple and robust approach is temperature scaling [8]. Temperature scaling utilizes a single parameter, the temperature κ, to soften (increase the entropy) of the model softmax distribution. Given a logit vector η_i from our model, we compute $p_i = \sigma(\eta_i/\kappa)$, where σ is the softmax operator. Noteably, $\lim_{\kappa \to \infty} p_i = \frac{1}{C}$. Since proper scoring functions reward correct calibration, we can tune κ on the validation data by optimizing a scoring function of our choosing, usually the logarithmic score.

Ultimately, our goal is to incorporate model uncertainty into downstream clinical tasks (such as assessing SVD severity). Numerous techniques exist to quantify the uncertainty of NN predictions [1,20,30], such as ensembling [25], sampling the latent space of conditional variational autoencoders [10], or modelling the covariance between voxels [21]. To assess the impact of loss function choice, we adopt a softmax entropy map over each image $\mathbb{H}(p_i)$ as a simple baseline. Softmax entropy captures the aleatoric uncertainty (the irreducible uncertainty inherint to the data) present in in-distribution samples [22]. For WMH, aleatoric uncertainty is introduced due to inter-rater disagreement and subjective definitions of WMH, such as at the borders of WMH where the exact boundary is usually unclear. At inference time we may select a threshold τ, with all voxels with uncertainty $> \tau$ flagged as uncertain during downstream tasks.

3 Materials and Methods

3.1 Dataset and Preprocessing

We validate each loss function on the WMH Segmentation Challenge 2017 dataset,[1]. This dataset provides a training dataset of 60 subjects and a test

---

[1] WMH Challenge Dataset is publicly available at https://wmh.isi.uu.nl/data/.

dataset of 110 subjects, collected across multiple different institutions and acquisition protocols. Supplementary A provides details. The images are provided with the following preprocessing: sagittal 3D FLAIR images are reoriented to axial and resampled to slice thickness of 3mm; T1w images are registered to the FLAIR using Elastix [16]; Bias field inhomogeneities for FLAIR and T1w are corrected with SPM12 [2]. We further applied the following preprocessing: brain extraction using ROBEX [11]; resampling images to $1.00 \times 1.00 \times 3.00$ voxel size (using cubic spline interpolation for images and nearest neighbours for labels); Z-score normalization to brain tissue, using intensities in the 5–95th percentile to calculate the mean and variance; centre crop/pad all axial slices to 224×192 voxels. Each voxel is labeled as either Background, WMH, or Other Pathology; however the Other Pathology class is not included in evaluation statistics.

3.2   Evaluation Metrics

To evaluate the segmentation performance of each loss function we employ the evaluation metrics from the WMH Challenge, detailed in Table 1. To assess calibration and usefulness of the softmax entropy uncertainty map we employ three metrics (Table 2). We use Expected Calibration Error (ECE) to measure calibration performance. However, a low ECE score across the test dataset can hide highly over or under confident segmentations on individual images [14], furthermore WMH Dice and lesion F1 score degrades for images with low WMH burden [5]. Therefore we also examine how ECE varies by individual according to WMH burden. Next, the uncertainty error overlap (UEO) metric assesses overlap between uncertainty and segmentation error rewarding uncertainty that is well localized (maximises the Dice metric between error and uncertainty). The unified uncertainty score (UUS) [20] assesses the quality of the remaining segmentation after voxels with uncertainty $> \tau$ are removed. UUS rewards methods that remove incorrectly segmented voxels (with higher Dice score when computed only on the remaining voxels) while penalizing the removal of correctly segmented voxels. WMH do not represent distinct, clearly identifiable anatomic abnormalities, but instead represent foci of (often subtle) white matter

Table 1. Evaluation metrics for assessing model performance. For **Recall** and **F1**-score, the metrics are defined across individual lesions, which are calculated as connected components in the predicted and ground truth WMH segmentations. Specifically, N refers to the number of connected components, where N_{TP} refers to the number of lesions where a predicted lesion overlaps with a true lesion by at least one voxel. TP refers to the number of true positive voxels. $V_{\hat{y}}$ and V_y are the predicted and true WMH volume respectively, **AVD** = Absolute Volume Difference. $\hat{d}(\hat{y}, y) = \max\limits_{\hat{y}_i \in \hat{y}} \min\limits_{y_i \in y} d(\hat{y}_i, y_i)$ where d is a distance function. **HD95** = Modified Hausdorff distance (95th percentile).

Dice($\uparrow$)	HD95($\downarrow$)	AVD($\downarrow$)	Recall($\uparrow$)	F1($\uparrow$)
$\frac{2TP}{2TP+FP+FN}$	$\max\{\hat{d}(\hat{y}, y), \hat{d}(\hat{y}, y)\}$	$\frac{\lvert V_{\hat{y}} - V_y \rvert}{V_y}$	$\frac{N_{TP}}{N_{TP}+N_{FN}}$	$\frac{2N_{TP}}{2N_{TP}+N_{FN}+N_{FP}}$

Table 2. Uncertainty quantification equations. **UEO** (Uncertainty Error Overlap [14]): Calculates overlap between the predicted segmentation error and the uncertainty map. Overlap is computed using Dice. We report the maximum attainable UEO score as the uncertainty threshold τ varies. $\hat{u}$ = uncertainty map, e = segmentation error. **UUS** (Modified Unified Uncertainty Score [20]): Computes the filtered Dice and filtered true/false positives/negatives as τ increases. Voxels with uncertainty $> \tau$ are removed from the computation. UUS computes the average of 5 AUC curves: filtered Dice, filtered False Positives (FFP)/Negatives (FFN) and 1 - filtered True Positives (FTP)/Negatives (FTN). Here FTP measures the ratio of filtered (remaining true positives (TP)) to the total true positives, i.e $1 - TP_\tau/TP$. Filtered Dice (FDice) calculates the Dice metric only on filtered voxels. **ECE** (Expected Calibration Error [8]): approximates the difference between model confidence and accuracy. Predictions are placed into equal width bins B, based on their confidence. ECE compares the weighted average of the difference between the mean confidence conf(B_w) and mean proportion of WMH in the ground truth acc(B_w), for the voxels in each bin.

max UEO($\uparrow$)	UUS($\uparrow$)	ECE($\downarrow$)
$\displaystyle\max_{\tau \in [0,1]} \mathrm{Dice}(\hat{u} > \tau, e)$	$\frac{1}{5}[\mathrm{AUC_{FDice}} + (2 - \mathrm{AUC_{FTP}}$ $-\mathrm{AUC_{FTN}}) + \mathrm{AUC_{FFP}} + \mathrm{AUC_{FFN}}]$	$\sum_{w=1}^{W} \frac{|B_w|}{n} \cdot$ $|\mathrm{acc}(B_w) - \mathrm{conf}(B_w)|$

changes [19]. Consequently, boundaries between normal appearing white matter and hyperintense tissue are difficult to delineate and annotators may disagree about the presence of small WMH. Hence, we would like to minimize silent failure, where uncertainty maps fail to highlight WMH in the annotation that is missing from the predicted segmentation. To assess the impact of loss function choice on detection of unsegmented WMH, we calculate the size and proportion of instances missed (no voxels in the instance have uncertainty $> \tau$) in the uncertainty map as we vary τ. We define instances as 2D connected components in axial slices.

3.3   Implementation Test Bench

We utilize a simple benchmarking system for each method, training using a single U-Net architecture for each loss. We use a resnet18 [9] backbone for our U-Net encoder, provided in Segmentation-Models Pytorch[2]. We train three models per loss function, using a different random seed for initializing each model. We report the mean results across the test set for all losses, averaged over each seed. We further evaluate a TopK variant per scoring function. WMH voxels occupy less than 1% of our 3D training images, hence we assess both the performance of k=10 recommended in prior work [17] and a more restricted $k = 1$, reporting the k that achieves the highest lesion F1 score. For Dice++ we first tune the γ parameter on the validation set, choosing the gamma from $\{2, 3, 4\}$ that yields the highest lesion F1 score. For post-hoc temperature scaling, we take the models trained on Dice loss and tune κ to maximise the logarithmic score on the

---

[2] https://github.com/qubvel/segmentation_models.pytorch

validation dataset. Models are optimized using Adam [15], with a learning rate of $3e-4$, multiplying by a factor of 0.1 if validation loss does not improve within 25 epochs, until $lr = 1e-6$. Early stopping on the validation set, with a patience of 50 epochs, is used to avoid over-fitting. Each epoch consists of 125 batches. To encourage robust, generalizable results with limited training data, we apply numerous augmentations during training, following the choices in nnU-Net [12]. We make our code publicly available.[3] Due to the high proportion of background voxels, where models are typically confident and accurate, $\mathcal{L}_S$ is pulled close to zero. To counter this, we re-weight $\mathcal{L}_S$ and $\mathcal{L}_{\text{TopK}}$ by 1 over the proportion of WMH voxels in the training data (which account for 0.28% of training voxels). This re-weighting is important for yielding strong performance for the logarithmic score. We refer to the logarithmic score as CE in the results. Uncertainty maps are normalized to $[0, 1]$ by dividing by $-\ln(\frac{1}{3})$.

Table 3. Performance Metrics for each loss function on the test set. Best performer per metric in bold. We denote significant improvements (two-tailed t-test comparing the three runs per method, $p < 0.01$) over: both Dice++ and Dice: †; over Dice only: *; over Dice++ only: ‡. CE: logarithmic score. TempDice: Model trained with Dice loss, with temperature scaling applied on the validation set.

Loss	UUS	ECE	Dice	F1	AVD%	HD95 mm	Recall	max UEO	prop. miss.
Brier	0.689*	0.076*	0.757‡	0.683	20.7‡	6.97*	0.637	0.427*	0.140*
Spherical	0.688*	0.076*	0.760†	0.700*	20.3‡	6.53*	0.673	0.433*	0.124*
CE	0.682*	0.074*	0.760†	**0.727†**	20.6‡	6.19*	**0.710**	**0.437†**	0.110†
Brier-TopK10	**0.695***	0.083*	0.760†	0.713†	20.9‡	6.43*	0.707	0.430*	0.108†
Sphere-TopK1	0.682*	**0.065***	**0.763†**	0.710†	**19.6†**	6.37*	0.700	0.433*	0.114†
CE-TopK10	0.685*	0.079*	0.760†	0.720†	19.9‡	**6.06†**	**0.710**	0.435*	**0.106†**
Dice	0.560	0.236	0.717	0.627	35.9	8.61	0.597	0.150	0.275
Dice++	0.684*	0.085*	0.740	0.660	28.0	6.60*	0.695	0.426*	0.144*
TempDice	0.527	0.092*	0.717	0.627	35.9	8.61	0.597	0.233	0.241

4   Results

The mean performance metrics per loss are shown in Table 3. Surprisingly, all scoring function variants yield significant improvements in Dice score over Dice/Dice++ loss, with the combination of Spherical and TopK yielding the highest Dice and best calibration. CE, or TopK variants of Spherical and Brier score, also show significant improvements over Dice/Dice++ loss for F1 score and in the proportion of instances missed. Furthermore, all scoring functions yield ECE scores less than that of Dice (0.236), or Dice++ (0.085) vs CE (0.068) or

---

[3] Code repository: https://github.com/BenjaminPhi5/Scoring_Functions_WMH

Spherical TopK (0.065), while temperature scaling makes only modest improvements (0.092). Figure 1c shows calibration curves for various loss functions. CE, SphericalTopk1, Dice++ and TempDice yield slightly overconfident distributions, with curves close to the optimum calibration. Dice loss yields arbitrarily accurate predictions regardless of confidences above zero, making differentiating model accuracy based on confidence difficult. Furthermore, examination of the ECE score when compared to ground truth WMH volume reveals Dice loss yields poor calibration at low volumes. Figure 1a shows correlation between individual ECE score and log WMH burden. Dice++ improves calibration over all volumes, but still degrades with log volume ($r = -0.5, p = 3.1e - 08$), while both SphericalTopk1 ($r = -0.12, p = 0.23$) and CE ($r = -0.0082, p = 0.93$) retain low ECE at low volumes. Similarly for AVD, while Dice++ improves performance over the Dice model, each scoring function substantially reduces the AVD score. Crucially, scoring functions yield less pronounced degradation in AVD performance for low burden patients (Fig. 1a); for CE mean ECE and AVD is almost half that of Dice or Dice++ in images with the lowest WMH burden. While high sample standard deviation (10.4) in average Dice loss AVD scores yields non-significant p-values when compared to scoring functions (Table 3), all scoring functions yield total separation in average AVD results compared to Dice loss.

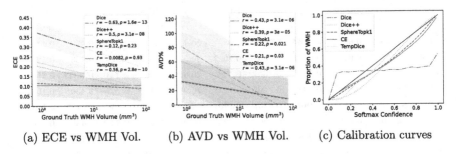

(a) ECE vs WMH Vol.	(b) AVD vs WMH Vol.	(c) Calibration curves

Fig. 1. (a), (b): Pearson correlation between (a) ECE or (b) AVD with log WMH volume for Dice, Dice++, SphericalTopk1, CE and TempDice. ECE and AVD scores are averaged for each individual over three runs. Shaded area: the standard deviation of the residuals, (c) Average calibration curves across three runs.

Figure 2 shows the uncertainty map performance as τ varies for different loss functions. Figure 2b shows scoring functions fail to detect lower proportions of WMH instances than Dice or Dice++ at any setting of τ. Notably, while choosing a τ below the max UEO point ($\hat{\tau}$) can improve the detection of missing instances, both SphericalTopK and CE miss less instances while retaining high UEO scores (Fig. 2a). For Dice++, UEO decreases sharply compared to CE as τ goes to zero, hence choosing a lower τ will yield uncertainty that is poorly localized to the segmentation error, increasing the true positives and negatives incorrectly identified as uncertain. Temperature scaling improves the maximum UEO Dice, but at $\hat{\tau}$ max UEO is less than half that of any other method except

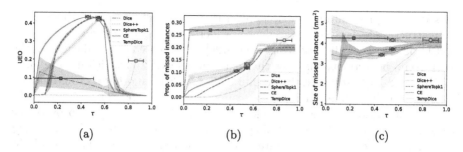

Fig. 2. Uncertainty map metrics, as uncertainty threshold τ increases. (a) UEO score, (b) Proportion of undetected (intersection over union = 0) WMH instances in segmentation and uncertainty map, (c) Size of undetected WMH instances in segmentation and uncertainty map. Bold line: mean, shaded area: standard deviation, square: mean τ that maximises UEO score, error bar: standard deviation in location of max τ.

Dice, while failing to detect double the instances of CE. Nonetheless, temperature scaling improves the useability of the uncertainty map, permitting meaningful tuning of τ to set the silent failure rate. Fig 2c shows the mean size of undetected lesions. Regardless of τ, Dice and Dice++ fail to capture some of the smallest instances, while SphericalTopK and CE permit trading UEO score for detection of very small instances. Supplementary B provides uncertainty map examples.

5 Discussion

We have shown that proper scoring functions can be effective and well calibrated loss functions for WMH segmentation. Spherical and Brier scores are understudied as segmentation losses, and when combined with TopK to counter class imbalance they can yield competitive performance. The TopK variants yield the same or improved results for Dice, HD95, Recall and the proportion of missed lesions at $\hat{\tau}$ across all scoring function losses. These variants could be fitted into existing compound losses that generalize well across datasets [29], and tuning of cutoff k could further enable generalization to other tasks with high class imbalance. Furthermore, alternative scoring rules such as generalized spherical or winklers score offer parameterized scoring functions that may be adjusted to the task at hand [7]. Greater attention should be paid to AVD divergence and poor calibration in low WMH burden patients, such individuals are poorly represented in average lesion-wise scores (e.g. lesion F1) or ECE scores due to the small lesion number and volume that they contribute overall. We find scoring functions yield models that are less prone to this degradation than Dice based methods, with no appreciable degradation in ECE at low volumes. This is especially important for downstream tasks such as identifying patients at risk of developing further manifestations of cerebral small vessel disease [24]. While Dice++ consistently outperforms Dice loss, performance still degrades at low WMH burdens, albeit to a lesser extent. Small WMH instances can often be missed by a segmentation model; however they often indicate areas where tissue microstructure is damaged, precedent of wider damage [6] and hence are important to detect - regardless of their size [18,26]. ECE score is not indicative of the most useful uncertainty maps, with BrierTopk and CETopK yielding the highest UUS and UEO respectively, despite higher ECE than other scoring function variants. Finally, while temperature scaling is effective and robust for improving the calibration of a given model [25], it alone is insufficient to overcome the drawbacks of Dice loss, yielding no significant improvement in any other metric. UEO and silent failure rates see only modest improvements, with ECE still degrading for low WMH burden. Global temperature scaling is not suitable in segmentation tasks (which commonly display spatial and heteroscedastic aleatoric uncertainty [21]) such as WMH segmentation. Dice loss encourages high confidence in both WMH instance centres and at ambiguous areas (edges and small WMH); hence the temperature parameter must vary spatially and per image. A separate model for predicting the temperature parameter [23] can achieve this, however this increases complexity and amount of validation data required [4] while still unable to improve over the segmentation performance of Dice loss.

References

1. Abdar, M., Pourpanah, F., Hussain, S., et al.: A review of uncertainty quantification in deep learning: techniques, applications and challenges. Inf. Fusion **76**, 243–297 (2021). https://doi.org/10.1016/j.inffus.2021.05.008

2. Ashburner, J., Friston, K.J.: Voxel-based morphometry-the methods. NeuroImage **11**(6), 805–821 (2000). https://doi.org/10.1006/nimg.2000.0582

3. Balakrishnan, R., Hernández, M.D.C.V., Farrall, A.J.: Automatic segmentation of white matter hyperintensities from brain magnetic resonance images in the era of deep learning and big data-a systematic review. Comput. Med. Imaging Graph **88**, 101867 (2021)

4. Balanya, S.A., Maroñas, J., Ramos, D.: Adaptive temperature scaling for robust calibration of deep neural networks. arXiv preprint arXiv:2208.00461 (2022)

5. Gaubert, M., et al.: Performance evaluation of automated white matter hyperintensity segmentation algorithms in a multicenter cohort on cognitive impairment and dementia. Front. Psychiatry **13**, 2928 (2023)

6. Ge, Y., Grossman, R.I., Babb, J.S., et al.: Dirty-appearing white matter in multiple sclerosis: volumetric MR imaging and magnetization transfer ratio histogram analysis. Am. J. Neuroradiol. **24**(10), 1935–1940 (2003)

7. Gneiting, T., Raftery, A.E.: Strictly proper scoring rules, prediction, and estimation. J. Am. Stat. Assoc. **102**(477), 359–378 (2007)

8. Guo, C., Pleiss, G., Sun, Y., Weinberger, K.Q.: On calibration of modern neural networks. In: Proceedings of the 34th International Conference on Machine Learning, pp. 1321–1330. PMLR, July 2017. iSSN: 2640-3498

9. He, K., Zhang, X., Ren, S., Sun, J.: Deep residual learning for image recognition. In: Proceedings of the IEEE Conference on Computer Vision and Pattern Recognition, pp. 770–778 (2016)

10. Hu, S., Worrall, D., Knegt, S., Veeling, B., Huisman, H., Welling, M.: Supervised uncertainty quantification for segmentation with multiple annotations. In: Shen, D., et al. (eds.) MICCAI 2019. LNCS, vol. 11765, pp. 137–145. Springer, Cham (2019). https://doi.org/10.1007/978-3-030-32245-8_16

11. Iglesias, J.E., Cheng-Yi Liu, Thompson, P.M., Zhuowen, T.: Robust brain extraction across datasets and comparison with publicly available methods. IEEE Trans. Med. Imaging **30**(9), 1617–1634 (2011). https://doi.org/10.1109/TMI.2011.2138152

12. Isensee, F., Jaeger, P.F., Kohl, S.A.A., Petersen, J., Maier-Hein, K.H.: nnU-net: a self-configuring method for deep learning-based biomedical image segmentation. Nat. Methods **18**(2), 203–211 (2021). https://doi.org/10.1038/s41592-020-01008-z

13. Jose, V.R.: A characterization for the spherical scoring rule. Theor. Decis. **66**, 263–281 (2009)

14. Jungo, A., Balsiger, F., Reyes, M.: Analyzing the quality and challenges of uncertainty estimations for brain tumor segmentation. Front. Neurosci. **14**, 282 (2020)

15. Kingma, D.P., Ba, J.: Adam: a method for stochastic optimization, January 2017. 10.48550/arXiv. 1412.6980, arXiv:1412.6980 [cs]

16. Klein, S., Staring, M., Murphy, K., Viergever, M.A., Pluim, J.P.W.: elastix: a toolbox for intensity-based medical image registration. IEEE Trans. Med. Imaging **29**(1), 196–205 (2010). https://doi.org/10.1109/TMI.2009.2035616

17. Ma, J., et al.: Loss odyssey in medical image segmentation. Med. Image Anal. **71**, 102035 (2021). https://doi.org/10.1016/j.media.2021.102035

18. MacLullich, A.M., Ferguson, K.J., Reid, L.M., et al.: Higher systolic blood pressure is associated with increased water diffusivity in normal-appearing white matter. Stroke **40**(12), 3869–3871 (2009)

19. Maillard, P., et al.: White matter hyperintensity penumbra. Stroke **42**(7), 1917–1922 (2011)

20. Mehta, R., Filos, A., Baid, U., et al.: QU-BraTS: MICCAI BraTS 2020 challenge on quantifying uncertainty in brain tumor segmentation-analysis of ranking metrics and benchmarking results. arXiv preprint arXiv:2112.10074 (2021)

21. Monteiro, M., Le Folgoc, L., et al.: Stochastic segmentation networks: modelling spatially correlated aleatoric uncertainty. In: Advances in Neural Information Processing Systems, vol. 33, pp. 12756–12767. Curran Associates, Inc. (2020)

22. Mukhoti, J., Kirsch, A., van Amersfoort, J., Torr, P.H., Gal, Y.: Deterministic neural networks with appropriate inductive biases capture epistemic and aleatoric uncertainty. arXiv preprint arXiv:2102.11582 (2021)

23. Ouyang, C., et al.: Improved post-hoc probability calibration for out-of-domain MRI segmentation. In: Sudre, C.H., et al. Uncertainty for Safe Utilization of Machine Learning in Medical Imaging. UNSURE 2022. LNCS, vol. 13563, pp. 59–69 Springer, Cham (2022). https://doi.org/10.1007/978-3-031-16749-2_6

24. Prins, N.D., Scheltens, P.: White matter hyperintensities, cognitive impairment and dementia: an update. Nat. Rev. Neurol. **11**(3), 157–165 (2015)

25. Rahaman, R., et al.: Uncertainty quantification and deep ensembles. Adv. Neural Inf. Process. Syst. **34**, 20063–20075 (2021)

26. Wardlaw, J.M., Valdés Hernández, M.C., Muñoz-Maniega, S.: What are white matter hyperintensities made of? Relevance to vascular cognitive impairment. J. Am. Heart Assoc. **4**(6), e001140 (2015)

27. Wu, Z., Shen, C., Hengel, A.V.d.: Bridging category-level and instance-level semantic image segmentation. arXiv preprint arXiv:1605.06885 (2016)

28. Yeung, M., Rundo, L., Nan, Y., Sala, E., Schönlieb, C.B., Yang, G.: Calibrating the dice loss to handle neural network overconfidence for biomedical image segmentation. J. Digit. Imaging **36**(2), 739–752 (2023). https://doi.org/10.1007/s10278-022-00735-3

29. Yeung, M., Sala, E., Schönlieb, C.B., Rundo, L.: Unified Focal loss: generalising dice and cross entropy-based losses to handle class imbalanced medical image segmentation. Comput. Med. Imaging Graph. **95**, 102026 (2022). https://doi.org/10.1016/j.compmedimag.2021.102026

30. Zou, K., Chen, Z., Yuan, X., et al.: A review of uncertainty estimation and its application in medical imaging. arXiv preprint arXiv:2302.08119 (2023)

Author Index

C. H. Sudre et al. (Eds.): UNSURE 2023, LNCS 14291, pp. 219–220, 2023.
https://doi.org/10.1007/978-3-031-44336-7

Printed in the United States
by Baker & Taylor Publisher Services